WORLD FORMULA ONE RECORDS
2026

This edition published by Welbeck
An Imprint of Headline Publishing Group Limited

1

Cataloguing in Publication Data is available from the British Library

ISBN 978-103542-472-6

Printed and bound in Dubai

HEADLINE PUBLISHING GROUP LIMITED
A Hachette UK Company
Carmelite House
50 Victoria Embankment
London EC4Y 0DZ

The authorised representative in the EEA is Hachette Ireland,
8 Castlecourt Centre, Dublin 15, D15 XTP3, Ireland (email: info@hbgi.ie)

2026 edition text update written by Phillip Horton

Editor: Conor Kilgallon
Design: Iain Fryer
Picture research: Paul Langan
Production: Rachel Burgess

www.headline.co.uk
www.hachette.co.uk

All stats and facts are correct as at December 2024.

WORLD FORMULA ONE RECORDS
2026

BRUCE JONES

WELBECK

CONTENTS

Contents pages (*main image*) Max Verstappen leads the field at the Saudi Arabian GP, one of Formula One's newest events; (*right*) Lewis Hamilton wins at Silverstone in 2024 for a record ninth victory at the circuit; (*below*) The late, great Ayrton Senna celebrates his first world title in 1988; (*bottom*) Peter Collins was victorious for Ferrari in the 1958 British GP; (*overleaf*) Lando Norris's victory in Abu Dhabi helped clinch the constructors' title for McLaren in 2024.

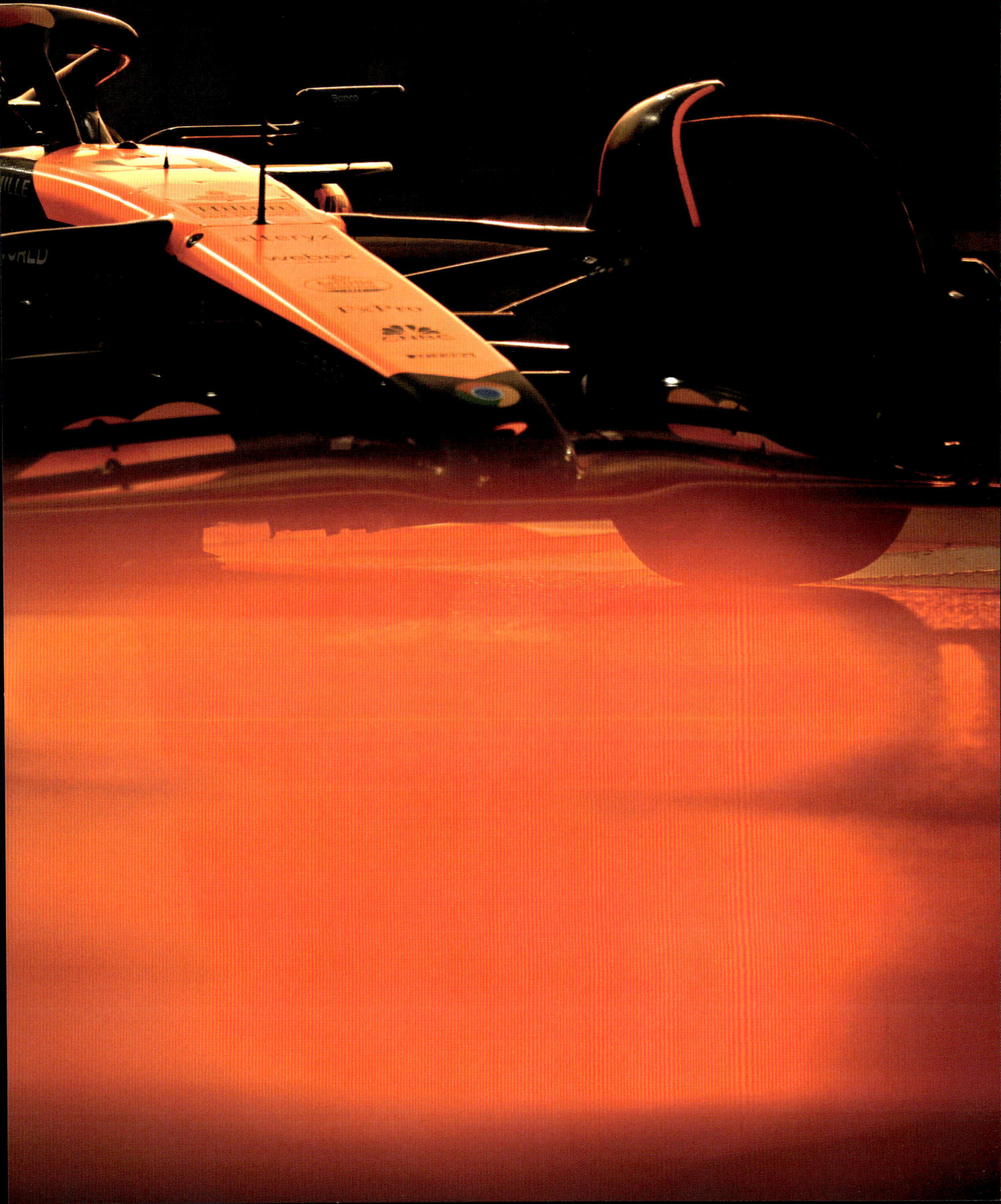
alteryx
webex

INTRODUCTION

Formula One is now speeding past its 75-year anniversary having produced an array of winners, champions and memorable moments, with motor racing transformed since the inaugural World Championship grand prix at Silverstone in 1950.

The best of the best work their way to the front, finding and developing the best machinery and building the strongest team around them, while laying down superlative drives that deliver them riches and a place within the all-time lists.

Each era has brought its own challenges, from the danger of the early decades – in which there were as few as eight grands prix per year on haphazard courses – to the multi-billion-dollar entity that now hurtles around the globe, to locations and circuits that dazzle and impress.

Icons have emerged, surpassing their predecessors, with Juan Manuel Fangio's tally of five world titles beaten by Michael Schumacher, and since matched by Lewis Hamilton, who was just one lap shy of moving clear of his fellow seven-time world champion. Hamilton's streak of success through the 2010s means he tops almost every records chart, becoming the first driver to reach 100 grand prix victories, with more individual wins than races started by great champions in decades gone by. Max Verstappen, who so far has a cast-iron grip on Formula One in the 2020s, is rapidly climbing the all-time lists and now Hamilton's victory tally no longer looks insurmountable.

Great teams have seen success come and go. Lotus, Tyrrell and Cooper have long since fallen by the wayside, Williams have slumped down the competitive order, and even Ferrari and McLaren have had leaner spells as Mercedes and Red Bull Racing emerged to exert a 15-year grip on both World Championships – at least until the renaissance of McLaren starting in 2024.

Drivers will come and go, and teams will rise and fall, and by the time Formula One reaches its century in 2050 there will be new additions and revisions to these lists, etching their names among the greats that they seek to emulate.

Right Max Verstappen celebrates his fourth Formula One drivers' title at the 2024 Las Vegas Grand Prix.

Formula One has been exciting and entertaining fans around the globe since the World Championship began in 1950. The drive to win is as strong as ever, but Formula One has changed dramatically over the past 75 years. The cars have been transformed into high-tech missiles with incredible acceleration, cornering and braking capabilities. The circuits are bigger, better and safer. So, with every grand prix, the records keep on being added to in a blaze of glamour and speed.

Above Formula One has been racing for more than seven decades – with Las Vegas among its newest venues.

DRIVERS

The likes of seven-time champions Michael Schumacher and Lewis Hamilton regularly find themselves in the record books owing to their achievements. But across Formula One's history over 100 drivers can call themselves a grand prix winner, over 30 have won a world championship and hundreds of others have contributed to the rich tapestry of the world's fastest and most prestigious motorsport.

Above Modern great Max Verstappen takes victory at the 2024 Saudi Arabian GP.

CHAMPIONS

WRAP IT UP EARLY

Michael Schumacher and Max Verstappen share the record of how early they've managed to win a world title. In 2002 Schumacher wrapped up his fifth world title at the French Grand Prix, Round 11 of 17, while Verstappen mathematically made sure of his third world title at the Sprint Race of the 2023 Qatar Grand Prix, when there were still six races left to run that season. In terms of dates Schumacher eclipses Verstappen, with his crown assured on the staggeringly early date of July 21st.

WINNER BY A FRACTION

Some champions win by a clear margin, others just scrape home. Lewis Hamilton (2008), Kimi Räikkönen (2007), James Hunt (1976) and Mike Hawthorn (1958) all edged home by one point, but Hawthorn's championship required an act of fair play from Stirling Moss who stopped Hawthorn from being disqualified from the Portuguese GP, verifying that Hawthorn's Ferrari hadn't been given a push-start. The closest championship finish was in 1984, when Niki Lauda beat his McLaren team-mate Alain Prost by half a point.

RULE BRITANNIA

British drivers are the most successful in F1 with 20 world titles – seven for Lewis Hamilton, three for Jackie Stewart, two apiece for Graham Hill and Jim Clark, and one for Mike Hawthorn, John Surtees, James Hunt, Nigel Mansell, Damon Hill and Jenson Button. Germany is next up with 12 – with seven for Michael Schumacher, four for Sebastian Vettel, and one for Nico Rosberg. Brazil is third, on eight titles.

Above Jenson Button is one of 10 Britons to be crowned world champion.

THREE TIMES TOGETHER

Through Formula One history there have been 23 occasions where team-mates have finished first and second in the standings. The drivers to have finished 1-2 most often are Lewis Hamilton and Nico Rosberg. During their spell together at Mercedes, Hamilton led Rosberg in 2014 and 2015, before Rosberg turned the tables in 2016.

WINNING FOR YOURSELF

To win the Formula One drivers' title is a huge honour. To win it in a car bearing your name is doubly so, and the late Jack Brabham is the only person to have managed this, in 1966. Team-mate Denny Hulme then became champion for Brabham in 1967.

Below McLaren's James Hunt took the 1976 drivers' title by a solitary point after an epic fight with Ferrari's Niki Lauda.

Above Jack Brabham celebrates after winning the 1959 British GP at Aintree, as Cooper came good.

PRIVATEERS STRIKE A BLOW

Jack Brabham and Cooper struck a blow for the little guys when they won both the 1959 World Drivers' and Constructors' Championships. This made Cooper the first specialist racing-car manufacturer to beat the established factory teams with their big budgets, such as Alfa Romeo, Ferrari, Mercedes and Maserati.

HOP, SKIP AND A JUMP

Aside from Giuseppe Farina's record in winning the inaugural World Championship in 1950, the smallest total number of grands prix contested by a driver before becoming world champion is Juan Manuel Fangio, who won the title in 1951 for Alfa Romeo after competing in just 12 grands prix – about half of the current season.

Above Max Verstappen pulverized the opposition in 2023 and finished 290 points ahead of Sergio Perez.

TWO HUNDRED AND NINETY

Formula One overhauled its points system in 2010, giving 25 points rather than 10 for a win, thus distorting lots of statistics. Sebastian Vettel's 2013 season ended with a 155-point buffer back to runner-up Fernando Alonso, but this record was obliterated by Max Verstappen in 2023. Verstappen finished 290 points clear of Sergio Perez – effectively an 11-round advantage.

TOP WORLD CHAMPIONSHIP-WINNING DRIVERS

1	Michael Schumacher	7
=	Lewis Hamilton	7
2	Juan Manuel Fangio	5
3	Alain Prost	4
=	Sebastian Vettel	4
=	Max Verstappen	4
6	Jack Brabham	3
=	Niki Lauda	3
=	Nelson Piquet	3
=	Ayrton Senna	3
=	Jackie Stewart	3
11	Fernando Alonso	2
=	Alberto Ascari	2
=	Jim Clark	2
=	Emerson Fittipaldi	2
=	Mika Häkkinen	2
=	Graham Hill	2
17	Mario Andretti	1
=	Jenson Button	1
=	Giuseppe Farina	1
=	Mike Hawthorn	1
=	Damon Hill	1
=	Phil Hill	1
=	Denny Hulme	1
=	James Hunt	1
=	Alan Jones	1
=	Nigel Mansell	1
=	Kimi Räikkönen	1
=	Jochen Rindt	1
=	Keke Rosberg	1
=	Nico Rosberg	1
=	Jody Scheckter	1
=	John Surtees	1
=	Jacques Villeneuve	1

KEEP IT IN THE FAMILY

The Hill family has a proud boast. Despite F1 being littered with sons following their fathers into the sport, Graham and Damon are the first father and son to both win the F1 title. Graham won in 1962 for BRM and in 1968 for Lotus while Damon was crowned with Williams in 1996. The Andrettis and Piquets failed to match their feat, before Nico Rosberg triumphed in 2016 to match his father Keke's feat in 1982.

Right In 1996, Damon Hill, son of Graham, leads Williams team-mate Jacques Villeneuve, son of Gilles, during the year he became the first second-generation world champion.

FROM GOOD TO BAD

World Champions can't win year in, year out, for a variety of reasons. Juan Manuel Fangio, Mike Hawthorn, Jochen Rindt, Nigel Mansell, Alain Prost and Nico Rosberg have failed to do so due to injury, death or retirement, but the following drivers failed to win a race in the year after claiming the title: Alberto Ascari (1954), Fangio (1958), Jack Brabham (1961), Phil Hill (1962), John Surtees (1965), Mario Andretti (1979), Jodi Scheckter (1980), Nelson Piquet (1988), Damon Hill (1997), Jacques Villeneuve (1998) and Sebastian Vettel (2014).

CHAMPION PAIRINGS

The pairing of Fernando Alonso and Jenson Button at McLaren from 2015 made it 14 seasons in which a team has run two world champions after Alberto Ascari and Giuseppe Farina at Ferrari in 1953 and 1954; Jim Clark and Graham Hill at Lotus in 1967 and 1968; Emerson Fittipaldi and Denny Hulme at McLaren in 1974; Alain Prost and Keke Rosberg at McLaren in 1986; Alain Prost and Ayrton Senna at McLaren in 1989; Lewis Hamilton and Button at Mercedes from 2010 to 2012; Kimi Räikkönen and Alonso at Ferrari in 2014, then Räikkönen and Sebastian Vettel from 2015 to 2018.

TWO WHEELS TO FOUR

John Surtees – who was the world champion for Ferrari in 1964 – has the distinction of being the only motorcycle world champion to hit world title-winning heights after transferring to car racing. Fellow motorcycle world champions Mike Hailwood and Johnny Cecotto also made the move to four wheels, but "Mike the Bike" peaked with a best finish of second place in the 1972 Italian GP, ironically racing for Surtees's team, while Cecotto's best result was a sixth position at Long Beach for Theodore in 1983.

Below Alberto Ascari failed to finish a single race in 1954 despite winning titles in both 1952 and 1953.

JUST ONE WILL DO

Anyone who watched Keke Rosberg race will know that he was a driver who raced to win, a driver full of on-the-limit aggression, yet he claimed his world title for Williams in 1982 with just one win. That was Mike Hawthorn's tally too when he was crowned in 1958. Jack Brabham (1959), Phil Hill (1961), John Surtees (1964) and Denny Hulme (1967) all managed to win the title with just two victories.

SUZUKA'S SUCCESSIONS

Suzuka is now an early season race, but between its arrival on the calendar in 1987 and 2023 it was regularly held towards the end of the campaign – sometimes as the finale. As a result it has been the circuit at which the world title has been secured a record 12 times, with Max Verstappen the most recent to be crowned there in 2022. Monza is next up on 11, with Interlagos on six.

Above Sebastian Vettel celebrates his second world title in 2011.

DRIVERS WHO COMPETED IN MOST RACES BEFORE WINNING FIRST WORLD CHAMPIONSHIP

1	Nico Rosberg	206
2	Nigel Mansell	180
3	Jenson Button	170
4	Max Verstappen	141
5	Kimi Räikkönen	121
6	Mika Häkkinen	112
7	Jody Scheckter	97
8	Alain Prost	87
9	Mario Andretti	80
=	Alan Jones	80
10	Ayrton Senna	77

THE FIRST WORLD CHAMPION

Giuseppe Farina was the first F1 world champion in 1950 at the age of 44. The Italian achieved his final win three years later just a few months short of his 47th birthday and, in so doing, became the second-oldest F1 race winner ever. These days, most of the drivers' fathers are younger than that.

I'LL TAKE THE FASTEST CAR

Juan Manuel Fangio was a master at making sure he had the right machinery beneath him and he moved teams to ensure this, which explains why he won the World Championship with more teams than any other driver. He was champion with Alfa Romeo, Mercedes, Ferrari and Maserati.

COMING BACK FROM RETIREMENT

Niki Lauda had two world titles when he quit before the end of the 1979 season. But he couldn't stay away and was back in 1982, racing for McLaren. In winning the title in 1984 he set the record for the longest gap between titles – seven years.

PERSEVERANCE PAYS OFF

Nico Rosberg set fastest lap on his grand prix debut in 2006, but didn't have a winning car until 2012. Mercedes team-mate Lewis Hamilton then kept him away from the title until 2016, when he struck after a record 206 grands prix before becoming World Champion.

Below Mario Andretti took 80 races to be champion, but Nigel Mansell took 100 more.

RUNNERS-UP

FIRST OF THE LOSERS

Nobody wants to finish second in a grand prix. In F1 it's referred to as "the first of the losers". So, imagine how drivers gnash their teeth at ending the year as the championship runner-up. It's even worse if they trip up in the final round and let the title slide from their grasp. The most extreme example of this was when Lewis Hamilton blew his chance of winning the title at his first attempt in 2007 at the Brazilian GP when gearbox problems affected his race and he could only finish seventh. Ferrari's Kimi Räikkönen powered to a race victory and the title.

LAUDA PIPS PROST

Being faster and scoring more wins is one thing, but master tactician Niki Lauda taught his McLaren team-mate Alain Prost a lesson in consistency in 1984. Prost settled in quickly after joining from Renault and won the opening round, then added six more wins, including three of the final four races. However, Lauda kept racking up the points, including five race wins. Lauda won the World Championship by half a point, courtesy of only half the points being awarded when the Monaco GP was stopped prematurely because of a heavy rainstorm when Prost was leading.

A RECORD NOT WANTED

Not only does Stirling Moss have the most years as runner-up to his name – four – but he also tops the chart for the driver with the most F1 wins without a title, at 16. David Coulthard is next on this list with 13 wins and Carlos Reutemann is third on 12, with Gerhard Berger, Ronnie Peterson and Valtteri Bottas having won 10 times each.

CHASING THE DREAM

Rubens Barrichello – runner-up in 2002 and 2004 – ran second behind Ayrton Senna in the 1993 European GP at Donington Park in his Jordan when a month short of his 21st birthday. It was only his third grand prix and yet he would end up contesting the most grands prix without clinching a World title, having raced 325 times by the end of the 2011 season. He then lost his ride for 2012 and turned to IndyCar racing.

Above Jim Clark took 25 wins, and was remarkably second just once in his career.

REMARKABLE CLARK

Jim Clark won 25 grands prix during his all-too-brief magnificent career in the 1960s. Quite astonishingly he was only runner-up once in his world championship career. That came at the Nürburgring in 1963, when Clark led from pole position only to be thwarted by his Lotus-Climax losing a cylinder from its engine. Conversely, 'Quick' Nick Heidfeld finished second eight times in his career in the 2000s and early 2010s, but never managed a race win.

Above Stirling Moss won four races in the 1958 World Championship – including the British GP – but lost the title to Mike Hawthorn, who won but once.

Below Valtteri Bottas won 10 races but never emerged with a world title.

ALWAYS THE BRIDESMAID

Stirling Moss will be remembered as the best driver never to have been world champion. Four times he finished as runner-up, three of those behind Juan Manuel Fangio, his one-time mentor at Mercedes. On the fourth occasion he lost out by a single point to Mike Hawthorn, despite winning more races that year. Alain Prost was also runner-up four times, but he could balance those against his four World Championships.

INSTANT IMPACT

Jacques Villeneuve and Lewis Hamilton are the only drivers to finish their debut seasons as World Championship runners-up. Villeneuve achieved this for Williams behind Damon Hill in 1996 and Hamilton for McLaren in 2007. However, both drivers did win the title a year later.

IF AT FIRST YOU DON'T SUCCEED...

Nigel Mansell would have been world champion in 1986 but for his blowout in the Adelaide finale that left him ranked second behind Alain Prost. But he persevered and was runner-up twice more, in 1987 and 1991, before it all came good and he finally landed his World Championship crown for Williams in 1992.

WHEN 10 WINS IS NOT ENOUGH

With seasons containing ever more grands prix, hitting 21 in 2016, a record was set for the most grands prix won in a season without winning a title, as Lewis Hamilton won 10 for Mercedes, three more than the previous unwanted record, but teammate Nico Rosberg won his title with one fewer wins.

Below Nigel Mansell had his first title in his sights in 1986, but had to wait to 1992 to claim it.

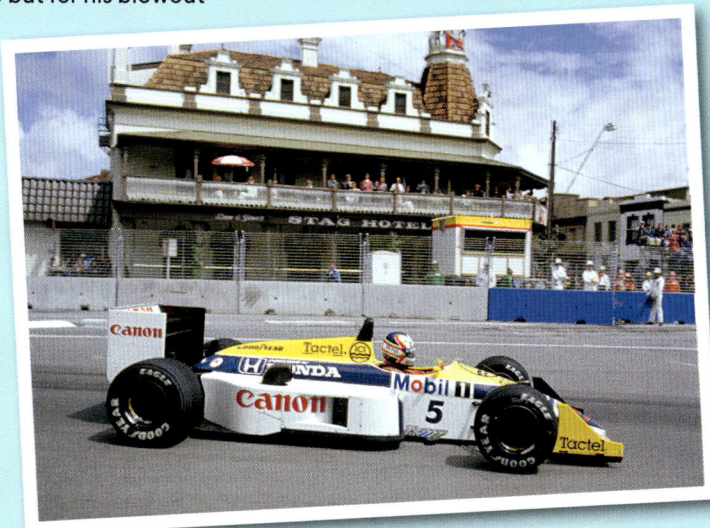

DRIVERS WITH MOST CAREER RACE WINS WITHOUT WINNING A WORLD CHAMPIONSHIP

1	Stirling Moss	16
2	David Coulthard	13
3	Carlos Reutemann	12
4	Rubens Barrichello	11
=	Felipe Massa	11
6	Gerhard Berger	10
=	Ronnie Peterson	10
=	Valtteri Bottas	10
9	Mark Webber	9
10	Jacky Ickx	8
=	Daniel Ricciardo	8
=	Charles Leclerc	8

WINS

I WANT TO BREAK THROUGH

Occasionally there are seasons where a couple of drivers win their first races – such as in 2024 – but there has never quite been a season like 1982. In total five different drivers logged a maiden victory in a tumultuous season laced by triumph and tragedy. Riccardo Patrese, Patrick Tambay, Elio de Angelis, eventual champion Keke Rosberg and Michele Alboreto all scored their first wins in this season.

CHECO-MATE

Sergio Perez had carved a reputation as a plucky underdog and came close to winning on a handful of occasions. But finally in 2020 his day came as he performed brilliantly for Racing Point, recovering from a lap one accident to rise to first place in Bahrain. It was Perez's 190th race, surpassing the 130 races it took for Mark Webber to end his drought in 2009. Carlos Sainz has since slotted into second place on the list, after taking exactly 150 races to score his maiden win.

Below It took 190 tries, but finally Sergio Perez won a race in Bahrain in 2020.

Above Sebastian Vettel winning in Monza 2008 for Toro Rosso.

WIN ONE, WIN TWO

Not many drivers take their first two victories for different teams, and fewer even manage to do it when it is their team's first victories too. Step forward Sebastian Vettel. His win at Monza in 2008 was his maiden victory, and the first for underdog Toro Rosso, while his next career win came at Shanghai in 2009, which was the first triumph for Red Bull Racing.

TEN THEN NINE

Max Verstappen broke a decade-old record in 2023 when he won 10 successive grands prix and, having been defeated in Singapore, went on to win the next nine grands prix – equalling the record previously held by Alberto Ascari and Sebastian Vettel that he had recently broken. It meant Verstappen won 19 grands prix out of 20 held. On both occasions his streak was ended by Ferrari driver Carlos Sainz.

WINS TOGETHER

Lewis Hamilton and Mercedes is the most successful partnership in F1 with 84 victories, with Michael Schumacher and Ferrari next on 72 wins. Max Verstappen has won 63 races with Red Bull, while McLaren's top driver is Ayrton Senna, on 35 wins. Williams' most successful operator, Nigel Mansell, took 27 victories.

Above Lewis Hamilton won 84 times in Mercedes colours.

SWEET SIXTEEN

Lewis Hamilton has the greatest number of victories so perhaps it isn't surprising that he has claimed a win across the most number of different seasons. Hamilton won at least one race in each of his first 15 years in Formula One, between 2007 and 2021, and after a two-year win-less streak returned to winning ways in 2024, making it 16 seasons in which the Briton has stood atop the podium.

COME IN NUMBER 115

Through Formula One history there have been 115 different drivers who can call themselves race winners. The century was brought up by Heikki Kovalainen, whose win at the 2008 Hungarian GP turned out to be his sole career triumph, while the latest new victor is Oscar Piastri. The Australian added his name to the list of winners in 2024, also at the Hungarian GP, and also while driving for McLaren.

EVERYONE HAS A GO

The 1982 season was extremely competitive as 11 drivers took at least one win in the 16 grands prix. Keke Rosberg ended the year as world champion ahead of Didier Pironi and John Watson (both of whom scored two wins), with Michele Alboreto, Rene Arnoux (two), Elio de Angelis, Niki Lauda (two), Riccardo Patrese, Nelson Piquet, Alain Prost (two) and Patrick Tambay also enjoying victories.

TOO GOOD TO BE A FLUKE

When a driver dominates, a lot of F1 fans point to the merits of the car. So, perhaps one of the best ways to prove that a driver's input is vital is to find the driver who has won for the most different teams. Step forward Stirling Moss, who won for five marques – Mercedes, Maserati, Vanwall, Cooper and Lotus. Juan Manuel Fangio and Alain Prost both won for four teams.

NO DISCERNIBLE PATTERN

The 1982 World Championship in which 11 drivers won grands prix also produced the longest run of different winning drivers. Riccardo Patrese's surprise win in the sixth round in Monaco triggered a sequence of wins for different drivers that ran through to Keke Rosberg's win in the 14th round in the Swiss GP. There's never been another year like it.

Left With his victory at Monaco in 1982, Riccardo Patrese started a historic run of nine grands prix with a different winner each time.

THE LAP THAT COUNTS

Jochen Rindt was an expert at leading the final lap rather than the first one, and he pulled off the trick to the greatest effect at Monaco in 1970 when he hunted down Jack Brabham and pressured him into a mistake at the first corner of the final lap. Brabham was pipped in another last-lap changeover later that year at Brands Hatch, when again Rindt demoted him as he coasted to the finish line, out of fuel.

FIRST TO 10

As F1 found its feet through the 1950s, drivers started to lay down markers of their excellence. The first to achieve 10 wins was not five-time champion Juan Manuel Fangio but Alberto Ascari, who had the good fortune to be leading Ferrari's attack when it had the pick of the cars. His victory in the 1953 Dutch GP made him the first driver to double figures.

HIT THE GROUND RUNNING

Nigel Mansell enjoyed the best start to a season when he won the first five grands prix in 1992. It could have been the first six but for a wheel issue at Monaco, and his subsequent charge just failed to overhaul Ayrton Senna's McLaren. Michael Schumacher matched this feat in 2004.

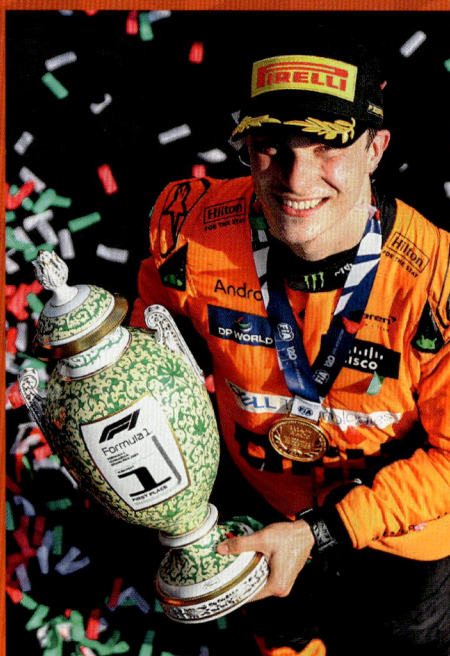

AND THE OSCAR GOES TO...

Oscar Piastri became the first driver born in the 21st century to win a grand prix when he scored his breakthrough win with McLaren in 2024. Piastri, born in 2001, led home McLaren team-mate Lando Norris to take his maiden victory at the Hungarian GP.

Left Oscar Piastri became the first driver born in the 21st century to win a grand prix.

COMETH THE HOUR, COMETH THE MAN

There are 25 drivers who have won just one solitary grand prix. How did it all go so right just the once then never again? In the case of Jean-Pierre Beltoise, a former French motorcycle racing champion who showed immense promise, he won in extremely wet conditions at Monaco in 1972. His BRM lacked the regular power of the other cars on the grid, but the rain negated this disadvantage and he never again had the equipment to add to that tally.

A LITTLE HELP FROM YOUR FRIENDS

Shared wins were allowed until 1957, when a team's lead driver might commandeer one of his team-mates' cars to complete the race. The points would be split between them. This happened three times for wins, and many more times for lower placings. Juan Manuel Fangio took over Luigi Fagioli's Alfa Romeo to win the 1951 French GP and did the same to Ferrari team-mate Luigi Musso in Argentina in 1956.

WHEN OVERTAKING IS ESSENTIAL

With overtaking becoming increasingly difficult, the possibility of a driver advancing from the rear of the grid is becoming less likely. Therefore, John Watson's record, set at the 1983 US West GP at Long Beach, California, of winning from 22nd on the grid, is probably guaranteed its place in the history books for ever. He also holds the record for the third best charge, from 17th to 1st at Detroit in 1982.

Left John Watson in fine form in a spectacular US West GP at Long Beach in 1983 when he drove his McLaren from 22nd to first.

Above Nico Hulkenberg has been around the block a few times, but has never finished higher than fourth place.

TOP 10 DRIVERS WITH MOST GRAND PRIX WINS

1	Lewis Hamilton	105
2	Michael Schumacher	91
3	Max Verstappen	63
4	Sebastian Vettel	53
5	Alain Prost	51
6	Ayrton Senna	41
7	Fernando Alonso	32
8	Nigel Mansell	31
9	Jackie Stewart	27
10	Jim Clark	25
=	Niki Lauda	25

WINLESS NICO

The record for the most races without a grand prix victory belongs to Nico Hulkenberg. The German, a stalwart of Formula One's midfield, has started 227 races without triumphing – his best result throughout his career has been fourth place.

BY THE SKIN OF HIS TEETH

A last-lap lead change in the Italian GP at Monza in 1971 produced the closest finish in F1 history. Peter Gethin nosed his BRM to the front of a five-car pack after a slipstreaming dash out of the final corner, doing his best to gain the stewards' confidence that he'd secured victory by punching the air ostentatiously as he crossed the line. His margin of victory was 0.01 seconds over March's Ronnie Peterson, with the first five covered by just 0.61 seconds.

FIRST IMPRESSIONS

Jacques Villeneuve and Lewis Hamilton share the record for the most grand prix wins in their maiden F1 seasons. Their tally is four apiece, with Villeneuve scoring the first of these with Williams on his fourth outing, at the Nürburgring in 1996, and Hamilton taking his McLaren first past the chequered flag at his sixth attempt, in Canada in 2007. Juan Manuel Fangio and Giuseppe Farina both won three grands prix in 1950, the inaugural year of the F1 World Championship.

GOLD AT SILVERSTONE

Lewis Hamilton grabbed another record in 2024 when he claimed victory at Silverstone. It was the ninth of his career at the British Grand Prix, the most times that a driver has won a single grand prix. Hamilton has won eight times at the Hungarian Grand Prix, while Michael Schumacher triumphed at the French Grand Prix on eight occasions as well.

Below Peter Gethin noses his BRM past Ronnie Peterson's March (25) for the closest grand prix finish ever.

BEATING YOUR RIVAL

Lewis Hamilton and Max Verstappen have raced together for a decade, and are first and third respectively on the all-time win list, so it shouldn't be a shock that they are the duo to have been 1-2 together most often. The pair have finished together on the top two steps of the podium 37 times between 2016 and 2024, 21 times in Hamilton's favour, and 16 times with Verstappen in front.

STARTING WITH A BANG

Two drivers hold the almost unbelievable record of winning a grand prix on their World Championship debut. Giuseppe Farina achieved this in 1950, in the first ever World Championship (he went on to win the title), but the more significant achievement was by Giancarlo Baghetti. Having been promoted through the Ferrari ranks in their search for a young Italian driver, in 1961 he won two non-championship races and then won a slipstreamer by 0.1 secs from Dan Gurney on his World Championship debut in the French GP at Reims. He never won again. Since then, only Jacques Villeneuve has come close to the same achievement, finishing as runner-up in Australia in 1996.

Below Ferrari's Giancarlo Baghetti holds off Dan Gurney to win on his debut in the 1961 French GP at Reims.

A QUARTET OF HAT-TRICKS

A grand slam is when a driver starts from pole position, leads every lap, sets the fastest lap and wins. Twenty drivers have achieved this, but four managed it three times in one season: Alberto Ascari, Jim Clark, Nigel Mansell and Lewis Hamilton, and all achieved this feat in a world-title-winning year. Ascari did it for Ferrari in 1952 at Rouen-les-Essarts, Nürburgring and Zandvoort. Clark was next in 1963 at Zandvoort, Reims and Mexico City. Mansell won for Williams at Kyalami, Catalunya and Silverstone. Mercedes' Hamilton did it in 2017, at Shanghai, Montreal and Silverstone.

TAKING ON SCHUEY'S MANTLE

When Sebastian Vettel scored his first victory at the 2008 Italian GP for Toro Rosso, he became the first German driver other than a Schumacher (Ralf six, Michael 91) to win a grand prix since Heinz-Harald Frentzen beat Ralf to the finish for Jordan in the 1999 Italian GP at Monza.

DUTCH DELIGHT

The Netherlands didn't have a race winner until 2016, when Max Verstappen triumphed, but the country is already fifth in the all-time win list by countries – and that's solely down to Verstappen. It is the country highest in the list to be carried by a single driver.

INDIAN SUMMER

The Indian GP at the Buddh International Circuit was short-lived but popular with Sebastian Vettel. The German ace won all three Indian GPs in 2011, 2012 and 2013, doing so from pole position every time. Vettel's victory in 2013 also ensured he sealed his fourth and final world title at the grand prix.

TOP 10 COUNTRIES WITH MOST GRAND PRIX WINS

1	Great Britain	316
2	Germany	179
3	Brazil	101
4	France	81
5	Netherlands	63
6	Finland	57
7	Australia	45
8	Italy	43
9	Austria	41
10	Argentina	38

Below Master of precision Jackie Stewart won the 1969 Spanish GP at Montjuich Park for Matra by two laps (4.711 miles).

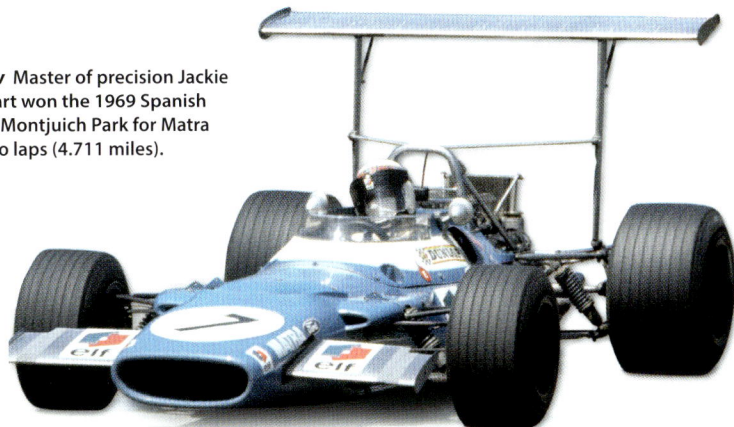

WHO'D HAVE THOUGHT IT?

Throughout F1 history there have been wins that have surprised everyone. Jo Bonnier's victory in the 1959 Dutch GP is a good example, as no one thought that a BRM would ever win. Vittorio Brambilla's win in Austria in 1975 came as a shock as no one expected that the wild Italian would be the one to stay on the track in the wet. However, Giancarlo Baghetti's win on his World Championship debut in France in 1961 was the most surprising as he had to work his way forward from 13th to do it, and it required his team-mates to retire to aid his progress.

WINNING BY A COUNTRY MILE

Jackie Stewart was always an exponent of "winning at the lowest speed possible". Risks weren't something he considered worthwhile but the policy paid off as he won 27 grands prix and three World Championships. Stewart also holds the record for the largest winning margin in F1 history – two laps. At the 1969 Spanish GP at Montjuich Park he won by 4.711 miles. Damon Hill also won by two laps in the 1995 Australian GP at Adelaide, but his winning margin was 4.698 miles.

MORE THAN THE CHAMP

There have been 13 seasons in history where a driver other than the eventual world champion won the most grands prix that year, and the driver to have won most races in a season without winning the title is Lewis Hamilton. In his 2016 battle against Mercedes team-mate Nico Rosberg, Hamilton won 10 grands prix but missed out on the title by five points to Rosberg, who won nine races.

MAGIC MONEGASQUE

Monaco became the 23rd nation to produce a Formula One race winner through Charles Leclerc. The Ferrari driver claimed his maiden victory at the 2019 Belgian GP, in turn becoming the third-youngest race winner in history, aged 21 years and 320 days.

SMALLEST WINNING MARGIN

MARGIN	WINNER	RUNNER-UP	GP	YEAR
0.010 sec	Peter Gethin	Ronnie Peterson	Italian	1971
0.011 sec	Rubens Barrichello	Michael Schumacher	US	2002
0.014 sec	Ayrton Senna	Nigel Mansell	Spanish	1986
0.050 sec	Elio de Angelis	Keke Rosberg	Austrian	1982
0.080 sec	Jackie Stewart	Jochen Rindt	Italian	1969
0.100 sec	Juan Manuel Fangio	Karl Kling	French	1954
0.100 sec	Giancarlo Baghetti	Dan Gurney	French	1961
0.174 sec	Michael Schumacher	Rubens Barrichello	Canadian	2000
0.179 sec	Max Verstappen	Lewis Hamilton	Australian	2023
0.182 sec*	Michael Schumacher	Rubens Barrichello	Austrian	2002
0.200 sec*	Stirling Moss	Juan Manuel Fangio	British	1955

* The win was donated to a team-mate due to team orders or benevolence

BEAT THE CLOCK

In terms of time, rather than laps, Stirling Moss holds the record for the greatest margin of victory. He took the chequered flag with his Vanwall 5 mins and 12.75 secs clear of Mike Hawthorn in the Portuguese GP at Oporto in 1958. Hawthorn half spun on the final lap and Moss, not wanting to embarrass his title rival by lapping him, slowed to let him rejoin, as he himself ambled around his slowing-down lap.

Left Stirling Moss was in a class of his own in his Vanwall in the 1958 Portuguese GP, winning by more than five minutes.

POLE POSITIONS

AS EASY AS ONE, TWO, THREE

Achieving pole position, setting the fastest lap and then winning the race has been achieved by Michael Schumacher on 22 occasions. Lewis Hamilton is next, on 19, followed by Max Verstappen, on 13, who did it a record six times in the 2023 season.

FOUR IN A ROW

British fans expected a home driver to be on pole at the British GP in the 1950s and 1960s. Stirling Moss was on pole for four straight years, 1955–58, as the race alternated between Aintree and Silverstone. Then Jim Clark matched that feat between 1962–65, at Aintree, twice at Silverstone and Brands Hatch. The Scottish Lotus driver didn't manage pole in 1966, but was at the front of the grid in 1967.

A QUARTER CENTURY

Juan Manuel Fangio knew that the best place from which to start a grand prix was from pole, which he first did at Monaco in 1950. Fittingly, he became the first driver to reach 25 poles, doing so at the same venue seven years later.

HAMILTON'S FAST NINE

Lewis Hamilton, Michael Schumacher and Ayrton Senna jointly held the record of most poles at one circuit, with eight. Hamilton's exploits came at Melbourne, Schumacher's at Suzuka and Senna's at Imola. But Hamilton moved clear in 2023 when he scored a ninth pole position around the Hungaroring.

Above Jackie Stewart gave March pole on its debut at Kyalami in 1970.

🏆 POLE AT THE FIRST ATTEMPT

Alfa Romeo had one of its cars qualify on pole position for its first F1 grand prix, as the Italian team dominated the inaugural 1950 event. So too then did Brawn, in Australia in 2009. More impressive was March filling the first two grid slots on its World Championship debut in South Africa in 1970, with Jackie Stewart ahead of Chris Amon.

Above Lewis Hamilton has proven to be the king of the Hungaroring, with nine poles.

NO ROMAIN EMPIRE

Romain Grosjean was rarely one to lift his right foot but the Franco-Swiss driver holds the record for the most grands prix without a pole position. Grosjean started 179 grands prix between 2009 and 2020 for Renault, Lotus and Haas, and while he managed one front row grid spot in Hungary in 2012, he was never able to take top spot.

PEREZ'S POLE

Sergio Perez has never had a reputation as a qualifying specialist so it should be little surprise that he holds the record for the most grands prix before taking a pole position. Perez finally fronted the pack at the 219th attempt, at Jeddah, in 2022. It did not exactly open the floodgates for Perez, and somewhat remarkably his second career pole came at the same track in 2023. That gave him a 66 per cent one-lap success rate at Jeddah, and 0 per cent at every other venue.

THE ICEMAN WAITETH

Kimi Räikkönen scored 18 pole positions during his career but had to wait eight years and 339 days between numbers 16 and 17!

Above Juan Pablo Montoya leads the field from pole position at the 2005 Italian GP.

TOP 10 DRIVERS WITH MOST POLE POSITIONS

1	Lewis Hamilton	104
2	Michael Schumacher	68
3	Ayrton Senna	65
4	Sebastian Vettel	57
5	Max Verstappen	40
6	Jim Clark	33
=	Alain Prost	33
8	Nigel Mansell	32
9	Nico Rosberg	30
10	Juan Manuel Fangio	29

THE FINE NINE

The 2005 season set a record for having the most drivers take pole position. The season started with an aggregate qualifying format – which was dropped – and had regulations that meant drivers qualified with their starting fuel onboard, thus leading to some distorted sessions. Fernando Alonso, Jenson Button, Giancarlo Fisichella, Nick Heidfeld, Juan Pablo Montoya, Kimi Räikkönen, Michael Schumacher, Ralf Schumacher and Jarno Trulli all claimed a pole position.

GR-EIGHT LAPS

Two drivers share the honour of managing to take eight successive pole positions. Ayrton Senna managed it between the Spanish GP of 1988 and USA GP of 1989, with Max Verstappen replicating the achievement between the Abu Dhabi GP of 2023 and Emilia Romagna GP of 2024.

I'M FEELING 32

It shouldn't be a shock that the driver with the most pole positions in history also holds the record for achieving them at the most number of different circuits. Lewis Hamilton has taken pole positions at 32 different venues during his career, failing to record pole at only six of the other circuits where he has raced. The 'least' successful track for Hamilton was Istanbul Park, where he competed seven times without taking pole position – but he did start from second, and win the race, twice.

POLES BUT NO WINS

Chris Amon holds the unwanted record of having the most pole positions – five – without a career victory. Amon at least contended for victories; Teo Fabi scored three pole positions in 1985 and 1986 but never led a single lap of a grand prix. Conversely there were two seasons – Denny Hulme in 1967 and Niki Lauda in 1984 – when the world champion that year did not claim a single pole position.

ELECTRIC LECLERC

Charles Leclerc has been known as a one-lap specialist since arriving onto the scene in 2018 and he has regularly pulled off a mind-bending qualifying lap. Consequently Leclerc now holds the accolade of setting the most pole positions without winning a world title. Leclerc has started up front 26 times in his career, meaning he is almost into the top 10 all-time list of all drivers.

A SHOOTING STAR

Sebastian Vettel holds the record for being the youngest pole-sitter, when he secured his place at the front of the grid at the 2008 Italian GP at the age of 21 years and 73 days. The previous holder of this record was Fernando Alonso at the 2003 Malaysian GP, at the age of 21 years and 236 days.

Below Sebastian Vettel scored the fourth of his poles at Silverstone in 2009.

FASTEST LAPS

HITTING DOUBLE FIGURES

Michael Schumacher and Kimi Räikkönen both gave Ferrari a return of 10 fastest laps in a single season, with the German achieving this impressive tally in 2004 and the Finn doing the same in 2008, both from 18 starts. Räikkönen also claimed 10 fastest laps for McLaren in 2005, although this percentage is slightly lower because there were 19 grands prix that season.

ASCARI'S DOMINANCE

Alberto Ascari's dominance of the 1952 World Championship left him with a tally of six fastest laps from seven rounds as he raced to the title for Ferrari. The Indy 500 was also a round of the World Championship then, but he, like other F1 drivers, gave it a miss. So, his tally was even better than the six from eight that some record books show.

Below Alberto Ascari drove his Ferrari to the fastest lap in every grand prix he contested in 1952.

Above Esteban Gutierrez set the fastest lap in Spain in 2013 – before he'd even scored a point.

NO ONE'S AN EXPERT

The Jarama circuit outside Madrid hosted nine Spanish GPs between 1968 and 1991, but not one driver was able to take the fastest lap more than once. A record nine different drivers set fastest lap times, starting with Matra's Jean-Pierre Beltoise in 1968 and ending with Williams's reigning world champion Alan Jones in 1981. Rival Spanish circuit Jerez ended up with a similar record, with seven drivers setting fastest laps there on F1's seven visits.

A FASTEST LAP BEFORE A POINT

There have been 138 different drivers to have recorded a fastest lap, and some unexpected faces crop up on the list. That includes Esteban Gutierrez, who adopted a different strategy at the 2013 Spanish Grand Prix. The Sauber driver not only led the race, but also set fastest lap, despite eventually finishing 11th. It meant the Mexican set a fastest lap before he'd even scored a point in Formula One.

START AS THEY MEAN TO GO ON

After the first 1950 season, just three drivers have set a fastest lap on their F1 debut. Masahiro Hasemi's amazing 1976 Japanese GP was the first, followed by Jacques Villeneuve in Australia in 1996. Only Nico Roseberg, at Bahrain in 2006, has achieved it since.

TOP 10 FASTEST LAPS BY DRIVER NATIONALITY

1	Great Britain	276
2	Germany	159
3	Finland	95
4	France	93
5	Brazil	88
6	Australia	64
7	Italy	51
8	Austria	49
9	Argentina	37
10	USA	36

Above Michael Schumacher set the first of his 77 fastest laps for Benetton in the 1992 Belgian GP.

TOP 10 DRIVERS WHO HAVE SET MOST FASTEST LAPS

1	Michael Schumacher	77
2	Lewis Hamilton	67
3	Kimi Räikkönen	46
4	Alain Prost	41
5	Sebastian Vettel	38
6	Max Verstappen	33
7	Nigel Mansell	30
8	Jim Clark	28
9	Fernando Alonso	26
10	Mika Häkkinen	25

AN HONOUR, BUT...

Kimi Räikkönen's 10 fastest laps in 2008 – six of them in succession – reflected well on his ability, but this was at a time of refuelling pit stops and it actually showed his ambition to impress rather than his Ferrari's speed over a race distance, and he ended the year third overall despite his 55.55 per cent strike rate. Jim Clark hit an identical figure for Lotus in 1962, also without becoming world champion.

WAS IT REALLY?

Every now and again a fastest lap is set by a driver that no one had expected to be so fast. This often happens when a driver with nothing to lose pits for fresh tyres. The most notorious example was Masahiro Hasemi setting the fastest lap on his F1 debut in the 1976 Japanese GP. There were mitigating circumstances in that he knew Fuji Speedway well and it was F1's first visit. Furthermore, it was incredibly wet and his Kojima chassis was on Dunlop wets that were superior to the Goodyears used by the regulars, but still...

A POINT TO PROVE

From 2019 until 2024, F1 awarded a bonus point to the driver who set the fastest lap – and also finished inside the top 10 of a race. That led to some more strategic variance during the closing stages of a race as sometimes drivers with a buffer behind them have stopped for fresh tyres. There have also been cases of teams using drivers to push for a fastest lap to try and take a bonus point away from a rival.

FASTEST AT THE MOST

Michael Schumacher still holds the record for the most number of fastest laps, at 77, 10 more than Lewis Hamilton, but the Briton has clocked the best time at the highest number of different circuits. While Schumacher's 77 fastest laps were set across 24 different venues, the 67 posted to date by Hamilton have come at 27 different circuits. The pair have both set a record seven fastest laps at one circuit, with Hamilton prolific at Monza, and Schumacher rapid around Barcelona.

Above Gerhard Berger claimed 21 fastest laps during his Formula One career.

WHAT A BERGER

Gerhard Berger had a couple of fast team-mates during his time in Formula One – most notably Ayrton Senna and Nigel Mansell – but the jovial Austrian held his own, scoring 10 wins across a lengthy career. He also recorded 21 fastest laps, the most achieved by a driver who never won the championship in Formula One. Berger opened his account at the 1986 German GP at Hockenheim and took his final fastest lap at the same venue 11 years later – which was also the race at which he claimed his final pole position and victory.

POINTS

JUST WHAT'S THE POINT?

Prior to the start of the 2009 season, Luca Badoer held an unwanted record: after 49 races he had not scored a single point. He hoped to put a stop to that when he stood in at Ferrari for the injured Felipe Massa. Unfortunately he didn't score, and he has extended that record to 51 races without a point. The closest he has come to a points finish was in the 1999 European GP, when he had to retire his Minardi while in fourth.

⏱ MAKING THE MOST OF EACH TIME OUT

With points having been awarded down to 10th place since 2010, it's easier to score now than in F1's early days. McLaren set a record in 2013, when it completed 64 consecutive scoring races before it failed at the Canadian GP, but Ferrari's run continued until the 15th race of the 2014 season, a total of 81 races.

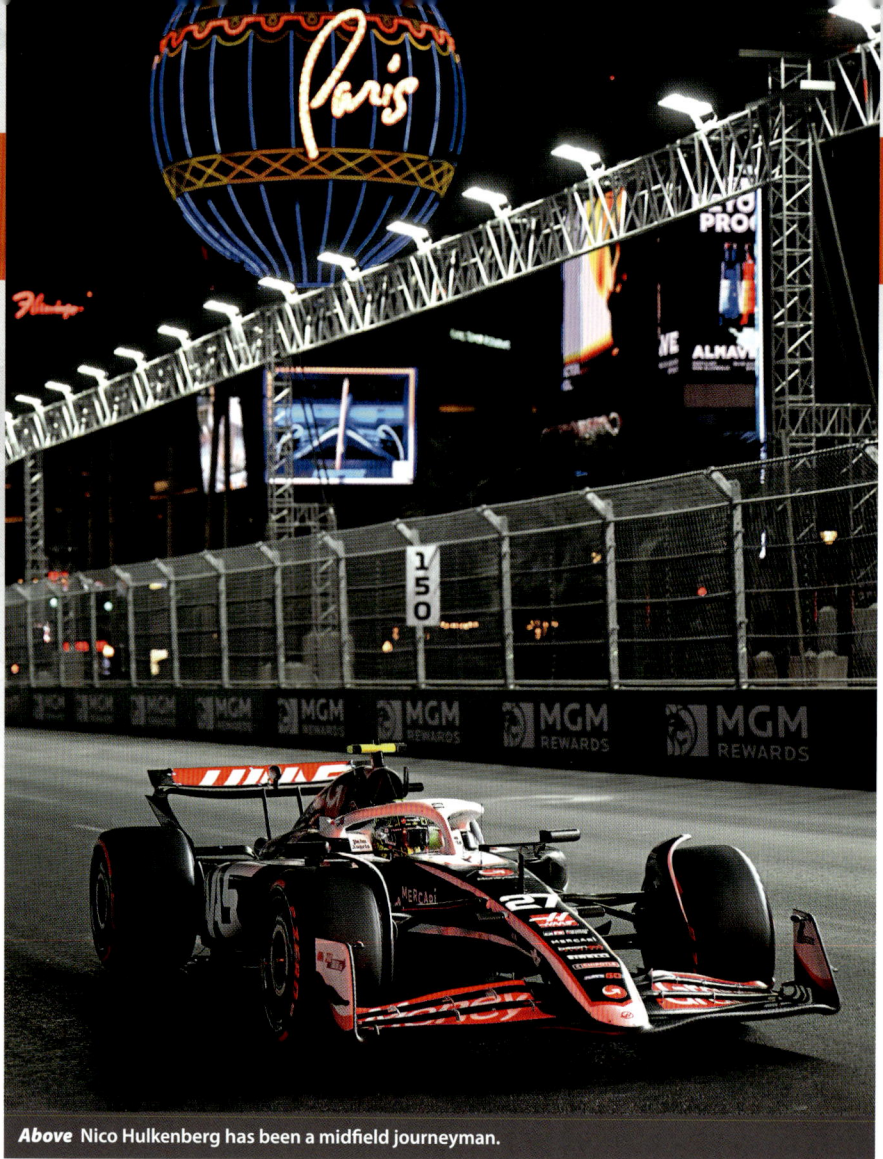

Above Nico Hulkenberg has been a midfield journeyman.

A HELPING HAND

The changes to the points system from the start of the 2010 season, when a win became 25 points (from 10) and the first 10 places scored points (it had been eight), had a dramatic effect on the all-time points table. By 2016, not one driver who raced mainly when it was nine points for a win, remained in the top 10. Most of Michael Schumacher's 1,566 points came when wins were worth 10 points.

HULKEN-POINTS

Nico Hulkenberg has started the most number of grands prix without a victory so naturally he also has the highest points total without the top accolade. Hulkenberg has scored 571 points across his career with spells at Williams, Force India, Sauber, Renault, Racing Point, Aston Martin and Haas. That puts him clear of the 391 amassed by fellow winless driver Romain Grosjean. Hulkenberg has also scored

those points across 111 different races, well clear of the 70 races in which Nick Heidfeld scored but failed to win.

KUBICA'S EIGHT-YEAR WAIT

Robert Kubica rounded out the 2010 season with points in Abu Dhabi but it proved to be his last race for eight years after sustaining life-altering injuries in a rally accident in early 2011. Kubica eventually embarked on a Formula One comeback, landing a race seat with Williams in 2019. Unfortunately the squad was in a competitive slump, but Kubica managed 10th in a rain-hit race at Hockenheim, setting a new record of eight years and 254 days between successive points finishes.

Left Robert Kubica's heroic Formula One return with Williams peaked with 10th place.

THE BEAR NECESSITIES

Oliver Bearman participated in three grands prix in the 2024 season and became the first driver to score points for different teams in his first two starts. Bearman was drafted in to Ferrari at Jeddah to replace Carlos Sainz, sidelined by appendicitis, and scored seventh place on his debut. Later the same season he was parachuted into Haas to take the spot of the suspended Kevin Magnussen in Baku, and claimed 10th position.

VERSTAPPEN'S MEGA HAUL

Max Verstappen's mercurial 2023 season set a new record both for the most points in a season and for the highest percentage of points accumulated. Verstappen gathered 575 of the 620 points available through the course of the season, equating to 92.74 per cent of the total possible score. That beat the previous percentage record of 84.71, held by Michael Schumacher, when he amassed 144 of the possible 170 points on offer in 2002.

MOST POINTS, NO TITLE

Lewis Hamilton has seven world titles and came agonisingly close to an eighth in 2021, when he was denied in a controversial finale. Hamilton claimed 387.5 points in 2021 to set a new record of the number of points accumulated in a season without winning the title. That eclipsed the previous record of 380, which was achieved by the runner-up of the 2016 season – also Hamilton.

ON DEBUT

353 drivers have scored points in Formula One – and a total of 79 have done so on their debuts. Lewis Hamilton is the driver to have had the longest points streak from debut, scoring in each of his first nine grands prix. The driver to have started the most number of grands prix is Nicola Larini, who finally broke his duck on his 44th start, taking second at the sombre 1994 San Marino GP.

TOP 10 DRIVERS WITH MOST GRAND PRIX POINTS

1	Lewis Hamilton	4,862.5
2	Sebastian Vettel	3,098
3	Max Verstappen	3,023.5
4	Fernando Alonso	2,337
5	Kimi Räikkönen	1,873
6	Valtteri Bottas	1,797
7	Sergio Perez	1,638
8	Nico Rosberg	1,594.5
9	Michael Schumacher	1,566
10	Charles Leclerc	1,430

Figures are gross, i.e. including scores that were later dropped

🏆 FROM CHAMPION TO SHORT RATIONS

America's first F1 world champion, Phil Hill, had a rapid fall from grace after his 1961 World Championship with Ferrari. Just over a year after winning the title he made a terrible mistake and

Above Phil Hill raced a red car in 1963, but it was an ATS not a Ferrari.

followed some of Ferrari's staff to ATS, a new Italian team that proved to be a disaster. So, shortly after he peaked, he plummeted and ended up with a career tally of 98 points, the fewest for a world champion.

POINTS FOR ALL

Even though points were allocated to only the first six finishers back in 1989, a record 29 different drivers made it onto the scoreboard that year, from world champion Alain Prost on 76 points, down to Philippe Alliot, Olivier Grouillard, Luis Perez Sala and Gabriele Tarquini on one point apiece. It was an incredible year, as 39 cars turned up for most races and a system of pre-qualifying had to be used to clear out the slowest before normal qualifying could start.

HAMILTON'S TWO LONG RUNS

Lewis Hamilton set a new record when he scored points for 33 successive races between the 2016 Japanese GP and 2018 French GP, before retiring in Austria due to an engine issue. Hamilton consequently started another run at the following event in Britain, and scored a top 10 finish through the 2020 Bahrain GP, after which he was sidelined due to Covid-19. Hamilton's new record run of 48 races in the points was also a record for successive races finished – with the one glitch nine laps from home denying him an 82-race streak!

Left Lewis Hamilton won the 2020 Bahrain GP, his record 48th successive race in the points, after which he was sidelined by Covid-19.

CAREER DURATION

NEVER GIVE UP!

Some drivers just never want to give up. Witness the haste with which the then 41-year-old Michael Schumacher jumped at the chance to end a three-year spell in retirement to return to F1 with Mercedes in 2010, racing through until the end of 2012. This is nothing compared to Jan Lammers, who returned to F1 in 1992 at the age of 36 after a break of 10 years and 114 days. He now runs the Dutch Grand Prix.

BLINK AND YOU MISSED IT

Marco Apicella was a decent driver, so it's odd that the Italian's spell in F1 remains the shortest on record. He had one crack at F1, with the Jordan team after Thierry Boutsen had been dropped, in his home race at Monza in 1993. He qualified 23rd out of 26 and, unfortunately, was unable to avoid the melee into the first chicane on the opening lap. His distance covered as an F1 racer was around ½ mile.

F1: IT'S A CAREER

Two-time champion Fernando Alonso is the face of longevity on the driving front, but Bernie Ecclestone clocked up 59 years from his first appearance as a driver-manager to his role as F1's ringmaster.

Above Fernando Alonso, a veteran of 21 seasons and over 400 races.

A-LONG-SO

Fernando Alonso holds nearly every record when it comes to career duration; Alonso has participated in 21 different Formula One seasons, became the first driver to start over 400 grands prix, and holds record for the longest time between scoring his first points and podium and most recent results. Alonso will enter the 2025 season lining up against five drivers who weren't born when he debuted in Formula One in 2001.

SILVER-HAIRED FLIER

Racer Luigi Fagioli showed that staying power is rewarded. Fagioli raced for Alfa Romeo in 1933, and was still with the team in 1951 when he took his one win in the World Championship, 22 days past his 53rd birthday, making him the oldest person to win an F1 race. The victory came in strange circumstances as he was pulled out of his car when he pitted and was forced to hand it over to team leader Juan Manuel Fangio, whose car was having mechanical difficulties. Fangio went on to win, but Fagioli was so unhappy, despite being credited with the win (shared with Fangio), that he quit.

Below Luigi Fagioli was still with Alfa Romeo 18 years after joining it when he raced to his final win in 1951.

TOP 10 LONGEST SERVERS

	NAME	YEAR	DURATION
1	Bernie Ecclestone	(1957–2016)	60 years
2	Frank Williams	(1969–2020)	51 years
3	Herbie Blash	(1968–2016)	49 years
4	Ron Dennis	(1966–2009, 2016)	47 years
5	Tyler Alexander	(1966–2009)	44 years
6	Luca Montezemolo	(1973–2014)	42 years
7	Jo Ramirez	(1961–2001)	41 years
=	Giampaolo Dallara	(1970–2010)	41 years
9	Max Mosley	(1970–2009)	40 years
10	Eric Broadley	(1960–1997)	38 years

Above Niki Lauda winning 1984 title for McLaren.

🏆 HAMILTON'S RECORD STAY

Lewis Hamilton has set a host of success records in his career, and most of them were achieved with Mercedes. Therefore it is perhaps inevitable that the Hamilton-Mercedes partnership has been the longest in Formula One history, stretching out across 12 seasons and 246 grands prix between 2013 and 2024. That eclipses the Max Verstappen-Red Bull partnership, which is at 186 grands prix, with the Michael Schumacher-Ferrari connection now shuffled down to third, having lasted 180 grands prix.

NO LOTTERY WIN

Apicella's record was almost matched a couple of decades later by Andre Lotterer. The three-times Le Mans winner was drafted in to race for Caterham at the 2014 Belgian GP and he outqualified team-mate and future Indianapolis 500 winner Marcus Ericsson. But Lotterer suffered an engine failure after the opening lap, forcing him to retire, in what proved to be his sole start.

YOUNGEST FAREWELL

Plenty of drivers have made their debuts at a young age and – assuming Ollie Bearman goes on to have a long and prosperous career – the youngest to start their last race is Esteban Tuero. The Argentine became one of the first teenagers to compete in Formula One, with Minardi, when he debuted in 1998. But Tuero walked away from Formula One at the end of his rookie campaign, starting his last grand prix at the tender age of 20 years and 193 days. Only 21 drivers in history have debuted at a younger age than Tuero was at his swansong.

A SEVEN-YEAR ITCH

Niki Lauda won three world titles and he holds the record for the longest wait between two titles. Lauda won the 1977 title, his second, and retired, before being brought back by McLaren, going on to win the 1984 crown – a gap of seven years. Both Jack Brabham, between 1960 and 1966, Graham Hill, between 1962 and 1968, and Lewis Hamilton, between 2008 and 2014, had a six-year gap between successive championship victories. Hamilton is the only driver to have won titles across three decades– the 2000s, 2010s and 2020s.

Above Alex Wurz spent years as a test driver before returning to racing in 2005 and finishing third at Imola.

PAYBACK TIME

Alex Wurz's lengthy period as a test driver was rewarded when he subbed for McLaren in the 2005 San Marino GP at Imola. He was standing in for the injured Juan Pablo Montoya, and he came away with third place. This gave him the record for the longest period of time between podium places, at seven years and 313 days. However, he didn't get to enjoy his moment in the sun this time as he was promoted to third after the podium ceremony had taken place because Jenson Button was subsequently disqualified.

YOUNGEST AND OLDEST

STILL A TEENAGER

Max Verstappen was aged 17 years and 180 days when he finished seventh in his second race in F1, the 2015 Malaysian GP, thus becoming the youngest driver ever to score World Championship points. The previous record belonged to Sebastian Vettel, at 19 years and 348 days, who had finished eighth for BMW Sauber in the 2007 US GP, his F1 debut. Philippe Etancelin is the oldest, at 53 years and 249 days, when he finished fifth in his Lago Talbot in the 1950 Italian GP.

Above Max Verstappen was still 17 midway through 2015 when he raced in Hungary.

YOUNG AND KEEN

In 2009, Jaime Alguersuari lowered the mark to just 19 years and 125 days when he made his debut for Scuderia Toro Rosso at the Hungarian GP. However, this was beaten comprehensively in 2015 when Max Verstappen made his first outing for the same Italian team at the opening race in Australia, aged just 17 years and 166 days.

A WEALTH OF EXPERIENCE

Luigi Fagioli was just short of 37 when he scored his second to last grand prix win, for Mercedes at Monaco in 1935. So, it must have been for his experience that he was added to Alfa Romeo's line-up at the start of the first World Championship in 1950, in which he ranked third overall. In his one race in 1951, at the French GP, he was forced out of his car mid-race as team leader Juan Manuel Fangio's car had mechanical difficulties. They shared the win. Luigi was aged 53 years and 22 days. Giuseppe Farina was next oldest when he won in Germany in 1953, at 46 years and 276 days.

RACING IS ONE THING...

Everyone thought Sebastian Vettel's record for being the youngest driver to win a grand prix, at 21 years and 73 days, was special, but Max Verstappen reduced it by two years and 210 days at the 2016 Spanish GP.

AFTER YOU, YOUNG SIR

The youngest driver to lead a grand prix had been Sebastian Vettel, who led the 2007 Japanese GP for Toro Rosso during a pit-stop sequence. He was 20 years and 89 days old. However, that record was smashed in the 2016 Spanish GP when Max Verstappen, at 18 years and 228 days, made the most of the Mercedes drivers clashing to win on his debut for Red Bull Racing after being promoted from Toro Rosso.

🏆 DELIVERING UNDER PRESSURE

it takes many drivers years to learn how to squeeze the maximum from themselves and their cars without pushing just that little bit too hard. The mercurial Sebastian Vettel is the youngest ever pole-sitter, being just 21 years and 72 days when he took first place on the grid at the 2008 Italian GP. Ferrari's Giuseppe Farina is the oldest pole-sitter, aged 47 years and 79 days at the 1954 Argentinian GP.

10 OLDEST DRIVERS IN F1

	NAME	TEAM	GP	YEAR	AGE
1	Eitel Cantoni	Maserati	Italian	1952	55 years 337 days
2	Louis Chiron	Lancia	Monaco	1955	55 years 292 days
3	Philippe Etancelin	Maserati	French	1952	55 years 190 days
4	Arthur Legat	Veritas	Belgian	1953	54 years 232 days
5	Luigi Fagioli	Alfa Romeo	French	1951	53 years 21 days
6	Adolf Brudes	Veritas	German	1952	52 years 292 days
7	Hans Stuck	AFM	Italian	1953	52 years 260 days
8	Bill Aston	Aston	German	1952	52 years 127 days
9	Clemente Biondetti	Ferrari	Italian	1950	52 years 15 days
10	Louis Rosier	Maserati	German	1956	50 years 273 days

Above Verstappen and Gasly shared the podium in Brazil in 2019, with Sainz later promoted to third place.

YOUNGEST PODIUM – BRAZIL 2019

The youngest podium line-up came at the 2019 Brazilian Grand Prix, when race winner Max Verstappen was joined by Pierre Gasly and Carlos Sainz – who was promoted to third post-race after a penalty for Lewis Hamilton. The race also marked a first podium finish for both Gasly and Sainz. The average age of the trio was 23 years and 253 days.

FROM FRESH-FACED TO VETERAN

The winner of the World Championship in 1950, Giuseppe Farina, was almost 44. Juan Manuel Fangio topped that, taking his final title in 1957 at 46 years and 41 days, making him the oldest-ever title winner. In 2006, Fernando Alonso – at 24 years and 58 days – become the youngest champion. Two years later Lewis Hamilton won the title aged 23 years and 300 days, but then Sebastian Vettel outdid him, aged 23 years and 134 days, in 2010.

CHAMPIONS BECOME EVER YOUNGER

One of the greatest differences between the F1 drivers of the 21st century and their forebears is that the drivers in the first decade of the World Championship were so much older. Inaugural champion Giuseppe Farina was 43 in 1950 and it wasn't until Mike Hawthorn lifted the crown in 1958 that F1 had its first champion still in his 20s.

10 YOUNGEST DRIVERS IN F1

	NAME	TEAM	GP	YEAR	AGE
1	Max Verstappen	Toro Rosso	Australian	2015	17 years 166 days
2	Lance Stroll	Williams	Australian	2017	18 years 144 days
3	Oliver Bearman	Ferrari	Saudi Arabian	2024	18 years 305 days
4	Lando Norris	McLaren	Australian	2019	19 years 124 days
5	Jaime Alguersuari	Toro Rosso	Hungarian	2009	19 years 125 days
6	Mike Thackwell	Tyrrell	Canadian	1980	19 years 182 days
7	Ricardo Rodriguez	Ferrari	Italian	1961	19 years 208 days
8	Fernando Alonso	Minardi	Australian	2001	19 years 218 days
9	Esteban Tuero	Minardi	Australian	1998	19 years 320 days
10	Chris Amon	Lola	Belgian	1963	19 years 324 days
=	Daniil Kvyat	Toro Rosso	Australian	2014	19 years 324 days

NB Andrea Kimi Antonelli will be 18 years 199 days when he debuts at the 2025 Australian GP

FROM ANOTHER CENTURY

Apart from Luigi Fagioli, Louis Chiron is the only other driver over 50 to step up on to the podium. He was aged 50 years and 289 days when he finished third for Maserati in his hometown of Monaco in 1950. Both drivers were born in the 19th century.

Below Being aged 50 didn't appear to slow Louis Chiron as he raced to third place in his native Monaco in 1950. Alberto Ascari, behind, would go on to finish second.

RACE STARTS

CHOPPING AND CHANGING

Jo Bonnier and Johnny Claes share the record for driving for the most teams in a World Championship season – four. Claes turned out for Gordini, Ecurie Belge, HWM and Vickomtesse de Walckiers in 1952. Bonnier raced for his own team, Giorgio Scarlatti's, Scuderia Centro Sud and BRM in 1958.

THE WRONG MOTTO

BAR was asking for trouble when the team was launched with the motto "A tradition of excellence". Firstly, it had no tradition. Secondly, its lead driver Jacques Villeneuve's run of retirements in the first 11 grands prix of the team's maiden season in 1999 set a record that is anything but excellent.

🏆 A FLYING START

Esteban Ocon finished a lap down in 16th place, when he made his F1 debut for Force India midway through 2016. He shattered Tiago Monteiro and Heikki Kovalainen's record of finishing their first 16 grands prix, making it 27 before he had his first F1 retirement at the penultimate round in 2017.

Below The 2020 Sakhir GP was the first Lewis Hamilton-less race in 13 years.

WELL, HE TRIED...

Claudio Langes seldom sported a smile and his one and only campaign in F1, in 1990, gave him every reason to look forlorn. The Italian had stepped up from F3000 to drive for the EuroBrun Racing team. But the car was not up to scratch and he failed to pre-qualify for all 14 races he entered. And that was the end of his F1 career.

Above Franco says relax – Colapinto joined the field in 2024.

DOOHAN JUST FINE

Up until the end of the 2024 season, 778 drivers have raced in Formula One, with Franco Colapinto and Jack Doohan debuting late in the year. Andrea Kimi Antonelli, Gabriel Bortoleto and Isack Hadjar made that 781 in 2025.

Above The wrong motto: Jacques Villeneuve had a torrid time in BAR's much-trumpeted maiden season in 1999.

THE MANY AND THE FEW

A record 75 drivers contested the 1952 season – aided by the Indianapolis 500 being part of the world championship – while in 2018 and 2019 there were only 20 competitors. They are the only two seasons in which every driver present has participated in every grand prix, with not a single in-season driver change at any team in either campaign.

LEWIS' RECORD RUN

Fernando Alonso may have started the most number of grands prix but the record for doing so consecutively belongs to Lewis Hamilton. Hamilton started every race between his debut in Australia, in 2007, before his streak came to an end when he was absent from the penultimate round of the 2020 season due to a Covid-19 diagnosis, a run of 265 grands prix.

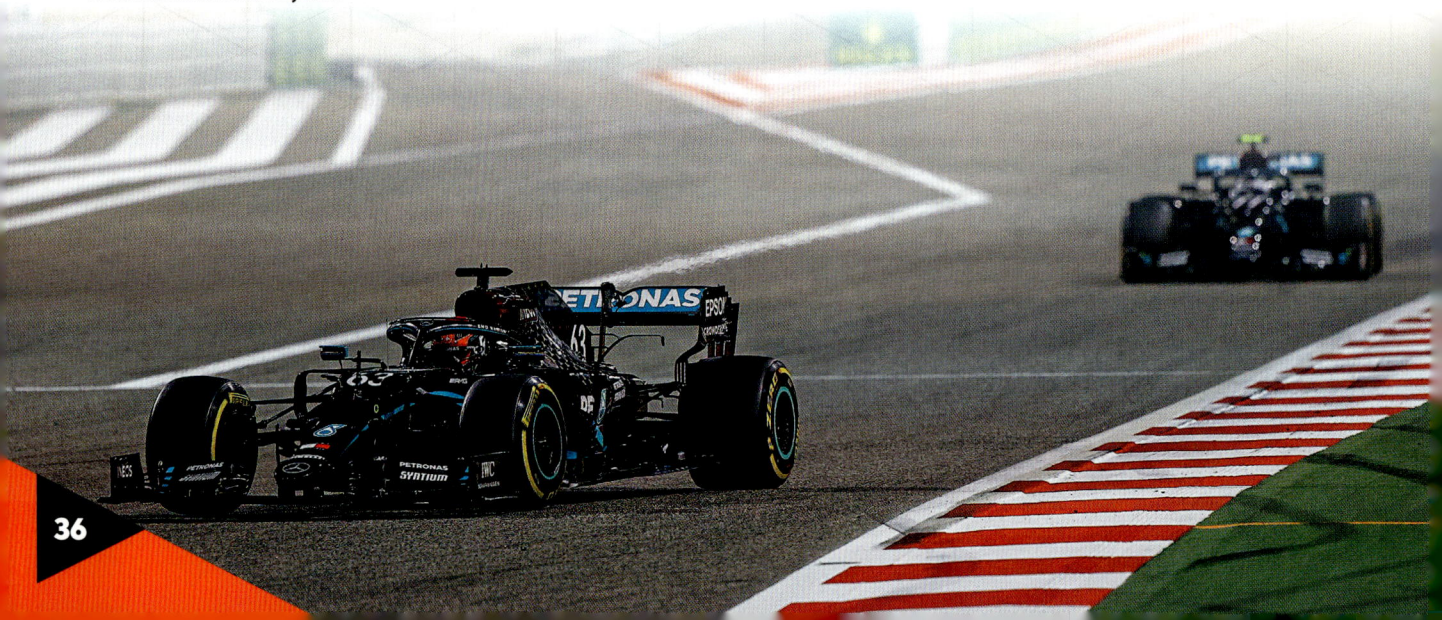

Above Lewis Hamilton has been at the front of the pack more often than any other driver.

⏱ HEADING THE PACK

Lewis Hamilton holds the record for leading the most number of grands prix, having hit the front at some stage in 190 different races. That puts him ahead of Michael Schumacher, on 142, and Sebastian Vettel, on 107. Hamilton also holds the record for leading the most number of grands prix uninterrupted, doing so at 23 separate races, and has the record for most laps led at one circuit – looping the Hungaroring atop the pack 487 times.

NOT FOR WANT OF TRYING

Andrea de Cesaris holds the record for the most grands prix contested without a win. In all, his F1 career stretched from 1980 (with Alfa Romeo) to 1994 (with Sauber), yet he did not produce one win from his 208 starts, not helped by Andrea retiring from 148 of these. His best results were a pair of second-place finishes in 1983.

NEW SEASON, NEW TEAM

Chris Amon is described as the best driver never to win a grand prix. One look at his F1 career shows that he wasn't worried about changing teams to chase his dream, as he raced for 12: Reg Parnell Racing, Ian Raby Racing, Cooper, his own team, Ferrari, March, Matra, Tecno, Tyrrell, BRM, Ensign and Walter Wolf Racing. In total he drove 13 different makes of car. Andrea de Cesaris, Stefan Johansson, Stirling Moss and Maurice Trintignant raced 10.

CLOSE, BUT NO CIGAR

Gabriele Tarquini holds the record for the most grand prix appearances that didn't result in a start. Forty times he turned up then failed to qualify. This was the price he paid for driving for uncompetitive teams when 39 cars fought for 26 grid spots and a pre-qualifying session was necessary. Luckily, he qualified on 38 other occasions.

TOP 10 TEAMS WITH MOST STARTS

1098 Ferrari

970 McLaren

834 Williams

770 Renault* (nee Toleman, then Benetton then, Renault, then Lotus-Renault (2012-15), then Alpine)

715 Visa Cash App RB (nee Minardi, then Toro Rosso, then AlphaTauri)

625 Aston Martin (nee Jordan then Midland then Spyker then Force India then Racing Point)

600 Sauber (+ BMW Sauber, Alfa Romeo Racing, Kick Sauber)

527 Red Bull (nee Stewart then Jaguar Racing)

492 Lotus

492 Mercedes GP (+ BAR + Honda Racing + Brawn)

430 Tyrrell

*Renault 1977–1985 classifies as a different team

THE RISKIEST LAP

All the efforts exerted to develop a car through practice and then to qualify it as far up the grid as possible can come to naught on the opening lap, when the cars are racing at their closest. Take the 1978 Italian GP, the worst ever example of wastage, as 10 cars were eliminated before they had reached the first corner. Sadly, Lotus ace Ronnie Peterson died of his injuries.

HOW NOT TO DO IT

Andrea de Cesaris retired from all 16 grands prix in 1987 while racing for Brabham; a record for F1's hall of shame. He was actually running third in Monaco, but was stationary when the chequered flag fell, his car having run out of fuel; and he was in eighth place in the Adelaide season finale, but spun off with four laps to go.

Above Andrea De Cesaris had a rotten run in 1987.

EARLY BATH

Jarno Trulli started 252 grands prix during his career – leaving him just outside of the top 10 most experienced drivers – peaking with a sole victory at the 2004 Monaco GP. Consequently he retired from a fair few, and he holds the record of having the most first-lap exits in history. On 14 occasions Trulli's race was run on the opening lap, and 12 of them were due to collisions, as the Italian often found himself in the thick of the frantic midfield action.

Right Jarno Trulli has had more first-lap exits than anyone else.

TRY, TRY AND TRY AGAIN

While Germany's Nico Hulkenberg holds the record for the most starts without a win (227 starts and counting), Arrows holds the team record. Founded by Jackie Oliver in 1978, the British–based team took part in 383 grands prix without achieving a victory. Arrows ran out of money and bowed out of F1 with five races remaining in the 2002 season.

TO FINISH FIRST...

On 11 occasions in Formula One history has a driver crossed the finish line first but not wound up winning the grands prix. Some of these have been due to time penalties or subsequent technical infringements. The most

Below George Russell crossed the line first in Belgium in 2024, but he didn't stay there for long.

recent incident befell Mercedes driver George Russell at the 2024 Belgian GP, who crossed the line in front, but was disqualified after technical checks discovered his car to be underweight. It was the first time in 30 years that a race winner was excluded.

MAKE A DATE

Grands prix have been held as early as January 1, and as late as December 29, but the most common date for a grand prix is July 16. A total of 11 grands prix have been held on July 16: nine times in Britain, once in Austria, and once in France. The most common date for crowning a champion is October 22, with four of the seven races held on that date resulting in a Drivers' title being clinched (1967, 1989, 1995, 2006).

SIX CHAMPS

The 2012 season featured the most world champions on the grid in F1 history. Michael Schumacher, Fernando Alonso, Kimi Räikkönen, Lewis Hamilton and Jenson Button were part of the field, as was reigning and eventual champion Sebastian Vettel. So too was Nico Rosberg, who went on to be crowned champion in 2016.

HIGHEST WIN RATE

Juan Manuel Fangio won 24 times from 51 starts to give him a record win rate of 0.471. Second is Alberto Ascari, who dominated for Ferrari in the early 1950s and ended up with a rate of 0.419 after winning 13 of his 31 races. Jim Clark ranks third on 0.347 and would certainly have ranked higher but for his Lotus often suffering from mechanical problems.

Above Riccardo Patrese used to hold the record for most starts – but now doesn't even make the top 10.

TOP 10 DRIVERS WITH MOST GP STARTS

1 Fernando Alonso	402
2 Lewis Hamilton	356
3 Kimi Räikkönen	349
4 Rubens Barrichello	322
5 Michael Schumacher	306
= Jenson Button	306
7 Sebastian Vettel	299
8 Sergio Perez	281
9 Felipe Massa	269
10 Daniel Ricciardo	257

PATRESE HOLDS IT FOR LONGEST

Riccardo Patrese became the most experienced driver when he started his 176th grand prix at the 1988 Australian GP, a record he pushed to 256 by the time of his retirement five years later. Patrese held the record until the 2008 Turkish GP, a run of almost 20 years, when he was surpassed by Rubens Barrichello, who pushed the record to 322, before Kimi Räikkönen and then Fernando Alonso extended their careers into the 2020s. Such is the longevity of careers nowadays, and the length of the calendar, that Patrese no longer features in the top 10 of most experienced racers.

WHAT'S A CHEQUERED FLAG?

From his 208 starts, Andrea de Cesaris failed to reach the finish of the race 137 times. There were certainly numerous mechanical failures when he raced for Alfa Romeo in the early 1980s, but he was equally responsible as there were many crashes too. Compatriot Riccardo Patrese clocked up 130 retirements from his 256 starts, but at least he scored six wins.

LEADING THE WAY

Lewis Hamilton and Michael Schumacher have both won seven world titles, but the Briton just edges his counterpart in having led the world championship for the most number of grands prix. Hamilton has left 126 events as leader in the title standings, narrowly ahead of Schumacher's 121, though neither hold the record for doing so consecutively. Max Verstappen has led the championship for 63 straight grands prix, between the 2022 Spanish GP and 2024 Abu Dhabi GP, surpassing Schumacher's record of 37 straight events.

39 AND RISING

By the end of the 2024 Formula One World Championship, drivers from 39 nations had taken part since its inception in 1950. Over those 75 seasons, there have been drivers from each and every one of the world's continents, apart from Antarctica.

WINKEL-SHOCK

Markus Winkelhock was drafted in to the Spyker team for the 2007 European GP at the Nürburgring. Local knowledge prompted Winkelhock to start from the pit lane on wet tyres, moments before a deluge soaked the track. As rivals skidded off on slicks, Winkelhock surged to the lead, prior to worsening conditions prompting the safety car and then a red flag. Winkelhock slipped back at the restart, then retired, and did not start another race. But of his 13-lap career, six were spent leading.

NEVER QUITE NICKED ONE

Nick Heidfeld gained a reputation for being very quick, and very reliable, during a respectable Formula One career – but he never quite managed the final push. Heidfeld took 13 podiums across 183 starts, with his strongest campaign coming in 2008, when he was runner-up in four grands prix. Stefan Johansson managed 12 career podiums without a victory, while Chris Amon was a visitor to the rostrum 11 times but failed to climb the top step.

Left Nick Heidfeld claimed 13 podium finishes but never managed a win.

MISCELLANEOUS DRIVER RECORDS

Above Peter Collins was victorious for Ferrari in the 1958 British GP, but would perish next time out, in the German GP.

KEVIN'S CONQUEST

Kevin Magnussen burst onto the scene in 2014 by finishing runner-up on his debut in Australia, but that proved to be the peak of his career, as he never again mounted the podium. Magnussen went on to start a total of 185 grands prix for McLaren, Renault and Haas, but the hard-charging Dane never managed to lead a single lap during his career – setting a record for the most races started without leading one.

Above Kevin Magnussen took his sole podium on his debut in 2014.

THE DARKEST DAYS

Death was a regular feature of F1 in the early years, with driver safety scarcely considered in the 1950s. Six drivers died at the wheel in both 1957 and 1958, with five being killed in other events and one in F1 testing in 1957. In 1958, Luigi Musso died in the French GP, Peter Collins in the German GP and Stuart Lewis-Evans from burns received in the Moroccan GP, with three others being killed in non-F1 events.

SPRINT SUCCESS

Formula One introduced Sprint races at three grands prix in 2021, and expanded its presence to six grands prix annually from 2022. At Sprint events a short race, of one-third distance, takes place on Saturday, ahead of Sunday's main grand prix. So far they have been the domain of Max Verstappen, as he won 11 of the 18 Sprint races held at the end of 2024.

FANCY SEEING YOU HERE

Lewis Hamilton, Valtteri Bottas and Max Verstappen were together on the podium at 20 different races – the most times the same trio have found themselves sharing the trophies. They shared the podium eight times during the 17-round 2020 season, but that is eclipsed by the nine podiums shared in one season – 2015 – by Lewis Hamilton, Nico Rosberg and Sebastian Vettel.

LEAPS AHEAD

Max Verstappen's dominant season included the most wins, the most points, and the biggest margin of title success – and he also got the record for leading the most laps. Verstappen held first place for 1,003 of the 1,325 laps (75.7 per cent), beating the previous record of Sebastian Vettel, who led 739 of the 1,133 laps (65.2 per cent) in 2011. Percentage wise, Verstappen's tally also put him clear of Jim Clark's prolific 1963 campaign, in which he led 506 of 708 laps (71.5 per cent).

YOU DON'T HAVE TO BE MALE

Only five female racers have entered World Championship grands prix, and only Lella Lombardi and Maria-Teresa de Filippis managed to qualify. Giovanna Amati, Divina Galica and Desire Wilson failed to make it on to the starting grid. Lombardi scored too, finishing sixth for March in the 1975 Spanish GP at Montjuich Park.

Left Lella Lombardi is the only female driver to have scored a point in F1.

THREE LAPS LED

Some drivers have led over a hundred laps without managing to win a grand prix – Chris Amon managed 183 laps atop the field – but others have triumphed without spending much time up front. Peter Gethin only led three laps during his entire career, all at Monza in 1971, but crucially he led the last one, ensuring he picked up a victory.

CHOPPING AND CHANGING

The most lead changes in a grand prix came in one of the cut and thrust races at Monza, where drivers slipstreamed the car in front down the long straights then dived out to overtake. The record isn't from the classic 1971 encounter in which the lead changed 25 times, but the race in 1965 in which the lead changed a staggering 41 times.

NO BROTHERLY LOVE

Quite a few brothers have competed in F1 at the same time, such as the Fittipaldis, the Scheckters, the Villeneuves and the less well-known Whiteheads. However, the Schumachers are the best known, with Michael taking 91 wins and Ralf six. Michael never cut Ralf any slack on track and was once accused of "trying to kill" him when he edged Ralf towards the wall.

THE MOST COSMOPOLITAN YEAR

The 1970s proved to be the decade when the most different nations had drivers competing in F1, with 18 countries being represented in 1978. They were: Argentina, Australia, Austria, Brazil, Canada, Finland, France, Germany, Great Britain, Holland, Ireland, Italy, Mexico, South Africa, Spain, Sweden, Switzerland and the USA.

ELEVENSES

Sergio Perez chose 11 as his permanent race number and so it's fitting he holds the record for finishing there most often in Formula One – the first position outside of the points. Perez has come home 11th a total of 23 times during his career.

TOP 10 DRIVERS WITH MOST MILES IN LEAD

1	Lewis Hamilton	17,377
2	Michael Schumacher	15,002
3	Sebastian Vettel	11,282
4	Max Verstappen	10,371
5	Ayrton Senna	8,345
6	Alain Prost	7,751
7	Jim Clark	6,282
8	Nigel Mansell	5,905
9	Juan Manuel Fangio	5,789
10	Jackie Stewart	5,692

FRONT ROW SEAT

Ayrton Senna was one of Formula One's finest qualifiers, as demonstrated by his 87 front row starts in 161 races. That included a streak of 24 successive races where he qualified either first or second between the 1988 German GP and 1989 Australian GP. Lewis Hamilton holds the record of front row starts, at 176, while he and long-time Mercedes sparring partner Nico Rosberg shared the front row at 44 races – more than any other driver combination.

Below Hamilton and Rosberg shared the front row of the grid in Australia in 2016.

TOP 10 DRIVERS WITH MOST LAPS IN LEAD

1	Lewis Hamilton	5,486
2	Michael Schumacher	5,111
3	Sebastian Vettel	3,501
4	Max Verstappen	3,418
5	Ayrton Senna	2,931
6	Alain Prost	2,683
7	Nigel Mansell	2,058
8	Jim Clark	1,940
9	Jackie Stewart	1,918
10	Fernando Alonso	1,773

CONSTRUCTORS

Every Formula One manufacturer wants to be the World Constructors' Champion, the ultimate accolade in team motorsport. Some entities have risen and fizzled out, others have enjoyed golden days before regressing, while a few have been mainstays at the competitive edge of Formula One for decades. It should be little surprise that stalwarts Ferrari are leading the way when it comes to titles, victories and pole positions.

Above Ferrari's longevity has put it at the top of many records, with Williams, McLaren, Red Bull and Mercedes all having spells of supremacy.

TEAM WINS

🏆 FERRARI – TITLES AND MORE TITLES

The team with the most constructors' titles to its name is Ferrari. It has 16, compared with the nine achieved by McLaren and Williams. Ferrari would have had a couple more, but the Constructors' Cup wasn't awarded until 1958.

⏱ THE JOY OF SIX

It's debatable whether Brawn GP can be viewed as a new team in 2009, as it was effectively a continuation of Honda Racing. Even if it was more of a new team name rather than a new team, its eight wins were the best haul from a team in its first season.

DECADE BY DECADE

Decade by decade, the 1950s belonged to Ferrari with 29 wins, the 1960s to Lotus with 36 wins, the 1970s to Ferrari with 37 wins, the 1980s to McLaren with 56 wins, the 1990s to Williams with 61 wins, the 2000s to Ferrari with 85 wins, and the 2010s to Mercedes with 93 wins. Across the opening half of the 2020s, Red Bull leads the way with 60 wins.

⚙ MANY WINS, NO PRIZE

As the Constructors' Championship was not contested until 1958, Alfa Romeo goes down in the history books as the marque with the most grand prix wins without a title. It dominated the 1950 and 1951 seasons, taking 10 wins. Mercedes-Benz, with five of its nine wins coming in 1955, and Maserati, four of its nine in 1957, were also denied official recognition. In the post-Constructors' Cup era, Ligier, who ran from 1976 to 1996, also scored nine wins, three of which came in 1979, its best season, is third overall.

DIFFERENT GUISES

The team currently existing as Alpine can trace its roots back to its days at Toleman, and despite its spells as Renault is considered as a different entity to the original Renault works team which raced from 1977 to 1985. Toleman never won a grand prix, but under its next phase as Benetton it claimed victories – and the world title – before it morphed into the new Renault works team, again winning races and titles. A brief spell as Lotus

Below Nino Farina (10) leads Alfa Romeo team-mate Juan Manuel Fangio (18) in the 1950 Italian Grand Prix, a race the former won to claim the first World Championship.

Racing yielded two more wins, before the Renault name returned, prior to its current guise as Alpine. It means the team has won under four different names throughout its history.

FERRARI HITS ITS STRIDE

Although Ferrari were beaten by Alfa Romeo in 1950 and 1951, it became dominant once the championship switched to F2 regulations, from 1952. A rash of wins, mainly by Alberto Ascari, made it no surprise that, despite the efforts of Maserati and Mercedes-Benz, Ferrari was the first to 25 wins when Juan Manuel Fangio won the 1956 German GP.

CLEAN SWEEPS ARE AS RARE AS HENS' TEETH

Only two teams have achieved 100 per cent win rates across a season. Alfa Romeo was the first to achieve this, winning all six grands prix in the first World Championship in 1950. Two years later Ferrari matched its national rivals, who quit after 1951, and won seven from seven. The closest any team has come since is when Red Bull won 21 from 22 in 2023.

TOP 10 TEAMS WITH MOST WINS

248	Ferrari
189	McLaren
138	Mercedes GP (+ Honda Racing + Brawn GP)
123	Red Bull (+ Stewart)
114	Williams
79	Lotus
49	Renault
35	Brabham
23	Tyrrell
17	BRM

Above Lewis Hamilton claimed McLaren's 164th win in Singapore in 2009.

WINS IN ONE SEASON

21	Red Bull	2023
19	Mercedes GP	2016
17	Red Bull	2022
16	Mercedes GP	2014
=	Mercedes GP	2015
15	Mercedes GP	2019
=	Ferrari	2002
=	Ferrari	2004
=	McLaren	1988
13	Mercedes GP	2020
=	Red Bull	2013
12	McLaren	1984
=	Mercedes GP	2017
=	Red Bull	2011
=	Williams	1996
11	Red Bull	2021
=	Mercedes GP	2018
=	Benetton	1995

THE TIFOSI'S FAVOURITE

Michael Schumacher was admired rather than liked by the Tifosi when he joined Ferrari in 1996, but they soon warmed to him when he and the team started winning on a regular basis. He is by far the most successful Ferrari driver, having won 72 times for the Scuderia. The next most successful is Niki Lauda on 15, just ahead of Sebastian Vettel, who won 14 times for Ferrari but was unable to add to its title tally.

WAITING POINT

Formula One teams have existed through different entities and tracking their history can be a little tricky on occasion. But the longest wait between successive victories belongs to 'Team Silverstone', which began life as Jordan in 1991, exists now as Aston Martin, and has had spells as Midland, Spyker, Force India and Racing Point. It triumphed in the 2003 Brazilian GP with Giancarlo Fisichella, but then had to wait 17 years and 8 months until its next victory, courtesy of Sergio Perez at the 2020 Sakhir GP.

PERSEVERANCE PAYS OFF

Scuderia Toro Rosso holds the record for the most races contested by a team before scoring its first win. It started life in 1985 as Minardi and never looked likely to score points on a regular basis. It took a change of ownership in 2005 and an injection of money to turn its fortunes around. Young flyer Sebastian Vettel did the rest, winning in the wet in the Italian GP at Monza in 2008, the team's first victory out of 372 starts.

RUSSIAN REVOLUTION

Mercedes set a new record by taking more successive wins at one venue than any other team. Mercedes won each race at the Sochi Autodrom between 2014 and 2021 – after which the event was discontinued – surpassing the six straight wins McLaren took in Monaco between 1988 and 1993, and its own run of six straight victories at Suzuka (2014–19) and Yas Marina (also 2014–19).

Above Red Bull won 15 straight races, the last of which was Max Verstappen's triumph at the 2023 Italian GP.

RELENTLESS RED BULL

McLaren held the record of 11 consecutive race victories for 35 years, before this was smashed in 2023 by Red Bull. The squad began its streak at the final round of the 2022 season in Abu Dhabi and went on to win 15 successive grands prix – 13 victories for Max Verstappen and two Sergio Perez – before it was defeated in Singapore. Red Bull responded by then winning the next nine grands prix.

TEAM POLE POSITIONS

FOR THE TIFOSI

It almost feels right that a Ferrari should take pole position in the Italian GP and the team has achieved this on 19 occasions, rising to the challenge even in years when its form has been patchy elsewhere. After Ferrari's qualifying glories at Monza, the next most pole positions set by a team at an individual circuit is shared by a group of three: Ferrari at the Nürburgring; McLaren at Hockenheim and Monaco; and Williams at Silverstone.

ALBORETO HITS A CENTURY

One hundred is always a landmark figure and Ferrari became the first team to claim 100 pole positions. Michele Alboreto helped the team achieve this century at Spa-Francorchamps in 1984. As this was in the team's 35th year of F1, its average was three per year.

TERRIFIC TWENTY

No team has completed a clean sweep of qualifying sessions but there have been eight seasons in which a marque has scored all but one pole position. In 2016, Mercedes took 20 pole positions from 21 attempts, with Lewis Hamilton leading the way 12 times, and Nico Rosberg starting up front on eight occasions. The streak was interrupted in Monaco, by Red Bull's Daniel Ricciardo, who beat Rosberg by just 0.169s.

THE CAR IN FRONT…

…probably wasn't a Toyota. The Japanese firm competed in Formula One between 2002 and 2009, but its handsome budget was not matched by its results. Toyota claimed three pole positions but no wins – the most times a manufacturer managed to start up front but not convert it into the same place by the end of the race.

HAAS' LONG WAIT

In terms of a single brand, Haas had the longest wait for its maiden pole position. The American team joined Formula One in 2016 but dazzled in São Paulo in 2022, as Kevin Magnussen profited from Haas' garage position and incoming rain to set a fast lap time before conditions quickly deteriorated. It was a first pole position for both Magnussen and Haas, coming in the team's 143rd event, though sadly thanks to that year's rules it was only for the Sprint Race and not for the main grand prix.

Below Pic: Kevin Magnussen, Haas, São Paulo in 2022, starting in pole position

A THREE-WAY TIE FOR POLE

The 1997 World Championship came to a crescendo at Jerez with the title being fought over by Ferrari's Michael Schumacher and Williams' Jacques Villeneuve. Then, at the end of qualifying for the race, Formula One was faced with a situation it had never witnessed before – the first three qualifying times were identical. Villeneuve claimed pole from Schumacher and his own team-mate Heinz-Harald Frentzen, all on 1m21.072s.

24 CARAT POLES

Williams controlled the 1992 and 1993 seasons, beginning its qualifying streak at the 1992 French GP which continued through the majority of the 1993 season, eventually beaten by McLaren's Ayrton Senna at the finale around the streets of Adelaide. The 24-event streak was carried out by Nigel Mansell, Riccardo Patrese, Alain Prost and Damon Hill.

Left and above Both Brawn (at the Australian GP) and Toyota (above at the Bahrain GP) claimed their first pole positions in 2009.

THE MORE THE MERRIER

The record for the greatest number of different teams to achieve pole position in one season is six. The ever-increasing number of rounds favours teams competing in recent years over those who raced in the early 1950s when there were sometimes only seven races in a season. So the record was first set in 1972, but then matched in 1976, 1981, 1985, 2005 and in 2009. In 2009 Brawn and Red Bull led the way in terms of the number of poles achieved, ahead of McLaren, Force India, Renault and Toyota.

FROM ZERO TO HERO

A number of teams have taken their first win without having previously achieved a pole position, including debutants Alfa Romeo in 1950, Mercedes in 1954 and Wolf in 1977, plus others who'd been racing a while, such as Cooper, Honda, Matra, McLaren and Porsche. Some teams, including BRM, Ferrari, Lotus, Toro Rosso, Vanwall and Williams, hit form and claimed their first pole and first win at the same race.

POLE POSITIONS

1	Ferrari	253
2	McLaren	164
3	Mercedes GP (+ Honda Racing and Brawn GP)	141
4	Williams	128
5	Red Bull (+ Stewart)	104
6	Lotus	107
7	Brabham	39
8	Renault (+ Toleman + Benetton + Alpine)	34
9	Renault	31
10	Tyrrell	14

AND, AT LAST...

The most pole positions achieved by a team before its first victory is just three. Shadow was on pole three times in 1975 through Jean-Pierre Jarier (twice) and Tom Pryce. However, the first win, in fact the team's only win, came two years later when Alan Jones raced from 14th to first on a damp track in the Austrian GP.

Above Alan Jones gave the Shadow team its one and only grand prix victory, at the Österreichring in 1977.

TEAM FASTEST LAPS

FERRARI FLIES

Michael Schumacher was peerless in 2004, setting 10 fastest laps from 18 rounds. But Ferrari's number-two driver, Rubens Barrichello, was also able to reel off fastest laps in his F2004, helping the Italian team to a record 14 fastest laps in a season. This is one more than its 2008 line-up of Felipe Massa (three) and Kimi Räikkönen (10) managed. Mercedes achieved 13 in 2015.

A BRITISH BONANZA

Italian teams started F1 with a bang, with Alfa Romeo, Ferrari or Maserati setting the fastest lap at each of the first 30 grands prix. However, this is no longer the record for the most successive fastest laps set by teams from one country. It was finally bettered between 1991 and 1995 when the British teams of Williams, McLaren, Benetton and Jordan set fastest laps for an incredible 62 races in a row.

SCARLET SUPREME

Ferrari's longevity in Formula One means it has many of the records and when it comes to fastest laps it's no different. Ferrari's most successful circuits are home venue Monza, and Silverstone, where it has registered the fastest lap on 19 occasions. It has been fastest around Monaco 17 times, meaning it is 1–2–3 on the record books when it comes to this particular accolade.

RED RACERS

An ample supply of horsepower has been a feature of Ferrari's engines over the years, and this is evident in the stats for which team has set the most fastest laps at an individual circuit. The Italian team tops the table with 19 at its home circuit of Monza, where the long, long straights require plenty of grunt. NB. It also has 19 FLs at Silverstone.

Above McLaren was fast in 2000 but missed out on the title.

FAST BUT NO CROWN

McLaren recorded the fastest lap at 12 of the 17 grands prix in the 2000 season but missed out on the Constructors' title to Ferrari by 18 points. It is the most number of fastest laps a team has taken in a single campaign without managing to win the championship.

FASTEST JUST THE ONCE

Twice in history has a Constructors' Champion recorded the race's fastest lap just once in a season – by Lotus in 1970, and McLaren in 1974. But on five occasions that year's Drivers' Champion didn't record a single fastest lap – though it hasn't occurred since Keke Rosberg's title in 1982.

A COMPETITIVE 2024

Eighty per cent of the Formula One teams in 2024 logged a fastest lap during a grand prix. McLaren's seven fastest laps led the way as it returned to the front of the field, but seven of its opponents also concluded a grand prix with a fastest lap, with just Williams and Sauber missing out.

THE LONGEST WAIT

Visa Cash App RB started life as underdog Minardi in 1985 and it rarely came anywhere near the sharp end of the grid. Minardi never set a fastest lap in its 340-event history, but brighter times arrived following Red Bull's takeover and its morphing into Scuderia Toro Rosso. Daniil Kvyat chalked up the team's first fastest lap at the 2016 Spanish GP, in what was the 531st race for the outfit, based in the charming Italian town of Faenza.

A YEAR OF VARIETY

The 1975 World Championship offered the greatest number of teams that set fastest laps across the 14 grands prix in the season. Eight teams got in on the act: Ferrari (six fastest laps), McLaren (two), Brabham, Hesketh, March, Parnelli, Shadow and Tyrrell (all with one).

HAAS JOINS THE FRAY

Haas ensured that each current Formula One team has recorded a fastest lap when Kevin Magnussen posted the fastest lap at the 2017 Singapore GP. Magnussen made it two at the same event a year later, then claimed Haas' third at the final round of 2024 in Abu Dhabi.

FAVOURING AMERICA

With a need to sell road-going sports cars as well as its range of racing cars, Lotus boss Colin Chapman was always delighted that his F1 cars seemed to shine in North America. The team has the most or equal most fastest laps at Detroit, Riverside and, most importantly, Watkins Glen in New York State.

RENAULT'S GLORY DAYS

Renault struggled when it arrived in the World Championship midway through 1977. The team had F1's first turbocharged engine, and while power wasn't a problem, reliability was. However, within two years the team's yellow and black cars were flying. Jean-Pierre Jabouille took the marque's first win at Dijon-Prenois and René Arnoux set the race's fastest lap. Renault again bagged the fastest lap on its return visit to the circuit in 1981.

Below Renault's glory days: René Arnoux set fastest lap for Renault at Dijon-Prenois, with team-mate Jean-Pierre Jabouille taking its first win in the same race.

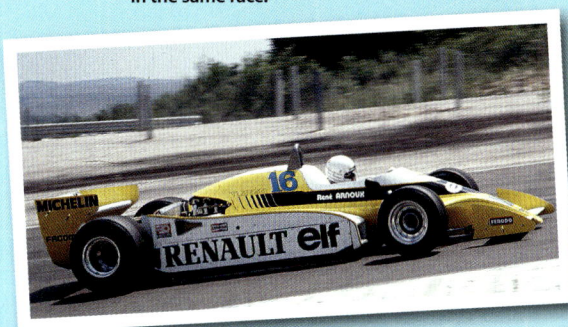

TOP 10 TEAMS WITH THE MOST FASTEST LAPS

#	Team	Fastest Laps
1	Ferrari	263
2	McLaren	172
3	Williams	133
4	Mercedes GP (+ Brawn GP)	104
5	Red Bull	99
6	Lotus	71
7	Renault (+ Toleman + Benetton + Lotus II)	61
8	Brabham	40
9	Tyrrell	22
10	Renault	18

TEAM POINTS

Above Ayrton Senna leads Alain Prost towards yet another one-two finish in 1988, this time in Hungary.

MAXIMUM POINTS HAULS

The quickest way for a team to rack up points is to have its cars finish in first and second places in a grand prix and Ferrari is the best at this, having achieved it 86 times, starting all the way back at the Italian GP in 1951. Mercedes GP is the next most successful, on 54, despite the first of the team's modern entity only coming in Malaysia in 2014.

🏆 SOMETHING FOR ALMOST EVERYONE

In 1989, 16 different teams scored points in the World Championship, the most ever. The scoring teams were, in points order: McLaren, Williams, Ferrari, Benetton, Tyrrell, Lotus, Arrows, Dallara, Brabham, Onyx, Minardi, March, Rial, Ligier, AGS and Lola. Only the Coloni, EuroBrun, Osella and Zakspeed teams failed to score.

LOTS OF TROPHIES

Finishing on the podium is a sure fire way of hoovering up the points, and Mercedes claimed 33 podiums in the 2016 season – 17 for Lewis Hamilton and 16 for Nico Rosberg – the most that one team has taken in a single campaign. That eclipsed the 32 Mercedes took in 2015, a number it replicated in 2019.

ONE AND TWO

F1's most successful teams all have periods when they manage to have the best chassis, engine, tyres and drivers at the same time. In 2015, Mercedes beat McLaren's record of 10 one-two finishes from 16 starts in 1988 when Lewis Hamilton and Nico Rosberg were first and second to the finish in 12 of the 19 rounds.

BUCKING THE SYSTEM

Haas F1 might have struggled when it made its bow in 2016. So people were stunned when Romain Grosjean not only finished on the team's debut in Australia but came home sixth. Then he backed this up with fifth next time out in Bahrain. Amazingly, Grosjean would score twice more to help the team rank eighth in the Constructors' Championship.

THE BEST WORST SEASON

There have been several seasons in which multiple teams have failed to score a single point but the raised professionalism of modern Formula One means even the slowest outfit can be a competitive proposition. In 2023 Haas was bottom of the 10-team Constructors' Championship but did so by amassing 12 points – the highest ever total by the statistically worst team.

COMING GOOD IN THE END

Benetton scored the most points before landing its first constructors' title. This came in 1995, by which time it had scored 663.5 points across 15 campaigns since starting life as the Toleman team back in 1981. Ironically, the team later became Renault in 2002. However, Mercedes GP passed this in the four years from its reinvention in 2010, collecting 881 points.

Left Benetton team boss Flavio Briatore and Michael Schumacher had plenty to smile about in 1995.

RED BULL MAKES A POINT

The change of the points system from 2010, when 25 points rather than 10 were awarded for wins, altered the landscape, and unsurprisingly that year's Constructors' Champions Red Bull set a new record of 498 points. That mark was subsequently bettered until Mercedes lifted the ceiling to 765 points in 2016. That record lasted for seven years until Red Bull reclaimed it with a whopping 860 points from a 2023 season, which included 22 races and six sprint events.

Right Red Bull dominated in 2023, and won in Las Vegas.

LOOKING DOWN FROM ABOVE

Ferrari holds the record for the most consecutive top-three finishes which resulted in podium finishes at an incredible 53 straight grands prix between the 1999 Malaysian GP and the final grand prix of 2002 in Japan. The team kept the stream of points flowing into 2003, but only for the next two grands prix. Disaster struck in the third race of the season at Interlagos when Ferrari went home empty-handed. It bounced back to finish first and third next time out.

FAILURE TO SCORE

Formula One welcomed three new teams in 2010 and one of them, confusingly, was Lotus Racing – though it had no connection to the original Lotus. The squad rebranded itself as Caterham for 2012, but the underwhelming results that had characterized Lotus Racing continued. The team eventually collapsed after the 2014 season, having failed to take a single point across its 94 entries. No outfit in history has started that many grands prix without taking a point.

FERRARI'S STREAK

Ferrari went title-less in the 2010s but it did still set one record, as its cars finished in the points for the most consecutive number of races. Between the 2010 German GP and 2014 Singapore GP there was always a red car in the top 10, a run of 81 grands prix. Mercedes managed 106 points finishes across 107 races between the 2012 Brazilian GP and 2018 French GP, but a collision between Lewis Hamilton and Nico Rosberg at the 2016 Spanish GP interrupted those two streaks.

Below Michael Schumacher and race winner Eddie Irvine started Ferrari's run of podium finishes at Sepang in 1999.

TEAM TITLES

FERRARI'S FLOP

There's no doubt that the worst follow-up season by a champion team was that of the inaugural constructors' champions, Vanwall, as it scaled down its involvement to almost nothing due to patron Tony Vandervell's ill health. However, of those who returned to defend their titles, Ferrari has had the worst time, scoring just eight points in 1980. As there was no driver change, 1979 world champion Jody Scheckter and Gilles Villeneuve staying on, the blame fell on the car.

TECHNOLOGY DELIVERS

The quest for advancement was what made Lotus the team to fear in the 1960s. Team owner Colin Chapman wouldn't rest if there wasn't a new idea that might make his cars faster. This earned the team its first constructors' title in 1963 and when this was backed up by titles in 1965, 1968 and 1970, Emerson Fittipaldi helped it to be the first team to five titles in 1972.

Below Lorenzo Bandini celebrates his only win, in Austria in 1964, to help Ferrari win the title by just three points.

WITH SIX TO GO

Red Bull's dominance through 2023 was such that it clinched the Constructors' championship earlier than any team had managed in history. Red Bull made sure of the crown at that year's Japanese GP, held with six of the 22 rounds left to run, and eventually finished the season on a record 860 points, a whopping 451 points clear of nearest rival Mercedes.

Below Red Bull celebrates its dominant Constructors' title in 2023.

COME IN NUMBER 15

Demonstrating a clear shuffling of the pack, four constructors have landed their first constructors' title since 2005. First it was Renault (formed from Benetton), duly repeating the feat the following year. Then in 2009 it was Brawn GP (formerly BAR and Honda Racing). In 2010, Red Bull Racing (formerly Stewart Grand Prix then Jaguar Racing) scored its first of four titles. Then, in 2014, Mercedes became the 15th constructor to be crowned.

SQUEAKING HOME

The narrowest title-winning margin is just three points, which was the result back in 1964 when Ferrari edged out BRM thanks to John Surtees and Lorenzo Bandini getting the better of Graham Hill and Richie Ginther. However, that season only had 10 rounds, making Ferrari's victory over McLaren by four points after 16 grands prix in 1999 statistically closer.

A HUGE MARGIN

The points system changing in 2010 has skewed the metrics of dominance but the performance gap between champions and runner-up was at its largest in 1988, a season in which only the best 11 results from the 16 grands prix were counted. McLaren swept to the title on 199 points, with nearest opponents Ferrari mustering 65 points. That tally of 32.6 per cent of the champion's points is the lowest percentage amassed by a runner-up in the title battle.

Above Jack Brabham won the Monaco GP to help Cooper be crowned after just 25 starts.

MCLAREN'S 26-YEAR WAIT

McLaren Racing won its first Constructors' title in 1974 and then added another seven across the next 24 years, before entering a fallow period. Finally in 2024, 50 years after its maiden triumph, it returned to the sport's summit, vaulting from fourth to first in the championship across successive seasons. Lando Norris and Oscar Piastri accrued six wins and 666 points to finish just 14 clear of Ferrari, ending McLaren's 26-year drought – the longest spell between Constructors' titles.

NEVER THE BRIDE

Two teams in history have secured second place in the world championship without ever winning the title. In 1980 Ligier finished a distant runner-up to champions Williams, while in 2007 BMW-Sauber was the third-best outfit through the year, but was promoted to second after McLaren was excluded from the standings due to the Spygate scandal.

TWENTY-ONE TIMES SECOND

Ferrari has won the most Constructors' Championships, 16, but it has actually finished runner-up on more occasions than it has emerged as champions. Ferrari has been second in the standings 21 times, including six times since the most recent of its world championships in 2008. In six of those 21 years its margin of defeat has been eight points or less, highlighting the fine margins at play in the sport.

Above Lando Norris and Zak Brown celebrate McLaren's 2024 title.

NEVER AT HOME

Despite the Italian GP taking place towards the end of the F1 racing calendar, not once has the Tifosi seen Ferrari claim the constructors' title on home ground. However, in two of those years – 2002 and 2004 – Ferrari had already won the title before heading for Monza, wrapping it up several rounds earlier at the Hungarian GP.

Above Michael Schumacher gave Ferrari a home win at Monza in 2000.

PARTICIPATION

44 YEARS AND COUNTING

Ferrari drivers are a regular presence on Formula One podiums and consequently the team has the longest streak of seasons in which it has taken home a trophy. Ferrari, and long-time rivals McLaren, both had a horrible 1980 season, but started a run of years always taking home at least one podium finish in 1981. McLaren's stint ended when it entered a downward spiral in 2013 but, despite a few leaner years, Ferrari is in a 44-year stint of podium finishes.

NEW TEAMS FAIL TO LAST

Having only 10 teams on the grid in 2009, and many of them struggling for budgets, four new teams were invited to join them for 2010. Team US F1 failed to step up, but the other three – HRT, Lotus F1 Racing and Virgin Racing – all gave it a good shot. Yet, by the end of 2016, they had failed and folded, even after name changes as more money was brought in to keep them going. The last to fall was Manor, the team that had begun life as Virgin Racing.

TO FINISH FIRST, FIRST YOU HAVE TO FINISH

The 1996 Monaco GP was an odd one. The Minardis took each other out before the first corner; Michael Schumacher took himself out further around the lap; and Rubens Barrichello spun out in his Jordan before the lap was over. At the end of it all, Olivier Panis scored his one and only win, for Ligier, and there were just four classified finishers, only three of which were still running at flag-fall. No race has come close to being as destructive.

Left Bruce McLaren founded his eponymous team, but was killed before it really thrived.

NEARLY ALL IN FRONT

Red Bull set a new record in 2023 when it led 1,149 laps (86.7 per cent), surpassing the 1,055 (86.2 per cent) fronted by Mercedes in 2016. But percentage wise both lag a little way behind McLaren's dominant 1988 season. Between them, Ayrton Senna and Alain Prost were at the front of the field for 1,003 of the 1,031 racing laps, an astonishing percentage of 97.3 per cent.

YOUR NAME ON THE NOSE

Winning is wonderful, and a handful of drivers have sought to do it in a car bearing their name. Most successful by far is Jack Brabham, who won seven grands prix in 1966 and landed both the drivers' and constructors' titles. His former team-mate Bruce McLaren founded a successful dynasty, although it flourished mainly after his death in 1970.

POINTS, BUT NO PRIZES

The Arrows team is no more, but at least it will never extend its record of being the team with the most grand prix starts without winning a grand prix – 382. It came close twice. Riccardo Patrese was leading until 15 laps before the end of the team's third race, in South Africa in 1978, when the engine failed and Damon Hill led the 1997 Hungarian GP until a lap before the finish when Jacques Villeneuve swept past to win and Hill came second.

THAT'S LIFE

Sometimes Formula One teams can be off the pace but when it comes to the worst team the short-lived Life operation tops the pile. Life entered the 1990 season with its terrible L190, a single car that lacked performance, while its heavy and underpowered engine was also terribly unreliable. When the car did finish a lap it was usually over a dozen seconds or so off the pace. In an era when there were an abundance of teams, Life failed to even pre-qualify for 14 grands prix before shutting up shop.

Above Bruno Giacomelli tried his best but could not get anywhere near to even getting the dreadful Life L190 through pre-qualifying.

Below Michael Schumacher and Rubens Barrichello were team-mates for 104 races at Ferrari, a record partnership.

Above All 24 starters finished the 2011 European GP – with HRT driver Narain Karthikeyan classifying in 24th position.

TEAM-MATES

Michael Schumacher and Rubens Barrichello were team-mates for longer than any other duo in F1 history. Schumacher and Barrichello teamed up together at Ferrari between 2000 and 2005, a spell in which Schumacher won five world titles, and Ferrari five Constructors' titles. The pair shared the red garage a record 104 times, eclipsing the partnership between Mercedes team-mates Lewis Hamilton and Valtteri Bottas by four races.

A FIRST AT THE BACK

There have been several occasions in Formula One history where all starters have finished and with stronger reliability it is a more frequent event with each passing season. The record for the most number of finishers – excluding the anomalous Indianapolis 500 – is 24, which happened at the 2011 European GP at Valencia's Street Circuit, in a year in which 12 teams competed. HRT's Narain Karthikeyan brought up the rear to become the first, and only, driver to finish a grand prix in 24th spot.

LOYAL LANDO

Lando Norris became the youngest British driver in history in 2019 when he debuted aged 19, and he is now already the driver with the longest spell exclusively at one team. Perhaps Norris will eventually seek pastures new, but he has spent the entirety of his career – which now stretches to 128 grands prix – with McLaren. No driver has competed in that many grands prix without ever changing teams.

TEAM PRINCIPALS

TIMBER MERCHANT TURNED CHIEF

Ken Tyrrell was a racing driver, financed by his family's timber business. Following the end of his driving career he ran the Cooper Formula Junior team in 1960, and advanced, with Jackie Stewart, to F2 in 1965. They switched to a Matra chassis for F2 and Ken moved into F1 with his own team in 1968, running a Matra-Ford for Stewart. They won the 1969 title. The first Tyrrell car appeared in 1970, and Stewart won titles in 1971 and 1973, but the team struggled after sponsor Elf quit, being taken over by BAR in 1998.

Right Timber merchant Ken Tyrrell and Jackie Stewart formed a great partnership, claiming their third title together in 1973.

PASSION HIDDEN BEHIND DARK GLASSES

Enzo Ferrari was drawn to the sport by a desire to compete. In the 1930s, he was put in charge of Alfa Romeo's racing activities. Fired in 1939, Enzo started building his own cars after the Second World War. His team's first World Championship win came at the 1951 British GP and the legend grew from there. Enzo was famously unemotional about his cars, which were broken up after they were superseded.

BUSINESS BRAIN

Twenty-first century F1 team principals are very different from their predecessors, who were often drivers turned engineers. Many of the new crop arrived from the business world, using their skills to run teams that have become large companies. One of these is Toto Wolff, a man who set up a private equity company. However, he was a former club racer and this drove him to get involved with Williams then Mercedes.

MID-ENGINES TO MINIS

John Cooper's father Charles got him interested in racing and they started building small chassis powered by motorbike engines after WWII. Stirling Moss gave Cooper its first F1 win in 1958 and Jack Brabham claimed the next two drivers' and constructors' titles for the team before Lotus stole its thunder. John ran the team in 1964 after his father died, but was then injured in a car crash and decided to sell the company, moving on to create the fast Mini Cooper car. John died in 2000.

Below Jack Brabham and John Cooper formed a great partnership.

FRANCE'S FIXER

Gerard Larrousse came to prominence in rallying, then turned to racing in 1966 and made his name by finishing second in the 1969 Le Mans 24 Hours. He went on to win this race in 1973 and 1974 for Matra. He then set up an F2 team and Jean-Pierre Jabouille won the 1976 crown, after which Gerard became Renault's competitions manager, managing its entry into F1 in 1977. After Renault closed in 1985, he set up his own F1 team for 1987, running Lola chassis.

McLAREN'S METICULOUS MAN

Ron Dennis started as a mechanic with Cooper. He moved to Brabham in 1968, before starting Rondel, with Neil Trundle in 1972. They were successful in F2 and built an F1 car that they had to sell when their sponsor pulled out. Back in F2, Ron gained management experience and, with backing from Marlboro, took over McLaren. Through his legendary attention to detail he turned it into the second most successful team in F1 history. In 2009 he stepped back from F1 to concentrate on the rest of the McLaren Group, before a final spell running the team from 2014 to 2016.

Right Ron Dennis looks proud rather than happy after Senna and Prost gave McLaren a one-two at Monaco in 1989.

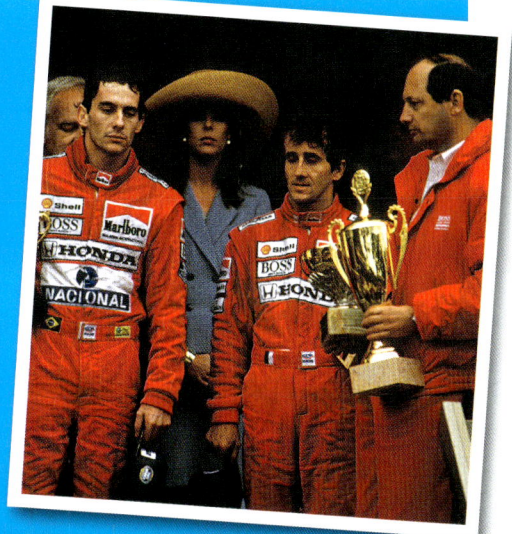

CAPTAIN AMERICA

Roger Penske started racing when at university and was competitive enough to enter the US GP in 1961 and 1962, ranking eighth at his first attempt. However, his skills as a businessman soon became more apparent as he built up a chain of car dealerships that is now the second largest in the USA. He also set up a team and ran Mark Donohue to success in TransAm in 1968 before branching into single-seaters. This was mainly in IndyCars, but he tried F1 from 1974–77 and took one win, with John Watson, at the Österreichring in 1976.

A RESTLESS, DRIVEN GENIUS

Colin Chapman probably shaped F1 more than any other team principal through his restless quest to find an engineering advantage. In 1962 his Lotus team was the first to use a monocoque chassis, and Jim Clark started to win. He made ground effects work for the 1978 season and Mario Andretti duly did the same. He tried to introduce a double chassis, but it was banned, infuriating this effervescent character. He died of a heart attack in 1988, leaving memories of a man hurling his cap in the air when his drivers won.

A SHARP BRAIN AND A STERN LOOK

Alfred Neubauer was the man who made the Mercedes team tick during its one-and-a-half-year stint in F1 in the mid-1950s. He joined Mercedes as a racing driver in 1923, but he quit after a team-mate was killed at the 1924 Italian GP and turned to team management. He guided the "Silver Arrows" through its glory years of the late 1920s and 1930s. Portly, serious and never without a jacket and tie, he was still at the helm after the Second World War and he encouraged the team back into racing in 1954 when it set new standards.

A TECHNICAL AND TACTICAL BRAIN

Ross Brawn joined March from the atomic industry. At Williams, he learned to be an aerodynamicist. After spells at Beatrice and Arrows, he designed Jaguar's sports cars but returned to F1 and Benetton. Ross started working with Michael Schumacher at Benetton, displaying great skill. The pair moved to Ferrari and won five more titles before Ross took a sabbatical. He came back with Honda, which became Brawn GP for 2009. His eponymous team won both titles, but was rebranded Mercedes GP for 2010. Ross retired after 2013, but returned in 2017 as Formula One's motorsport boss.

Below Ross Brawn hugs Jenson Button after he'd won on the team's debut in Australia in 2009.

DRIVEN BY PATRIOTIC FERVOUR

A racer up to F3 level, Frank Williams turned to running cars for others, most notably for Piers Courage in 1969 and 1970. Some lean years followed as Frank fought on in F1. In 1977 he formed Williams Grand Prix Engineering with Patrick Head. It developed into F1's third most successful team, winning nine constructors' titles, despite the setback of Frank being paralysed in a car crash in 1986. Williams remained involved in Formula One until 2020, a year before his death.

Right Frank Williams and partner Patrick Head watch the action at the 1980 British GP.

FERRARI'S FIERCE LITTLE NAPOLEON

Jean Todt was a successful rally co-driver through the 1970s before being given his break in management in 1982 when he was asked to set up Peugeot Talbot Sport. Wins and world titles soon followed through Ari Vatanen, before Peugeot sought success in sports car racing, and got it in 1992. After Peugeot declined to enter F1, Todt joined Ferrari in 1993, making it more clinical in its approach. The team won its first constructors' title under Todt's leadership in 1999 and then, in conjunction with Michael Schumacher, won title after title from 2000 until 2004. Todt became FIA President in 2009, a role he held for 12 years.

Below Racing was always fun when Lord Hesketh (left with James Hunt and "Bubbles" Horsley) was around.

ONE BIG TEDDY BEAR

Lord Hesketh made quite a splash in F1 in the mid-1970s when he rolled in with a plain white car daubed with patriotic red and blue stripes and a teddy bear on the nose. There was no sponsorship to be seen. "The Good Lord", as driver James Hunt called him, was bankrolling his foray into F1 from his considerable inheritance. They raced a March in 1974, but soon built their own car and had their day of days when Hunt won the Dutch GP at Zandvoort in 1975. Then Hesketh sold the team and moved into politics, leaving F1 all the poorer without his flamboyance.

FLAMBOYANT BUT FLAWED

Flavio Briatore became involved in racing through the Benetton family after he'd headed up their clothing chain's push into the USA. He was asked to be commercial director of their team in 1988 and brought in Tom Walkinshaw to help run it. Signing Michael Schumacher was the key to success and titles followed in 1994 (drivers') and 1995 (drivers' and constructors'). He has since been involved with supplying teams with Renault engines and then ran Renault's F1 return until he was banned in 2009 for his role in the "Singaporegate" race-fixing scandal. However, that ban was overturned, and in 2024 he returned as an advisor to the Alpine team.

A STELLA JOB

McLaren appointed Andrea Stella as its Team Principal in December 2022, marking the first top job for the Italian. He swiftly put in place a revised technical structure, and calmly fronted McLaren's revival. Stella, who was previously race engineer at Ferrari for Michael Schumacher, Kimi Räikkönen and Fernando Alonso, returned McLaren to the top of the Constructors' standings, ending in 2024 its 26-year wait for another world title.

Above Andrea Stella guided McLaren to the 2024 championship.

DRIVER THEN TEAM CHIEF

Jack Brabham landed three F1 drivers' titles and also set new standards by becoming the first F1 driver to win a grand prix in a car bearing his name. Decades later, Christian Horner also transferred to running race teams after starting off as a racing driver. As a driver, he didn't make it to F1, stopping short in F3000, but many feel that it is Christian's insight into a racer's psyche that has helped him take Red Bull Racing forwards after its transformation from Jaguar Racing, including overseeing Sebastian Vettel's four F1 drivers' titles.

THE ULTIMATE ENTREPRENEUR

Bernie Ecclestone made his first fortune selling motorbike parts. A club-level car racer, Bernie was busier away from the tracks, establishing a business empire. He bought the Connaught F1 team in 1958 and even tried to qualify a car himself at Monaco. His attempt was unsuccessful so he settled for driver management. After the death of charge Jochen Rindt in 1970, he bought Brabham in 1972 and ran that until he sold it in 1987. His role as the F1 rights holder through his Formula One Management company gave him both power and wealth before he sold it to CVC in 2005. Ecclestone remained in charge of F1 until it was sold to Liberty Media in 2017.

FROM RACER TO PRESIDENT

Max Mosley spent his life being referred to as the son of fascist politician Sir Oswald Mosley, precluding any dreams of a political career. Instead, Max tried racing, reaching F2 before becoming one of the founder members of March in 1969. He quit March in 1977 and moved into helping the teams form a united front through the Formula One Constructors' Association (FOCA), working with Bernie Ecclestone. He then became president of the Fédération Internationale de l'Automobile (FIA) in 1986 and held the position until late 2009 when he stood down and was replaced by the newly elected Jean Todt. Mosley died in 2021.

A MODEL PROFESSIONAL

Jackie Stewart achieved far more in F1 than winning 27 grands prix and three World Championships. He pushed for driver safety when it was far from fashionable to do so, his efforts no doubt saving many lives. He also sought a more professional level than his contemporaries and, after a spell commentating for American TV, returned to F1 as a team owner in 1997, in conjunction with older son Paul. Stewart GP won once, at the Nürburgring in 1999, but was sold on to Ford, who rebranded it as Jaguar Racing and it later became Red Bull Racing.

A RACER WHO TURNED TO MANAGEMENT

Christian Horner had hoped to make it as a driver, but wasn't able to progress beyond Formula 3000. At this point, he started his own team, Arden Motorsport, and it would become increasingly competitive until it achieved title success with Bjorn Wirdheim in 2003 and Vitantonio Liuzzi in 2004. Christian's big break came with the formation of Red Bull Racing for 2005 from what had been Jaguar Racing. Installed as team principal, he has run the team ever since as it has moved to the top and claimed drivers' and constructors' titles.

Right Sebastian Vettel and Christian Horner celebrate in the paddock after yet another Vettel win in 2013.

TYRE MANUFACTURERS

🏆 GOODYEAR'S BREAKTHROUGH

F1's most successful tyre supplier, Goodyear, had no clue what lay ahead when it did a deal with Honda in 1965 and driver Richie Ginther guided the combination to its first win in the last round of the World Championship in Mexico City. No one then would have predicted that this famous American tyre manufacturer would go on to become F1's leading supplier, achieving a further 367 wins.

Left Jacques Villeneuve claimed seven wins for Williams in 1997 as he became Goodyear's 24th and most recent F1 World Champion.

NO TREAD REQUIRED

The tyres used in the World Championship have changed in many ways since 1950, but few changes have been as great as the arrival of slick tyres in 1971, when tread was dispensed with to provide extra grip. These lasted until 1998 when, to slow the cars, grooved tyres became obligatory. It wasn't until 2009 that slick tyres returned.

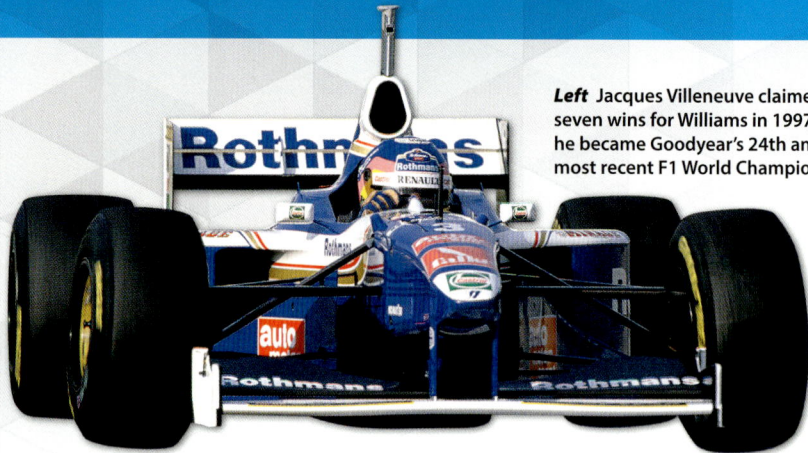

MADE TO LAST

Goodyear is the tyre company with the longest F1 association. Its involvement began in 1959 and finished in 1998 after its tyres had been used in just short of 500 grands prix. Bridgestone edged past Michelin (215 grands prix) in 2009, to become the second most-used tyre, with 244 races by the end of 2010. Both were then passed by Pirelli, which quit at the end of 1991 before coming back in 2011, and moving ahead of rival manufacturer Bridgestone in 2013.

THEY SHOOT, THEY SCORE

Goodyear has scored more World Championship points than any other tyre manufacturer, its tally standing at 9,474.5 when it packed up its tyre trucks for the final time after the 1998 Japanese GP, two races after Michael Schumacher gave the American company its final F1 win at Monza. That tally represents just over 19 points for each grand prix that it attended. This would have been much higher still had the current scoring system been in operation during those years.

Below Bridgestone passed Michelin in 2009 to become F1's second most prolific tyre company. Pirelli has been the sole supplier since 2011.

Above Esteban Ocon carried out a zero-stop strategy for Alpine during the 2021 Turkish GP.

TYRE MANUFACTURER WITH MOST WINS

1	Goodyear	368
2	Pirelli	329
3	Bridgestone	175
4	Michelin	102
5	Dunlop	83
6	Firestone	38
7	Continental	10
8	Englebert	8

YET ANOTHER GOOD YEAR

Cars fitted with Goodyear tyres have started more grands prix than those fitted with any other tyre brand by a factor of two. Goodyear-shod cars have claimed 24 titles between 1966 and 1997, though Pirelli, sole supplier since 2011, is fast catching up!

NO STOPPING OCON

Under Formula One regulations drivers must pit at least once in a grand prix and run two different compounds of tyre – assuming the race is held in dry conditions. At the 2021 Turkish GP, held in wet conditions, Alpine's Esteban Ocon coaxed life out of his wet tyres and did not make a single pit stop, profiting to finish in 10th position. He is the only driver to have not made a pit stop in a full-distance race, with no red flags, in the Pirelli era.

A CHANGING OF THE GUARD

Tyre manufacturers have come and gone and Bridgestone's exclusive spell as rubber supplier closed at the end of the 2010 season, with Pirelli returning for 2011 after 20 years away. As it is now the World Championship's sole tyre supplier, the Italian company has boosted its tally of wins from 44 race wins to 329.

FORMULA FARCE

The 2005 US GP at Indianapolis remains the biggest farce in F1 history. Following tyre failure on Ralf Schumacher's Toyota as it went through Turn 13, the only high-speed banked turn on an F1 circuit, during Friday practice, Michelin declared that it couldn't guarantee the safety of the tyres that it was supplying for BAR, McLaren, Red Bull, Renault, Sauber and Williams. So, the 14 cars on Michelin tyres peeled into the pits after the formation lap and refused to start, leaving just the six cars with Bridgestone tyres to race.

IN THE BLACK CORNER

The most tyre manufacturers to go head-to-head in a season is six. This happened in 1958 when Avon, Continental, Dunlop, Englebert, Firestone and Pirelli all sought glory.

TYRE MANUFACTURER WITH MOST POLE POSITIONS

1	Goodyear	358
2	Pirelli	331
3	Bridgestone	168
4	Michelin	111
5	Dunlop	76
6	Firestone	49
7	Englebert	12
8	Continental	8

Above It was a busy pit lane at a rain-hit Dutch GP in 2023.

A BUSY PIT LANE

F1 races typically feature a single pit stop, a more aggressive strategy may result in a two-stopper, while on occasion drivers will come in for a third time. The busiest pit lane action happened at the 2023 Dutch GP, when the 20 drivers pitted a record 89 times overall, as showers swept through the coastal Zandvoort circuit during the course of the afternoon. Race winner Max Verstappen had six visits to the pit lane!

ENGINE MANUFACTURERS

MORE THAN JUST A BADGE

After Renault's pioneering turbo years in the late 1970s more and more horsepower was produced. The arbitrary 1.5-litre equivalency allowed against the 3.0-litre normally aspirated engines soon gave the turbo teams a big advantage and they won race after race. Turbos were back for 2014.

ENDING UP ON TOP

Renault can be delighted by the 173 grand prix wins achieved by cars carrying its engines, but its ability to develop its engines until they are the best of their age is shown by the fact that Renault-powered cars won the final races of the 3.5-litre formula in 1994, the V10 era in 2005 and the 2.4-litre formula in 2013.

STRAIGHT EIGHT OR IN A VEE?

When F1 began in 1950, the dominant Alfa Romeos were powered by supercharged straight-eight engines, with their rivals using straight-six or even four-cylinder engines. Since then, the V8 engine has been most successful, with 451 grand prix wins, with V10 engines, used from 1995 to 2005, on 240 wins.

Above Teo Fabi's Benetton enjoyed prodigious BMW turbo horsepower in 1986.

TOP 10 ENGINE MANUFACTURERS WITH MOST STARTS

1	Ferrari	1100
2	Renault	747
3	Mercedes	587
4	Honda	543
5	Ford	523
6	BMW	270
7	Alfa Romeo	222
8	BRM	189
9	Mugen Honda	147
10	Hart	145

THE MOST BANGS FOR YOUR BUCK

F1 technical regulations have changed constantly since the World Championship began in 1950 and the most recent engines are not the most powerful. That honour goes to the turbocharged engines when their boost was wound up for qualifying for a burst of one lap. The BMW turbo used by Benetton racers Gerhard Berger and Teo Fabi in 1986 is estimated to have pushed out 1400bhp.

THE HEARTBEAT OF AMERICA

The V8 engine is still the heartbeat of America, but the first winning V8 in F1 was fitted to Luigi Musso's Lancia Ferrari in the 1956 Argentinian GP. That said, Ford put its name to F1's most successful V8 of all, the Cosworth DFV, which claimed a record 155 F1 wins.

TOP 10 ENGINE MANUFACTURERS WITH MOST WINS

1	Ferrari	249
2	Mercedes	222
3	Renault	178
4	Ford	176
5	Honda	136
6	Coventry Climax	40
7	Porsche	26
8	BMW	20
9	BRM	18
10	Alfa Romeo	12

FORZA FERRARI

Ferrari has been around for the longest so it's little surprise that its engines have claimed the most wins, at 249, with Mercedes next on the list, scoring 222 victories – despite a 42-year gap between successive wins in 1955 and 1997.

SPINNERS CAN BE WINNERS

BMW took peak revs per minute to a new level in 2003 when its V10-format engines revved up to 19,200rpm and pushed out more than 900bhp in the back of the Williams. Within two years, engine capacity was cut back from 3.0 litres to 2.4 to reduce performance in the name of driver safety.

FERRARI POWERS TOP DRIVERS

Ferrari's prancing horses have powered drivers to the most World Championship titles – 15 in all, between Alberto Ascari in 1952 and Kimi Räikkönen's title in 2007. Ford is next on 13, from 1968 to 1994, with the first 12 of those up to 1982 won with the most successful F1 engine ever: the Ford Cosworth DFV.

THE PACE OF CHANGE

There is no more testing arena for technical development than F1, so it's not surprising there have been many developments since the World Championship began. The most visible ones have been to the car, but the engines have changed too (*see* box right).

Above Kimi Räikkönen was the most recent Ferrari world champion, when he pipped Lewis Hamilton and Fernando Alonso in 2007.

ENGINE DEVELOPMENT TIMELINE

1950	Cars allowed 4500cc normally aspirated or 1500cc supercharged engines.
1952	Engine capacity restricted to 2000cc or 500cc supercharged engines as F2 rules adopted.
1954	Capacity boosted to 2500cc or 750cc supercharged.
1958	Use of commercial fuel made mandatory.
1961	Supercharged engines banned and engine size reduced to 1500–1300cc.
1966	Engine capacity enlarged to 3000cc.
1972	Maximum of 12 cylinders imposed.
1987	Engine capacity enlarged to 3500cc.
1989	Turbocharged engines banned.
1995	Reduction of maximum engine capacity to 3000cc.
2006	Engines restricted to eight cylinders and 2400cc.
2014	Engines changed to 1600cc turbocharged V6 hybrids.

Above Williams racer Ralf Schumacher enjoyed an incredible 19,200rpm from his BMW engine in 2003.
Left Ferrari's Luigi Musso races towards the first win for a V8, chased by Stirling Moss's Maserati in 1956.

TRACKS

Across the globe 78 different venues have welcomed the Formula One World Championship. Some have been fleeting partnerships while other circuits have long rubber-stamped their way into the hearts of multiple generations of drivers, thanks to their challenging nature and ability to regularly produce exciting racing. There are also newer kids on the block, as Formula One continues to expand its horizons.

Above Formula One laid down a marker in Las Vegas when it took over the famous Strip in 2023.

TRACK LENGTHS

GOING ROUND AND ROUND

The greatest number of laps in a grand prix was the 110 laps covered by the winning entrants in the US GP at Watkins Glen between 1963 and 1965. This equated to a race distance of 258.5 miles. In 1966, maximum race distances were cut back to 248.5 miles.

NOT THE BEST OF STARTS

The Monaco street circuit had been hosting races since 1929, but its World Championship debut in 1950 was a near disaster as there was an accident at Tabac at the end of the opening lap after Giuseppe Farina triggered a shunt that eliminated nine cars. The wreckage was spread across the track, but Juan Manuel Fangio was able to thread his way through and race clear to score his first win for Alfa Romeo.

WILL IT BE OVER SOON?

Grands prix up to 1957 were run to a target time of three hours, although some went on for even longer. The 1954 German GP held at the 14.167-mile-long Nürburgring Nordschleife was the longest grand prix in terms of time. It took winner Juan Manuel Fangio 3 hrs 45 mins 45.8 secs to cover the 22 laps, and he was rewarded with victory by 1 min 36.5 secs.

Above A gaggle of midfielders climb the sloping approach to Shell Kurve at the Nürgburgring in 1996 with the Dunlop Kehre in the background.

THE CRUELLEST CUT OF ALL

Once it ran for a full 14.189 miles through the Eifel Forest, the second longest circuit ever in the World Championship, but its Nordschleife lay-out was dropped by F1 after 1976 and when it next hosted a World Championship round in 1985, it had been hacked back to just 3.199 miles, leaving the forest loop to club racers.

GOING ON AND ON

The longest circuit is the Pescara circuit on Italy's Adriatic coast, which held a grand prix in 1957. The 15.894-mile lap ran uphill, through villages and over level crossings before returning for a blast along the seafront. Stirling Moss beat Juan Manuel Fangio by more than three minutes.

OVER IN A FLASH

Because the Monza circuit produces such a high average speed, it is usually the shortest race on the F1 calendar in terms of duration. The drivers know that if they don't clash and the safety car doesn't have to be involved they can have their afternoon's work completed in just 1 hr 15 mins.

Below The circuit's endless twists – this is Turn 2 – keep speeds in check.

HUNGARORING

Grand prix years: 1986 onwards

No. of grands prix held: 39

Lap length: From 2.494 miles to 2.466 miles to 2.722 miles

Fastest qualifying lap: 1 min 13.447 secs, Lewis Hamilton (Mercedes, 2020)

Fastest race lap: 1 min 16.627 secs, Lewis Hamilton (Mercedes, 2020)

Driver with most wins: Lewis Hamilton – eight (2007, 2009, 2012, 2013, 2016, 2018, 2019, 2020)

TRACKS WITH LONGEST LAP LENGTHS

1	Pescara	(Italy)	15.894 miles
2	Nürburgring	(Germany)	14.189 miles
3	Spa-Francorchamps	(Belgium)	8.774 miles
4	Monza	(Italy)	6.214 miles
5	Sebring	(USA)	5.200 miles

Right Tracks with longest lap lengths: Masten Gregory points his Maserati around Pescara's 15.894-mile lap in 1957.

BONKERS BAKU

The Baku City Circuit is unusual and includes one section where the apex of a corner is actually the edge of the Old City's walls. Baku arrived on the schedule in 2016 and the circuit has the longest full-throttle section on the calendar. When drivers exit Turn 16 they have a couple of kinks taken flat out, which leads them onto the main straight. By the time they brake for Turn 1 drivers have had their foot to the floor for almost 1.4 miles.

ARE YOU GOING VERY FAR SIR?

Discounting the 500-mile Indianapolis 500 that was nominally a round of the World Championship from 1950–60, the longest grand prix in terms of distance was the 1951 French GP at Reims, with its 77 laps equating to 373.912 miles. It's no surprise that Juan Manuel Fangio's Alfa Romeo started to fail, forcing him to take over the sister car that started the race in the hands of Luigi Fagioli. Fangio's winning time was 3 hrs 22 mins 11 secs.

JUST FOUR LEFT RUNNING

It seems inconceivable, but two grands prix since 1950 have finished with just four cars still running. Less hard to imagine is that both of these were at Monaco, where the walls can bite. The first occasion was in 1966 when Jackie Stewart won for BRM, albeit with two further finishers not being classified as they were so far behind. The second was 30 years later when Olivier Panis won a wet/dry race for Ligier as others crashed out.

THE SHORTEST POLE LAP

Bahrain's Outer Circuit doesn't quite make the top five shortest laps – at 2.2 miles – but it holds the record for the shortest pole time thanks to its high average speed. The Outer Circuit was used just once, in the 2020 season, when two grands prix were held in Bahrain. Mercedes driver Valtteri Bottas set a time of 53.377s to claim pole.

TRACKS WITH SHORTEST LAP LENGTHS

1	Monaco		1.954 miles
2	Zeltweg	(Austria)	1.988 miles
3	Long Beach	(USA)	2.020 miles
4	Dijon-Prenois	(France)	2.044 miles
5	Jarama	(Spain)	2.058 miles

Below Modern Formula One laps usually last around 70–90 seconds, but Bahrain's Outer Circuit featured a rare sub-minute lap time.

LOCATIONS

DOES ANYONE WANT TO FINISH?

A heavy burst of rain that hit the far side of the circuit led to carnage in the 1975 British GP, when car after car slid off to bring the race to a premature halt. Race leader Emerson Fittipaldi managed to guide his McLaren through the corners, but Carlos Pace and Jody Scheckter, who were classified second and third, did not, along with 10 others.

HOTSPOT LOCATIONS

Three F1 circuits have volcanic connections: Fuji Speedway in Japan is situated on the side slopes of Mount Fuji; France's Clermont-Ferrand is built among volcanic outcrops; and the Mexico City circuit is actually located in a volcanic basin.

UNDER THE SEA

F1 first visited Azerbaijan in 2016, with a street circuit laid out around capital city, Baku. It is one of several circuits next to a body of water, with the Caspian Sea just a few minutes' walk away. As the Caspian Sea is actually a low-lying lake, it means that the lowest point of the Baku City Circuit sits around 25 metres below sea level.

EUROPE LEADS THE WAY

Europe has hosted grands prix at 41 circuits. They are: A1-Ring, Aintree, Anderstorp, Avus, Brands Hatch, Bremgarten, Catalunya, Clermont-Ferrand, Dijon-Prenois, Donington Park, Estoril, Hockenheim, Hungaroring, Imola, Jarama, Jerez, Le Mans Bugatti, Magny-Cours, Monaco, Monsanto, Montjuich Park, Monza, Mugello, Nivelles, Nürburgring, Österreichring, Paul Ricard, Pedralbes, Pescara, Portimao, Porto, Red Bull Ring, Reims, Rouen-les Essarts, Silverstone, Sochi, Spa-Francorchamps, Valencia, Zandvoort, Zeltweg and Zolder.

HOW NOT TO FINISH THE FIRST LAP

Jody Scheckter was looking to impress when he made his fourth grand prix appearance for McLaren at the 1973 British GP. Starting sixth, he was up to fourth when he ran wide out of Woodcote at the end of the first lap, went on to the grass, then took out a third of the field as he scattered the cars behind. Only 19 of 28 starters were able to take the restart 90 minutes later.

Below Cars scatter in all directions at Silverstone in 1973 after Jody Scheckter spun in front of them at the end of the opening lap.

Above Aerial view of the MIA campus/Hard Rock Stadium.

STADIUM SUCCESS

The Miami International Autodrome, which made its debut in 2022, is entirely located on the campus of the Hard Rock Stadium, home to American football team Miami Dolphins.

ITALY FIRST TO 100

Italy is the only country to have hosted more than 100 grands prix. It has been a mainstay of the calendar since 1950, and while Monza has long held the country's national race, Imola has hosted races under the San Marino and Emilia Romagna guise, while Pescara in 1957 and Mugello in 2020 have also been visited by Formula One. Italy has now held 107 races, while (to the end of 2024), the USA, Britain and Germany have all hosted 79 races.

NUMBER OF F1 CIRCUITS BY CONTINENT

1	Europe	41
2	North/Central America	16
3	Asia	15
4	Africa	3
=	South America	3
6	Australasia	2

Above Saudi Arabia joined the calendar in 2021 with the Jeddah Corniche Circuit.

NARROWING THE GULF

Formula One did not race in the Middle East for the first five decades of the championship, before Bahrain joined the party in 2004. The United Arab Emirates came along in 2009, with Abu Dhabi welcoming Formula One, while Qatar and Saudi Arabia were both added to the schedule in 2021. Qatar and Bahrain are the two closest locations on the schedule, with the Lusail and Sakhir circuits just 71 miles apart, separated by the Persian Gulf.

TWICE THE PLEASURE

During the pandemic-hit 2020 season both Red Bull Ring and Silverstone hosted two grands prix apiece, with its alternative races called the Styrian GP and 70th Anniversary Grand Prix respectively. It marked the first time the same circuit was used twice in one season. Bahrain also held two rounds, though one was held on its 'Outer Layout', with Turns 4 to 13 bypassed by a short section. The Red Bull Ring hosted two grands prix once more, in 2021, as the pandemic continued.

A RACER'S DOZEN

No country has held more races at different venues than the USA. There have been 12 different circuits, and they are Indianapolis, Sebring, Riverside, Watkins Glen, Long Beach, Caesars Palace, Detroit, Dallas, Phoenix, Austin, Miami and Las Vegas. Miami joined in 2022, with Las Vegas following suit in 2023, a stone's throw from the Caesars Palace track which was only visited twice in the 1980s. The USA's dozen puts it above the seven locations F1 has raced at in France.

HANOI-NO

Vietnam was added to Formula One's 2020 calendar, and a hybrid circuit, of purpose-built permanent sections meshed with the city's streets, was built in capital Ha-Noi. But three weeks out from the debut event it was cancelled due to the pandemic, and by the time restrictions were lifted the main organiser had been charged with corruption. There was no appetite in Vietnam to continue the project, so the fully built circuit has never been used.

Above Suzuka is revered among Formula One drivers.

SUZUKA

Grand prix years: 1987–2006, 2009–2019, 2022 onwards

No. of grands prix held: 34

Lap length: From 3.641 miles to 3.644 miles to current 3.608 miles

Fastest qualifying lap: 1 min 27.064 secs, Sebastian Vettel (Ferrari), 2019

Fastest race lap: 1 min 30.983 secs, Lewis Hamilton (Mercedes), 2019

Driver with most wins: Michael Schumacher – six (1995, 1997, 2000, 2001, 2002, 2004)

LAP RECORDS

MONZA, THE FASTEST OF THEM ALL

The home of the Italian GP, Monza, remains the circuit with the highest race lap speed recorded – 159.909mph set in 2004. Those circuits ranked behind Monza in terms of lap speed are: Silverstone, Spa-Francorchamps, the Österreichring, Hockenheim, Avus, Suzuka, A1-Ring, Reims and Melbourne. Of these, only Monza, Suzuka and Melbourne have a similar track configuration to when these fastest laps were set.

ALMOST ALL STRAIGHTS

The Avus circuit in Berlin had a remarkably simple layout. It was an up-and-down dual carriageway, with a corner at its southern end that made its shape look like a hairclip and at the northern end there was a high, banked corner. These were its only features. As a result, lap speeds were high, with Tony Brooks' winning average speed for Ferrari being 143.342mph all the way back in 1959.

LOOKING FOR SPEED

When the Silverstone circuit was reshaped for 2010 and beyond, as part of its modernization project, there was talk that its average lap speed would soar. However, such headlines had to be forgotten when the new Arena infield section failed to boost average lap speeds. Indeed, Fernando Alonso's fastest race lap equated to 145.011mph, falling short of the 146.059mph lap average that Michael Schumacher set on the previous layout in his Ferrari F2004 back in 2004.

Below Mercedes' W11 holds the distinction of being the fastest machine in Formula One history, especially in the hands of Lewis Hamil

FAST, FASTER, FASTEST

Monza and Spa-Francorchamps used to vie for the fastest average race-winning speed – a mind-boggling 150mph. Then chicanes were inserted. But the cars kept getting faster and the winning average speed for Michael Schumacher's Ferrari in the 2003 Italian GP at Monza was 153.842mph. The fastest Spa average is from 1970 on the old circuit, when Pedro Rodriguez lapped his BRM in a race-winning average of 149.942mph.

LIGHTNING LEWIS

The fastest laps in Formula One come during qualifying, when the engine modes are turned up, cars are equipped with fresh soft tyres, and there is just enough fuel to get the car around the lap. The fastest-ever qualifying lap was set at Monza, in 2020, and Formula One's pole king Lewis Hamilton achieved it. Hamilton hurtled the W11 around the circuit in a time of 1:18.887, at an average speed of 164.267 mph.

RUBENS' RECORD

Lap records are officially recorded during grands prix, so they tend to be slightly slower than the overall circuit records, which are set in qualifying. Rubens Barrichello still holds the overall fastest lap record, a 1:21.046s, at an average speed of 159.892mph, at Monza in 2004. That was during an era of in-race refuelling, and super grippy Bridgestone tyres. Lando Norris came just a few tenths away from the record in 2024, but Barrichello's honour remains in tact for now.

Above Jeddah is one of F1's newest circuits but has gained a reputation for its high-speed nature.

WONDER WALLS

By their nature, street circuits in Formula One have tended to be slightly slower than their road course counterparts, but the Jeddah Street Circuit bucks this trend. The wall-lined circuit joined Formula One's calendar in 2021 and immediately became a driver favourite owing to the fast-paced nature of the lap, and that year Lewis Hamilton set the lap record at an average speed of 152.212mph, with Max Verstappen's pole lap in 2024 resulting in a circuit record of 157.888mph.

Above A narrow track littered with hairpins slows drivers at Monaco, as shown by Juan Manuel Fangio in 1950 as he recorded the slowest ever fastest lap.

GET A MOVE ON

Not all circuits produce average lap speeds that are double what you'd normally travel at in the fast lane of a motorway. The tight confines of Monaco limit drivers to average speeds in double rather than treble figures. However, the slowest fastest lap in a grand prix was set by Juan Manuel Fangio at Monaco in 1950, at 64.085mph. Detroit's street track is second on this list.

BARCELONA

Grand prix years: 1991 onwards	
No. of grands prix held: 34	
2.875 miles to current 2.894 miles	
Fastest qualifying lap: 1 min 11.383 secs, Lando Norris (McLaren), 2024	
Fastest race lap: 1 min 16.330 secs, Max Verstappen (Red Bull Racing), 2023	
Driver with most wins: Michael Schumacher – six (1995, 1996, 2001, 2002, 2003, 2004)	
Lewis Hamilton – six (2014, 2017, 2018, 2019, 2020, 2021)	

TOP 10 CIRCUITS WITH FASTEST LAP RECORDS

1	Monza	159.892mph
2	Silverstone	153.053mph
3	Jeddah	152.212mph
4	Spa-Francorchamps	152.049mph
5	Österreichring	150.509mph
6	Hockenheim	150.059mph
7	Avus	149.129mph
8	Mugello	148.830mph
9	Melbourne	147.928mph
10	Red Bull Ring	147.200mph

Note: All circuit layouts from history, so old Silverstone & old Spa rather than current layouts

Below The downhill run past the pits.

VICTORY ROLLS

THAT SPECIAL RELATIONSHIP

British drivers grew to love their forays across the Atlantic to the US GP because they enjoyed remarkable success. There was a run of nine straight US wins for British drivers between Stirling Moss' triumph in 1960 and Jackie Stewart's in 1968.

STREETS AHEAD

British teams experienced significant success in Monaco in the 1950s, 60s and 70s. The drivers tended to come up trumps, winning there 16 times in a row from Maurice Trintignant's win in Rob Walker's Cooper in 1958 to Ronnie Peterson's victory for Lotus in 1974.

HIGH FIVE

Ayrton Senna and Lewis Hamilton both have the distinction of winning the same grand prix for five successive years. Monaco king Senna won around the streets of the Principality five times in a row from 1989 through 1993, having also won for Lotus in 1987, with his shock crash from the lead denying him the win in 1988. Hamilton made it five on the bounce at the Spanish GP from 2017 through 2021, following on from his first Barcelona triumph in 2014.

HAMILTON'S ROLL CALL

Lewis Hamilton has won at more circuits than any other driver. He has won at 31 different circuits (in order of accomplishment): Montreal, Indianapolis, Hungaroring, Fuji Speedway, Melbourne, Monaco, Silverstone, Hockenheim, Shanghai, Singapore, Istanbul Park, Spa-Francorchamps, Nürburgring, Yas Marina, Monza, Austin, Sepang, Sakhir, Barcelona, Suzuka, Sochi, Red Bull Ring, Mexico City, Interlagos, Baku, Paul Ricard, Mugello, Portimao, Imola, Lusail and Jeddah. Max Verstappen is next, having won at 26 different circuits.

Right Lewis Hamilton has stood on the top step of the podium at 31 different venues

FERRARI'S MONZA MAGIC

The Italian GP is one of the originals and it is here above all other venues that Ferrari wants to win, right in front of its fans (the Tifosi). The team, whose scarlet cars bear the famous prancing horse emblem, has done just that on 20 occasions, from Alberto Ascari's victory in 1951 to Charles Leclerc's in 2024.

FOUR STARTS, THREE WINS

Alfa Romeo all but swept the board in the first two years of Formula One before it quit and Ferrari came on strong in 1952. As a result of this, it was Ferrari that collected records through the 1950s and Ferrari that became the first team to win three times at any circuit, doing so at Silverstone in 1954.

BUENOS AIRES

Grand prix years: 1953-1958, 1960, 1972-1975, 1995-1998

No. of grands prix held: 20

Lap length: From 2.431 miles to 3.708 miles to 2.646 miles

Fastest qualifying lap: 1 min 24.473 secs, Jacques Villeneuve (Williams), 1997

Fastest race lap: 1 min 27.981 secs, Gerhard Berger (Benetton), 1997

Driver with most wins: Juan Manuel Fangio – four (1954, 1955, 1956, 1957)

THE MOST DANGEROUS PLACE TO RACE

The Nürburgring Nordschleife had the reputation as the sport's most deadly circuit, as it claimed the lives of seven F1 drivers: Onofre Marimon in practice in 1954, Erwin Bauer in a sports car race in 1958, Peter Collins in the 1958 grand prix, Carel Godin de Beaufort in practice in 1964, John Taylor in 1966, Georges Berger in an endurance race in 1967 and Gerhard Mitter in practice in 1969. Niki Lauda was almost added to that list in 1976.

Right Niki Lauda was lucky to survive this fiery crash in 1976.

HOME COMFORTS

British drivers have won their home event on 29 occasions, split across 12 different racers, with Stirling Moss starting the roll call at Aintree in 1955, through to Lewis Hamilton's most recent triumph at Silverstone in 2024. In addition, Nigel Mansell won the European Grand Prix, in 1985, which was held at Brands Hatch.

WINNING IN YOUR BACKYARD

Red Bull acquired the old A1-Ring circuit in Austria, rebranded it the Red Bull Ring, and restored it to the calendar in 2014. In 2018 Max Verstappen claimed victory, the first for a team at a circuit which bears its name. Red Bull has since added further wins at the Red Bull Ring in 2019, two during the pandemic-hit 2021 season, and again in 2023.

UNPREDICTABLE BARCELONA

The Circuit de Barcelona-Catalunya had, perhaps unfairly, earned a reputation for producing a predictable snoozefest. But between 2007 and 2016 Barcelona's race produced 10 different winners. Felipe Massa started the streak in 2007, followed by Kimi Räikkönen, Jenson Button, Mark Webber, Sebastian Vettel, Pastor Maldonado, Fernando Alonso, Lewis Hamilton, Nico Rosberg and Max Verstappen. That streak was firmly snapped, with Hamilton winning in 2017, 2018, 2019, 2020 and 2021, before Verstappen's triumphs in 2022, 2023 and 2024.

UNB-EIGHT-EN

Mercedes had several successful streaks throughout its dominant phase in F1 in the 2010s and this was best witnessed at Russia's uninspiring Sochi Autodrom. The venue, a former Winter Olympics host, joined the calendar in 2014, and Mercedes won all eight grands prix held there, before it dropped off the schedule after 2021. Lewis Hamilton won there five times, Nico Rosberg once, while Valtteri Bottas emerged as a two-time winner – including his maiden victory in 2017.

TEAMS WITH MOST WINS AT ONE CIRCUIT

1	20	Ferrari	Monza
2=	15	McLaren	Monaco
2=	15	Ferrari	Silverstone
4=	14	Ferrari	Nürburgring
4=	14	Ferrari	Spa-Francorchamps
6=	12	McLaren	Silverstone
6=	12	McLaren	Spa-Francorchamps
6=	12	McLaren	Hungaroring
9=	11	Ferrari	Hockenheim
9=	11	Ferrari	Montreal
9=	11	McLaren	Monza

Below The refurbished Red Bull Ring has been back in action for over a decade, and Max Verstappen has delivered home victories for the outfit.

NUMBER OF RACES HELD

⊙ HONOUR OF OPENING THE SEASON

Australia holds the record for hosting the most opening grands prix of the season, having done so on 22 occasions at Melbourne's Albert Park. Second is Buenos Aires in Argentina, which has hosted 15 openers. South Africa's Kyalami circuit is third, having held the opening race eight times.

MOROCCAN ROLL

Several circuits have been raced on only once throughout Formula One history but they have been frequented in countries that the championship regularly visits. The only country to have ever held just one Formula One world championship grand prix is Morocco. The Ain-Daib road circuit near Casablanca held the 1958 finale, with Sir Stirling Moss victorious, while Mike Hawthorn secured the world title with second place.

THREE TIMES IN ONE YEAR

Italy and the United States are the only countries to have hosted three grands prix in a single season. Long Beach, Detroit and Caesars Palace all hosted races in 1982, while from 2023 Austin, Miami and Las Vegas all feature on F1's calendar. Italy's Monza, Imola and Mugello all welcomed Formula One in 2020.

CURTAIN CLOSER

The location of Formula One's season finale has varied across the years. Australia's Adelaide, Japan's Suzuka and Brazil's Interlagos have all held the honour of rounding out the campaign, but Abu Dhabi's Yas Marina Circuit has now held more finales than any other circuits. Yas Marina first hosted the finale in 2009 and 2010, and after a brief return to Interlagos, Yas Marina was shifted back to the curtain-closer in 2014, where it has remained ever since, reaching 13 in 2024.

SOMETHING ON THE SIDE

The World Championship was augmented by non-championship races in the early years, with the six championship grands prix in 1950 supported by 16 non-championship events. Juan Manuel Fangio won four of them, earning prize money.

Below The sun sets on both the Abu Dhabi Grand Prix, and the Formula One season, with Yas Marina now the location for the finale.

Above The purpose-built Circuit of the Americas has hosted the US Grand Prix since 2012, and has now been joined by Miami and Las Vegas.

TOP 10 MOST-USED CIRCUITS

1	Monza	74
2	Monaco	70
3	Silverstone	59
4	Spa-Francorchamps	57
5	Montreal	43
6	Nürburgring	41
7	Interlagos	40
8	Hungaroring	39
9	Hockenheim	37
10	Zandvoort	34
=	Suzuka	34
=	Barcelona	34

VARIETY APLENTY

The Long Beach street circuit in California has been used just eight times as a second US GP, but its tricky, bumpy course is one that no individual driver conquered as pole position went to a different driver each time, from Clay Regazzoni in 1976 to Patrick Tambay in 1983, both driving for Ferrari.

BACK-TO-BACK

In 1995 the Pacific Grand Prix at Japan's TI Aida was postponed from March due to an earthquake, and was instead held a week before the Japanese Grand Prix at Suzuka. The final round of 1995 took place at Australia's Adelaide circuit, the last time the venue was used, and the opening event of 1996 was Melbourne's inaugural race.

WHAT'S IN A NAME?

The Nürburgring has hosted 41 grands prix – and has done so under four different monikers. On 26 occasions it has been as the German Grand Prix but when that name was unavailable – with the race held at Hockenheim or licensed elsewhere – it has adopted the name of the European Grand Prix 12 times, and was twice called the Luxembourg Grand Prix. In 2020 the Nürburgring came back for a one-off race under the title of the Eifel Grand Prix, in deference to the surrounding region.

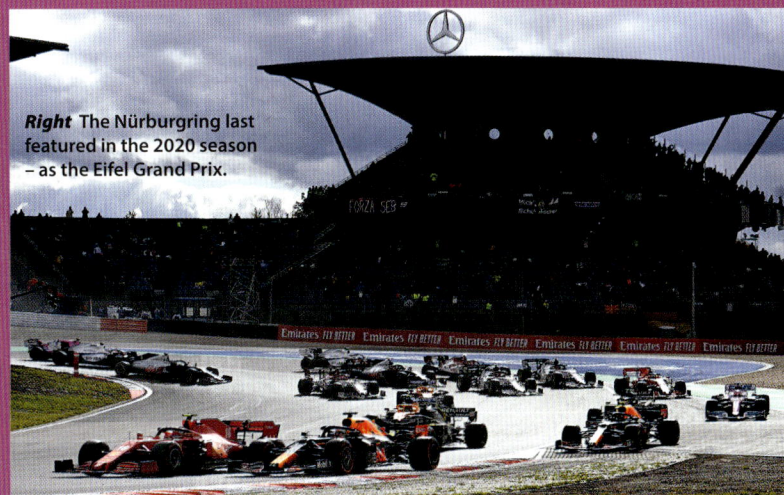

Right The Nürburgring last featured in the 2020 season – as the Eifel Grand Prix.

TWENTY-FOUR RACES

Formula One's calendar has gradually expanded through the years, aiding its revenue, and the 2024 season set a new record for the most number of grands prix, with 24. The average number of grands prix per year in the 1950s (excluding the Indianapolis 500 that then counted as a round of the World Championship) was 7.4. It rose to 9.9 in the 1960s, then 14.4 in the 1970s, 15.6 in the 1980s, 16.2 in the 1990s, 18.3 in the 2000s, and 19.8 in the 2010s. The current average for the 2020s is 21.4 – and that average will no doubt increase by the end of 2029.

Above The drop then climb from the start to Sunset bend.

KYALAMI

Grand prix years: 1967–1980, 1982–1985, 1992–1993

No. of grands prix held: 20

Lap length: From 2.544 miles to 2.550 miles to 2.648 miles

Fastest qualifying lap: 1 min 15.486 secs, Nigel Mansell (Williams), 1992

Fastest race lap: 1 min 17.578 secs, Nigel Mansell (Williams), 1992

Driver with most wins: Niki Lauda – three (1976, 1977, 1984)

HIGHEST AND LOWEST SPEEDS

SURPRISE, SURPRISE

One glance at the tight layout of the Monte Carlo street circuit and it comes as no surprise that it's the slowest circuit used by F1. Its first World Championship grand prix in 1950 was won by Juan Manuel Fangio in his Alfa Romeo, doing an average speed of just 61.331mph. There have been circuit modifications since, but not appreciable ones, yet the highest winning average rose to 98.074mph when Max Verstappen won for Red Bull in 2021.

TAKING IT TO EXTREMES

Honda Racing decided to show what its F1 car could do if it was given every opportunity to go for the max, not constrained by the limits of circuits. In 2006, test driver Alan van der Merwe drove its RA106 on the Bonneville salt flats and clocked a top speed of 246.908mph on an early morning run over the flying mile, making it the fastest F1 car ever, but falling just short of its 248.5mph (400km/h) target.

Below Aerial shot of Albert Park with its attractive lakeside setting.

QUICK QATAR

Lusail joined the F1 calendar in 2021, returning on a long-term deal from 2023, and immediately cemented a reputation as a high-speed, high-energy track. The majority of the 16 corners are taken at rapid speed, including a flat-out triple-apex right-hander, and across the course of a qualifying lap the drivers drop below fourth gear just once.

Above Lusail sits in the middle of the desert – and is home to some rapid segments of tarmac.

BOTTAS BOLTS

Formula One cars are inherently fast, of course, but the requirement for downforce means set-up compromises are often made. But the quickest speeds in different conditions were both recorded by Valtteri Bottas.

The then Williams driver clocked 234.9mph along the two-kilometre full-throttle section at the Baku City Circuit in 2016, while in the Mexican Grand Prix – where high speeds are regular due to the thinner air at altitude – Bottas registered 231.5 mph in the race that year.

MELBOURNE

Grand prix years: 1996–2019, 2022 onwards

No. of grands prix held: 27

Lap length: 3.280 to 3.295 miles

Fastest qualifying lap: 1 min 15.195 secs, Max Verstappen (Red Bull Racing), 2024

Fastest race lap: 1 min 19.813 secs, Charles Leclerc (Ferrari), 2024

Driver with most wins: Michael Schumacher – four (2000, 2001, 2002, 2004)

IT NEVER HAPPENED

Having spent his childhood in his family home overlooking Interlagos, Rubens Barrichello always dreamt that one day he would be crowned winner of the Brazilian GP. However, he seemed to be "cursed" at his home race and, by the end of 2009, had a best result of only third, despite having led the race in 1999, 2000, 2002, 2003, 2004 and 2009.

Left Rubens Barrichello did everything but win at his home circuit, Interlagos, even after starting from pole position in 2009.

FOR THE FANS

Interlagos has a proud boast of being a good track for Brazil's F1 stars, as both Emerson Fittipaldi and Carlos Pace won there during the circuit's first spell of hosting the Brazilian GP in the 1970s, sending the partisan crowd home happy. Ayrton Senna and Felipe Massa have won there since it took over the race again from Rio de Janeiro's Jacarepagua circuit in 1990, but Rubens Barrichello was never able to manage a victory.

FOOT TO THE FLOOR

Several circuits on the calendar have longer straights than Monza, and higher top speeds, but the fabled Italian venue is where the foot is on the throttle more than any other venue. For an average qualifying lap drivers spend 76 per cent of the time, and 84 per cent of the lap distance, on the throttle – meaning there's plenty of time to breathe and think about the next braking point.

PACEY PIASTRI

McLaren driver Oscar Piastri set the fastest top speed during the 2024 season. At Mexico City the Australian reached a DRS-assisted top speed of 225.2mph along the main straight at the Autódromo Hermanos Rodríguez, faster than any other driver achieved all year.

FULL LOCK

Several circuits feature flat-out corners nowadays, where drivers hustle cars at 200mph in the full knowledge that they will stick to the tarmac, but the challenge can often come at the opposite end of the spectrum, where they have to wrestle the cumbersome machines around the slow turns. The hairpin in Monaco – now named after the overlooking Fairmont Hotel – is the slowest corner on the calendar, barely wide enough for two cars, and which drivers navigate at only 30mph.

Below The hairpin at the Circuit de Monaco is the slowest corner on the calendar.

TOP 10 HIGHEST SPEEDS IN 2024

1	Mexico City	225.2mph
2	Baku	222.2mph
3	Monza	221.9mph
4	Las Vegas	221.4mph
5	Miami	220.6mph
6	Austin	216.7mph
7	Montreal	215.9mph
8	Shanghai	215.9mph
9	Barcelona	213.2mph
10	Jeddah	212.0mph

PART 2

LEGENDARY DRIVERS

Formula One is into its eighth decade and each era has featured its legendary drivers. Comparing generations in terms of achievements is often futile, given the evolving nature of the cars and the calendar. Juan Manuel Fangio and Jim Clark were heroes in a different landscape, with the baton of greatness passed down to the likes of Ayrton Senna and Michael Schumacher, and now to drivers such as Lewis Hamilton and Max Verstappen, who are already icons for the youngsters seeking to emulate them.

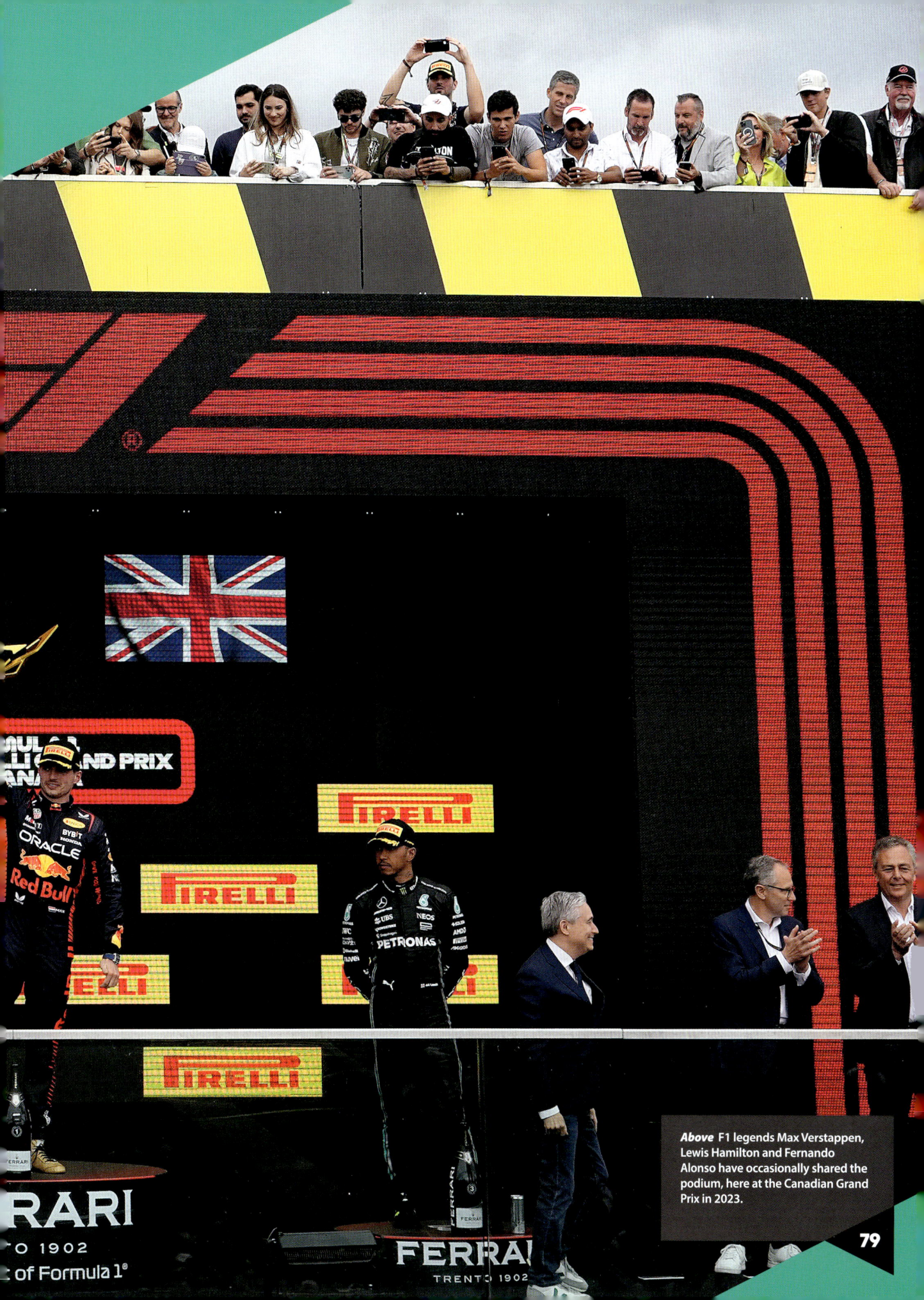

Above F1 legends Max Verstappen, Lewis Hamilton and Fernando Alonso have occasionally shared the podium, here at the Canadian Grand Prix in 2023.

MICHAEL SCHUMACHER

Michael Schumacher won two titles for Benetton in the mid-1990s before striving to return Ferrari to the top of the pile. After four years of near-misses and setbacks, Michael and Ferrari broke through, sparking wild celebrations, and setting the groundwork for the glory days of the early 2000s. Sadly, he has retreated from public life after sustaining severe injuries in a skiing accident in 2013, only one year after his retirement.

FACT FILE

Name:	Michael Schumacher
Nationality:	German
Date of birth:	3/1/69
F1 career span:	1991–2006, 2010–2012
Teams:	Jordan 1991, Benetton 1991–1995, Ferrari 1996–2006, Mercedes 2010–2012
Races contested:	308
Wins:	91
Poles:	68
Fastest laps:	76
Points:	1566
Championships:	1994, 1995, 2000, 2001, 2002, 2003, 2004

Above When Michael Schumacher won the Japanese GP at Suzuka for Ferrari in 2000 his normal podium delight was taken to a new level as it gave him the first of his five world titles with Ferrari.

A TITLE IN JULY

Michael's dominance of the 2002 season was such that he finished all 17 races on the podium, with 11 of those victories – which then was a record for one year. Michael's advantage over the field, combined with no rival putting up a consistent challenge, enabled him to clinch his fifth world title at the French GP at Magny Cours. Michael's title win came at the 11th of 17 rounds, on July 21st, making it the earliest in a calendar year that the championship has been mathematically done and dusted.

Right Michael was able to celebrate his fifth world title in 2002 as early as July.

KART BLANCHE

Michael was given the flying start of which other aspiring racers can only dream. His father Rolf ran a kart circuit, so Michael spent all his spare time during his childhood in Kerpen behind the wheel.

A HAPPY ANNIVERARY

Michael's first win came at his 18th start, on the anniversary of his debut, at the 1992 Belgian GP. After qualifying his Benetton third behind Nigel Mansell and Ayrton Senna, he enjoyed three slices of luck. Senna's gamble to start on slicks on a damp track backfired. Mansell's engine lost power. Finally, he slid off the circuit and rejoined behind team-mate Martin Brundle, noticed his tyres were blistering and changed his own at the optimum moment.

Below One year on from his debut at Spa-Francorchamps, now driving for Benetton, Michael raced to his first victory there in 1992.

BROTHER AND SON

A decade of Michael's career was spent racing alongside younger brother Ralf, with the pair on the grid together between 1997 and 2006. They shared the podium 16 times, including at the Canadian Grand Prix in 2001, when Ralf led Michael to take the first 1-2 finish for siblings. Michael's son, Mick, then raced for Haas in Formula One in 2021 and 2022.

MAKING AN IMPRESSION

Michael got his F1 break during 1991 when Jordan driver Bertrand Gachot was jailed. He qualified seventh for the Belgian GP, but burnt out his clutch at the start. By the next race, he had been snapped up by Benetton.

Right Michael was on the pace on his F1 debut for Jordan in Belgium, but his race was a short one.

A FINAL FLING WITH MERCEDES

Michael returned to Formula One in 2010 after a three-year absence and did so with Mercedes, with whom he competed in sportscars in the early years of his career. Michael's success was limited, but he set the fastest lap during qualifying in Monaco, in 2012, before a grid penalty denied him the official stat. Michael nonetheless added one more podium finish, in Valencia in 2012, to mount the podium aged 43 – the oldest to do so since 1970.

A YEAR OF CONTROVERSY

With wins in the first three races of 1994, and the death of chief rival Ayrton Senna, it was clear that Michael was heading for his first F1 title. Damon Hill stepped up for Williams and challenged him, but the matter was settled at the final round in Adelaide when Michael swerved his damaged car into Hill's Williams, after a year that had already seen Schumacher's disqualification from the British and Belgian GPs and a subsequent two-race suspension.

WHO NEEDS FULL POWER?

Perhaps Michael's greatest race performance came at the 1996 Spanish GP. This was in his first year with Ferrari, coming off the back of two consecutive title-winning seasons with Benetton, and the team was at a low ebb. However, Michael produced an extraordinary drive at a very wet Circuit de Catalunya. His Ferrari dropped onto only nine of its 10 cylinders at mid-distance, but he was still able to press on at scarcely abated speed for his first win for Ferrari.

CAREER STATS

YEAR	TEAM	RACES	WINS	POINTS	RANKING
1991	Jordan & Benetton	6	0	4	12th
1992	Benetton	16	1	53	3rd
1993	Benetton	16	1	52	4th
1994	Benetton	14	8	92	1st
1995	Benetton	17	9	102	1st
1996	Ferrari	16	3	59	3rd
1997	Ferrari	17	5	78	Not placed*
1998	Ferrari	16	6	86	2nd
1999	Ferrari	10	2	44	5th
2000	Ferrari	17	9	108	1st
2001	Ferrari	17	9	123	1st
2002	Ferrari	17	11	144	1st
2003	Ferrari	16	6	93	1st
2004	Ferrari	18	13	148	1st
2005	Ferrari	19	1	62	3rd
2006	Ferrari	18	7	121	2nd
2010	Mercedes	19	0	72	9th
2011	Mercedes	19	0	76	8th
2012	Mercedes	20	0	49	13th

*Removed from championship ranking for driving into Jacques Villeneuve in the final round at Jerez

IN FRONT AT LAST

It was only the pace of the Williams drivers that kept Michael Schumacher from pole position in 1992 and 1993, but he finally claimed his first pole position in the 1994 Monaco GP, the fourth race of the season and the one after which that arch pole qualifier Ayrton Senna had died at the San Marino GP. Michael would go on to score 67 more before he took his sabbatical from F1 at the end of 2006, but none since his return in 2010.

Right Monaco yielded the first pole position of Michael's F1 career, for Benetton in 1994, and the 2006 French GP for Ferrari the last.

Above Alain rounded out his illustrious career in 1993 by claiming his fourth title with Williams thanks to wins like this one at the German GP at Hockenheim, which proved to be his last.

ALAIN PROST

Alain Prost was extremely fast but seldom looked it as he wasn't flamboyant. It was the way that he used his head to drive supremely tactical races that earned him the sobriquet "Le Professeur". This cerebral driving style guided him to his four world drivers' titles for McLaren and then Williams.

FACT FILE

Name:	Alain Prost
Nationality:	French
Date of birth:	24/2/55
F1 career span:	1980–1991 & 1993
Teams:	McLaren 1980, Renault 1981–83, McLaren 1984–89, Ferrari 1990–91, Williams 1993
Races contested:	200
Wins:	51
Poles:	33
Fastest laps:	41
Points:	798.5
Championships:	1985, 1986, 1989, 1993

FINISHING THE JOB

Having been runner-up in 1983 and 1984, Alain was desperate to go one better in 1985, his second year with McLaren. And so he did, thanks to a good mid-season run of results. By the time he reached Brands Hatch for the European GP, Alain was in touching distance. An evasive move at the start of the race dropped him to 14th and it took a solid run to fourth to end the title bid of closest challenger Michele Alboreto, whose Ferrari's turbo failed.

FIRST PAST 50

Alain now has less than half of Lewis Hamilton's career tally of 105 wins, but he was once clear at the top of the list of winners. His victory in the 1993 British GP made him the first driver to score 50. Alain added one more to that tally at the next race at Hockenheim, but this proved to be his last as his Williams team-mate Damon Hill came on strong and won three of the remaining six grands prix.

Below Alain's victory for Williams at Silverstone in 1993 made him the first to top 50 grand prix wins.

CAREER STATS

YEAR	TEAM	RACES	WINS	POINTS	RANKING
1980	McLaren	11	0	5	15th
1981	Renault	15	3	43	5th
1982	Renault	16	2	34	4th
1983	Renault	15	4	57	2nd
1984	McLaren	16	7	71.5	2nd
1985	McLaren	16	5	76	1st
1986	McLaren	16	4	74	1st
1987	McLaren	16	3	46	4th
1988	McLaren	16	7	95	2nd
1989	McLaren	16	4	81	1st
1990	Ferrari	16	5	73	2nd
1991	Ferrari	15	0	31	5th
1993	Williams	16	7	99	1st

THE CLOSEST MISS

After quitting Renault at the end of 1983, Alain had a fruitful year with McLaren in 1984, starting with victory first time out at the Brazilian GP (above). After adding wins at Imola, Hockenheim, Zandvoort and the Nürburgring, Alain went to the final round at Estoril just 3.5 points down on team-mate Niki Lauda. Alain did all he could, passing Nelson Piquet for the lead. However, Lauda gained second place when Nigel Mansell spun out and that was enough to clinch the title by half a point.

FALLING AT THE LAST

Renault was so confident that Alain would clinch the title in 1983 that the manufacturer flew out plane loads of journalists to South Africa to cover the occasion. Alain held a two-point lead over Nelson Piquet but wasn't confident as he felt Brabham was still pushing on with its development. Piquet vaulted from second into the lead at the start and Alain could run only fourth, which wasn't going to be enough. When he felt his turbo start to fail, Alain quit the race.

Above Alain's win for Williams at Hockenheim in 1993 helped him to claim a fourth world title.

Below The first of Alain's 51 grand prix wins came in 1981, at his home grand prix.

FRESH FROM A YEAR OUT

After quitting F1 in 1991 after two years with Ferrari, Alain came back from his year's sabbatical to prove his ability yet again, this time with Williams. The car was very much the class of the field in 1993. Alain claimed seven wins (equalling his record haul for a season as recorded in 1984 and 1988) to land his fourth title, wrapping it up with second place at the Portuguese GP at Estoril.

SCORING TO THE VERY END

When Alain Prost came home second in his final race, the 1993 Australian GP at Adelaide, he cemented his position as the scorer of the highest tally of points, reaching 798.5 points, a total that Michael Schumacher passed in 2001. Michael went on to score 1,566 points after his return with Mercedes. But Lewis Hamilton (4,862.5) topped the chart by the start of 2025 season, helped by the introduction of 25 points for a win in 2010.

STEPPING UP IN STYLE

Back in the days when outstanding Formula 3 drivers could leap direct to F1, Alain Prost demonstrated that the skills that landed him the 1979 European F3 crown were more than good enough for F1. On his debut in the 1980 Argentinian GP, Alain qualified his McLaren midgrid and advanced from there to sixth place. When he finished fifth next time out, Prost emphasized the talents that would land him four world titles.

FOOTBALL GETS THE BOOT

Alain had other sporting pretensions before he settled on racing. He was a handy football player, good enough to be given trials, but after trying karting when he was on holiday aged 14 he made up his mind on the matter.

ALAIN'S ARRIVAL

Impressed by his maiden season with McLaren, Renault snapped up Alain for 1981. He was soon proving that he was the best French driver of his generation by claiming his first podium, coming third in the third round in Argentina. Alain went better still at his home grand prix at Dijon-Prenois (right) by not only setting his first fastest lap but going on to secure his first win, heading home John Watson.

Right The first of Alain's 51 grand prix wins came in 1981, at his home grand prix.

Above Ayrton Senna celebrates his first world title with McLaren in 1988.

AYRTON SENNA

The late Ayrton Senna was a driver who polarized opinions. He was supremely fast but spoiled that, for some, by his 'win at all costs' approach. No-one, though, could deny his presence and unswerving focus. His career with McLaren was synonymous with winning, but shortly after a move to Williams his life came to a sudden end at Imola.

FACT FILE

Name:	Ayrton Senna
Nationality:	Brazilian
Date of birth:	21/3/60
Date of death:	1/5/94
F1 career span:	1984–1994
Teams:	Toleman 1984, Lotus 1985–1987, McLaren 1988–1993, Williams 1994
Races contested:	161
Wins:	41
Poles:	65
Fastest laps:	19
Points:	614
Championships:	1988, 1990, 1991

A FALSE START

Anyone who had watched Ayrton Senna trounce his rivals in the junior single-seater formulae knew that he was special. However, when he made his break into F1 with Toleman in 1984, not much was expected as the team was midfield at best. Having qualified 17th out of 27 starters for his first grand prix, at home in Brazil, he climbed three places in the opening few laps before retiring with turbo failure.

A NATION MOURNED

Such was the impact of Ayrton's death in the 1994 San Marino GP that Brazil declared three days of national mourning. It was estimated that a million people lined the streets of São Paulo for his funeral.

WET WEATHER MASTERPIECE

Ayrton produced some mesmerizing performances among his 41 runs to grand prix victories, but his greatest race of all was the 1993 European GP at Donington Park. Conditions were wet and he lost a place at the start, falling to fifth. However, with a singular focus and outstanding car control, Ayrton picked off each and every one of the drivers ahead to take the lead before lap 1 was complete and then raced ever further clear.

IN A CLASS OF HIS OWN

Ayrton could be untouchable in qualifying, as you would imagine from someone who claimed 65 poles. His day of days in qualifying came at the 1989 Japanese GP, when he was fastest by 1.730s. His speed advantage was greatest at Monaco and he qualified on pole there by more than one second in 1988 and 1989, also enjoying that massive margin at Detroit in 1985, Phoenix in 1989 and the Hungaroring in 1991.

Above Ayrton dominated qualifying at Suzuka in 1989, but team-mate Alain Prost got a grippier start and led.

Below Ayrton was untouchable in the wet at Donington Park in 1993 and was soon lapping his rivals, including Riccardo Patrese and Fabrizio Barbazza.

TWO SETS OF FOUR

Ayrton Senna was far more than the king of the qualifying lap, as his world titles in 1988, 1989 and 1991 attest. Indeed, he claimed 41 wins. His best winning sequence was four in a row, which he managed twice by winning the British, German, Hungarian and Belgian GPs in 1998 then the US, Brazilian, San Marino and Monaco GPs in 1991.

PICKING OFF THE POLES

Acknowledged as the supreme qualifier, Ayrton Senna notched up 65 pole positions, at an average that the more long-serving Michael Schumacher was never able to match. Ayrton achieved the remarkable tally of 13 pole positions in a season twice. Once in 1988 and again in 1989 when he guided his McLaren to 13 poles, starting 1988 with six straight poles and rounding out 1989 with the same sequence.

THWARTED BY A RED FLAG

Having scored points on his second and third outings, Ayrton produced a stunning drive at his sixth attempt, at the 1984 Monaco GP. Conditions were extremely wet but the Brazilian rookie was still able to reel in experienced race leader Alain Prost's McLaren. But, just as Ayrton latched onto Prost's tail, the race was red-flagged and brought to a premature conclusion by Clerk of the Course, Jacky Ickx.

Left Ayrton waves the flag for Brazil after victory at the 1988 Japanese GP was enough for him to become world champion.

MIND OVER MATTER

Winning in a competitive car is one thing, but doing so in one that is not the pick of the pack deserves even more respect. In 1993, his final season with McLaren, Ayrton drove some of his greatest races. And, in the final race of the campaign, at Adelaide, he managed to manhandle his Ford-powered MP4/8 around faster than the dominant Williams-Renaults for his only pole of the year. He then outraced Prost for what proved to be the last of his 41 wins.

CAREER STATS

YEAR	TEAM	RACES	WINS	POINTS	RANKING
1984	Toleman	15	0	13	9th
1985	Lotus	16	2	38	4th
1986	Lotus	16	2	55	4th
1987	Lotus	16	2	57	3rd
1988	McLaren	16	8	94	1st
1989	McLaren	16	5	60	2nd
1990	McLaren	16	6	78	1st
1991	McLaren	16	6	96	1st
1992	McLaren	16	3	50	4th
1993	McLaren	16	5	73	2nd
1994	Williams	3	0	0	-

AYRTON'S TREBLE BREAKTHROUGH

Joining Lotus for his second year in F1, after his rookie season with the Toleman team, was a great move for Ayrton Senna. He claimed his first pole position on his second outing at the 1985 Portuguese GP. Better than that, he was then able to set the fastest lap in the race around a very wet Estoril circuit and lead every lap through the deluge to record his first grand prix win.

Left The Estoril circuit was streaming with water at the 1985 Portuguese GP, but Ayrton was in control from start to finish.

NIGEL MANSELL

Right Mansell celebrates in his title-winning campaign in 1992.

Nigel Mansell never had a quiet race. They were all packed with drama, malady or performances of dogged brilliance. When all was right, he would wring every last drop of speed out of the car and out of himself in a flamboyant, entertaining style. Then, when his chance came in 1992, he grabbed it.

FACT FILE

Name:	Nigel Mansell
Nationality:	British
Date of birth:	8/8/53
F1 career span:	1980–1992, 1994 & 1995
Teams:	Lotus 1980–1984, Williams 1985–1988, Ferrari 1989–1990, Williams 1991–1992 & 1994, McLaren 1995
Races contested:	187
Wins:	31
Poles:	32
Fastest laps:	30
Points:	482
Championships:	1992

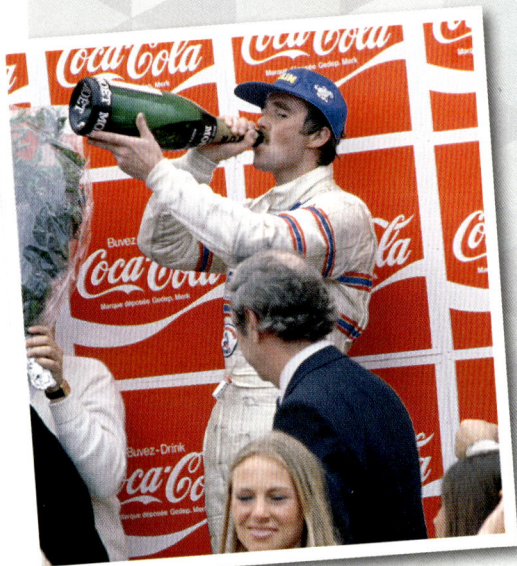

Above Nigel savours his first grand prix podium after finishing third in the 1981 Belgian GP.

CAREER STATS

YEAR	TEAM	RACES	WINS	POINTS	RANKING
1980	Lotus	3	0	0	-
1981	Lotus	14	0	8	14th
1982	Lotus	13	0	7	14th
1983	Lotus	15	0	10	13th
1984	Lotus	16	0	13	9th
1985	Williams	16	2	31	6th
1986	Williams	16	5	72	2nd
1987	Williams	15	6	61	2nd
1988	Williams	14	0	12	9th
1989	Ferrari	15	2	38	4th
1990	Ferrari	16	1	37	5th
1991	Williams	16	5	72	2nd
1992	Williams	16	9	108	1st
1994	Williams	4	1	13	9th
1995	McLaren	2	0	0	-

LOOKING DOWN ON OTHERS

All aspiring racing drivers conjure images of themselves smiling down from the podium. Obviously, mounting the top step as a winner would be best, but Nigel would have been happy enough to claim his first podium finish. This came in the 1981 Belgian GP at Zolder when he brought his Lotus home behind Carlos Reutemann's Williams and Jacques Laffite's Ligier. For his first win, he'd have to wait another four years and more.

MOVING TO THE FRONT

To top timesheets or win grands prix, a driver needs a really competitive car. Nigel Mansell never really had that in his first few years of F1. However, by 1984, with Renault turbo power, he was on the pace and duly delivered his first pole position halfway through the season on the World Championship's one and only visit to the Dallas street circuit. This didn't result in his first win, though, as Nigel could finish no higher than sixth.

NO RESPECT FOR YOUTH

The best way to augment one's reputation after retiring is to pop back for a cameo performance and stick it to the young guns. Nigel Mansell achieved this in 1994 when the fourth of his stand-in outings for Williams resulted in victory. This happened at the Australian GP when third place turned into first place after Michael Schumacher collided with Damon Hill while fighting over the lead. It was Nigel's final F1 win.

INSTANT AFFECTION

The Tifosi don't immediately warm to Ferrari's new signings, but Nigel Mansell gave them every reason to love him when he joined in 1989. How? By winning on his first outing. He did this at the Brazilian GP at Jacarepagua when he qualified sixth alongside team-mate Gerhard Berger. Nigel was up to third on the opening lap before working his way past Thierry Boutsen's failing Williams and then Alain Prost's McLaren. He would win just once more in 1989.

Above Nigel showed how to win friends with the tifosi by winning on his first outing, in Brazil.

DOGGED DETERMINATION

Nigel Mansell had had to fight more than almost any of his rivals to get his break in F1 and, because of this, he was not going to give up when the going got tough. This it did on his F1 debut at the 1980 Austrian GP. Petrol leaked into the cockpit of Nigel's Lotus, causing him extreme pain. He soldiered on until the car's engine failed, earning Nigel increased respect from team boss, Colin Chapman, and first degree burns to his back.

Right Nigel was soaked with fuel, burning his back, but he kept going on his F1 debut for Lotus in the 1980 Austrian GP until his car's engine failed.

A SEASON TO FORGET

The loss of the Honda engine cost Williams dear in 1988 when it had to replace them with Judd engines. Nigel Mansell dropped from second in the 1987 title race to ninth in 1988 – his worst ever year in terms of retirements, failing to finish in 12 of the 14 rounds, albeit four of these were due to driver error. Showing the thwarted promise, he came home second in each of the races he finished.

CROSSING THE ATLANTIC

After not being kept on by Williams for 1993, Nigel headed instead to the USA, where he became the only driver to win the F1 and Indycar titles in successive years.

Below Supplied with a pace-setting car by Williams in 1992, Nigel did the rest to record nine wins and land the title.

PLEASING THE HOME CROWD

There can be no better place to secure your first win than on home ground and Nigel did just that in the 1985 European GP at Brands Hatch. He qualified his Williams behind Ayrton Senna and Nelson Piquet but lost a place to Keke Rosberg at the start. Nigel moved into second when Rosberg spun while attacking Senna and Piquet hit him. Three laps later, Nigel took a lead he was never to lose when he passed Senna. With the monkey off his back, he won the following race at Kyalami.

MAKING THE MOST OF IT

Having been so close to landing the world title in 1986, only to be robbed by a blow-out, Nigel must have felt that he deserved the crown, and his 1992 campaign finally produced it. That year's Williams FW14B was the pick of the pack and Nigel made the most of it, starting with a run of five straight wins, in the South African, Mexican, Brazilian, Spanish and San Marino GPs. This provided the largest part of his tally of nine wins that landed him the title with five rounds to spare.

Right Jackie Stewart won three titles and was a pioneer for improved safety standards in F1.

JACKIE STEWART

The immaculate Jackie Stewart was a driver who raced by the principle of wanting to win grands prix by the lowest speed possible. He had all the pace in the world but, in an age when cars were fragile and drivers died if they slipped up, he calculated his victories and earned himself three world titles.

FACT FILE

Name:	Jackie Stewart
Nationality:	British
Date of birth:	11/6/39
F1 career span:	1965–1973
Teams:	BRM 1965–1967, Matra 1968–1969, Tyrrell 1970–1973
Races contested:	99
Wins:	27
Poles:	17
Fastest laps:	15
Points:	360
Championships:	1969, 1971, 1973

STARTING IN THE POINTS

Jackie Stewart made his F1 debut in 1965 after strong seasons in F3 then F2. Driving for BRM, after turning down the chance to join fellow Scot Jim Clark at Lotus, Jackie qualified 11th out of 25 on his debut in the South African GP at East London. Jackie advanced to sixth place and claimed points first time out. This feat remains something of a rarity, even with points extended first to the top eight then the top 10 finishers.

LEAVING HIS MARK

Victory in the 1973 Dutch GP put Jackie clear as the driver with the most grand prix wins, exceeding the record held by fellow Scot Jim Clark. Then, at the Nürburgring, not only did Jackie head home Tyrrell team-mate Francois Cevert for his 27th win, but this final win would leave him at the top of the list until Alain Prost passed this mark in 1987. The Frenchman would go on to win 51 times, a record bettered only by Michael Schumacher with 91.

Above Having scored points on his F1 debut in South Africa, Jackie would claim his first victory in just his eighth race, at Monza in the 1965 Italian Grand Prix.

Right Jackie races through Monaco's narrow streets in his BRM in 1965, heading for third place for his first podium finish.

IN FRONT AT THE FINISH

Having been in the points on his debut in the South African GP and scored his first podium finish next time out at Monaco, it seemed likely that Jackie Stewart would take his first win in his maiden season. And so he did at the 1965 Italian GP. Jackie started the race third on the grid and worked his way up to enjoy a typical Monza slipstreaming battle with BRM team-mate Richie Ginther before taking the lead with two laps to go.

Below Jackie jumps his Tyrrell 006 over one of the Nürburgring's many brows en route to his 27th and last grand prix win.

A PAIR OF THREES

Jackie Stewart twice enjoyed a hat-trick of wins, taking three wins in a row at the Dutch, French and British GPs in his Ken Tyrrell-run Matra in 1969, his first title-winning year. In 1971 he achieved the feat again at the French, British and German GPs in his Elf-sponsored Tyrrell to claim the second of his three F1 titles.

Left Jackie savours Stewart GP's first podium with son Paul after Rubens Barrichello finished second at Monaco in 1997.

MISSING OUT ON A CENTURY

Jackie Stewart was a driver of immense precision and he would have liked the fact that the last race before he quit driving would have been his 100th. However, the death of his Tyrrell team-mate Francois Cevert in practice for the 1973 United States GP at Watkins Glen led to the team withdrawing, and so Jackie remains eternally with 99 not 100 grands prix starts to his name.

A FAMILY ENTERPRISE

Jackie retired from F1 in 1973, but he returned full-time in 1997 when he and elder son Paul established Stewart GP after running teams in F3 and F3000. The team took one win, in 1999, before being sold to Jaguar in 2000, later becoming Red Bull Racing.

A DOUBLE VICTORY

To win an F1 drivers' title is a feather in any driver's cap, but to do so with a victory adds immeasurably, and this is what Jackie Stewart managed when he claimed the first of his three titles in 1969. He lined up his Matra third on the grid for the Italian GP behind Jochen Rindt's Lotus and Denny Hulme's McLaren, then jumped both and raced clear before holding off a slipstreaming pack to land his sixth win of the year and the title.

NO DRIP IN THE WET

The Nürburgring Nordschleife sorted the men from the boys, especially when it rained. At the 1968 German GP, Jackie Stewart produced his greatest-ever drive to jump from sixth on the grid to lead the race before the end of the first 14-mile lap. His Matra was then never headed again and he won by an amazing four minutes from Graham Hill's Lotus.

Above Jackie splashes his Matra around the Nürburgring to score a famous win in 1968, crossing the finish line just over four minutes clear of Graham Hill's second-placed Lotus.

CAREER STATS

YEAR	TEAM	RACES	WINS	POINTS	RANKING
1965	BRM	10	1	34	3rd
1966	BRM	8	1	14	7th
1967	BRM	11	0	10	9th
1968	Matra	10	3	36	2nd
1969	Matra	11	6	63	1st
1970	Tyrrell	13	1	25	5th
1971	Tyrrell	11	6	62	1st
1972	Tyrrell	11	4	45	2nd
1973	Tyrrell	14	5	71	1st

Below Jim Clark was effortlessly fast and broke multiple records before his untimely death.

JIM CLARK

Jim Clark was a driver who was so effortlessly quick in whatever type of car he drove that he appeared to be in a different class to even his closest rivals. In the years when his flying Lotus was strong enough for the job, he was crowned World Champion, but then a freak accident in an F2 race claimed his life.

FACT FILE

Name:	Jim Clark
Nationality:	British
Date of birth:	4/3/36
Date of death:	7/4/68
F1 career span:	1960–1968
Teams: Lotus	1960–1968
Races contested: 72	
Wins:	25
Poles:	33
Fastest laps:	28
Points:	274
Championships:	1963, 1965

Above Jim powers through the field to regain the lead at the 1967 Italian GP at Monza.

OVERTAKING NO PROBLEM

One of Jim Clark's most remarkable drives came at the 1967 Italian GP at Monza. He started from pole position and was leading before his Lotus had to pit to have a flat tyre replaced on the 13th of 70 laps, dropping him to 15th of the 16 remaining runners. Clark then tore through the field, making up an entire lap to retake the lead with seven laps to go, only to suffer fuel pump problems on the final lap and fall to third.

CONQUERING HIS FEAR

Spa-Francorchamps in the 1960s was a circuit to be feared. It was ultra-fast with little to stop cars from flying off into the trees. Jim Clark loathed it after his first visit in 1958 saw Archie Scott-Brown killed, followed by team-mate Alan Stacey and Chris Bristow in 1960. However, he managed to win there each year from 1962 to 1965, with his 1962 victory the first of his 25 grand prix wins.

Above Jim loathed Spa-Francorchamps, but still managed to win there on four occasions, including this run in 1964.

ARISE PRINCE JIM THE FIRST

Jim Clark was always going to be World Champion and an improvement in Lotus' reliability in 1963 allowed him the tools to do the job. Such was his form, winning four of the first six races, that the Scot was able to clinch his first title at the Italian GP with three rounds still to run. To become champion, he raced to his fifth win by 35s over Richie Ginther's BRM.

A TOURING CAR STAR

All F1 drivers in Jim's day would race everything they could for money, often on the same weekend as a grand prix. Jim was so good at this that he was also British Touring Car Champion in 1964.

THE BEGINNING OF THE END

Going into 1968 the second campaign in which Lotus was powered by Ford's pace-setting Cosworth DFV engine, Jim Clark laid down his marker by dominating the season-opening South African GP at Kyalami. Such was Clark's advantage that he started from pole, demoted Jackie Stewart's fast-starting Matra on the second lap and led every remaining lap to beat team-mate Graham Hill by 25.3s. Tragically, he died in an F2 race before the second round.

Left Winning at the 1968 South African GP.

A FALSE START

Jim Clark didn't take long to reach F1. When Aston Martin scrapped its F1 project for 1960, Clark bounced back to sign for Lotus to race in F2. His pace was such that he was granted his F1 debut in the season's third round, the Dutch GP. The Scot qualified 11th out of 21, but his Lotus 18 retired from fifth when the transmission failed. He scored his first points next time out, at Spa-Francorchamps.

🏆 IT COULD HAVE BEEN FOUR STRAIGHT

Jim Clark's death in 1968 scuppered any hopes of a third F1 title but, had his luck been better, he could have had four titles to his name by the end of 1965. All set to land the title in 1962, Jim's Lotus was sidelined by oil line failure in the final round. Although champion in 1963 and 1965, Clark came within an ace of taking the 1964 crown too, but suffered another oil line failure in Mexico City.

CAREER STATS

YEAR	TEAM	RACES	WINS	POINTS	RANKING
1960	Lotus	6	0	8	8th
1961	Lotus	8	0	11	7th
1962	Lotus	9	3	30	2nd
1963	Lotus	10	7	73	1st
1964	Lotus	10	3	32	3rd
1965	Lotus	9	6	54	1st
1966	Lotus	9	0	16	6th
1967	Lotus	11	4	41	3rd
1968	Lotus	1	1	9	11th

⚙ STARTING FROM THE FRONT

The predominance of Jim Clark and the Lotus 25 in 1963 led to his best seasonal tally of pole positions when he claimed the top spot in qualifying seven times in 10 rounds. He took pole position at Monaco, Zandvoort, Reims, Silverstone, the Nürburgring, Mexico City and East London. They didn't all result in wins, but he still managed seven of those that year.

AN AIR OF INVINCIBILITY

When Jim Clark was in his pomp, his rivals might have felt that second place behind his Lotus was the best that they could hope for. This would certainly have been the case in 1965 when Jim achieved his best winning sequence, following victory in the opening round in South Africa with five more wins in the next five races in Belgium, France, Britain, Holland and Germany.

Below Jim shows his smooth style as he guides his Lotus 25 to victory at Silverstone in 1965, as the fourth of six wins in a row.

Right Juan Manuel Fangio won five titles in the 1950s during the early days of Formula One racing.

JUAN MANUEL FANGIO

Although approaching 39 when the World Championship kicked-off in 1950, Juan Manuel Fangio showed that skill counted more than age as he rattled off five F1 titles between 1951 and 1957 (and he didn't even compete in 1952 after a life-threatening accident before the opening round).

FACT FILE

Name:	Juan Manuel Fangio
Nationality:	Argentinian
Date of birth:	24/6/11
Date of death:	17/7/95
F1 career span:	1950–1951 & 1953–1958
Teams:	Alfa Romeo 1950–1951, Maserati 1953–1954, Mercedes-Benz 1954–1955, Ferrari 1956, Maserati 1957, Scuderia Sud Americana 1958, own team 1958
Races contested:	51
Wins:	24
Poles:	29
Fastest laps:	23
Points:	277.14
Championships:	1951, 1954, 1955, 1956, 1957

FAST TO THE VERY END

With Maserati closing its operation after his 1957 title, Juan Manuel raced on with independently-entered Maseratis. He raced in only two World Championship events in 1958 and in the second of these, the French GP at Reims, he finished fourth after completing the entire race without the benefit of a clutch. Showing great respect, winner Mike Hawthorn backed off on the final lap rather than lap the great ace.

CAREER STATS

YEAR	TEAM	RACES	WINS	POINTS	RANKING
1950	Alfa Romeo	6	3	27	2nd
1951	Alfa Romeo	7	3	37	1st
1953	Maserati	8	1	29	2nd
1954	Maserati & Mercedes	8	6	57.14	1st
1955	Mercedes	6	4	41	1st
1956	Ferrari	7	2	33	1st
1957	Maserati	7	4	46	1st
1958	Scuderia Sud Americana & Fangio	2	0	7	14th

THE GREATEST CHASE

Juan Manuel Fangio's final win was his most dramatic. It came in 1957 at the German GP around the 14-mile Nürburgring Nordschleife. Despite qualifying his Maserati on pole, he completed the opening tour in third behind the Ferraris of Mike Hawthorn and Peter Collins. Two laps later, he was leading, but his gamble to stop for fresh tyres did not pay off when a slow pitstop dropped him to third. He then had to claw back 48s before passing both Ferraris on the penultimate lap to take victory and claim his fifth world title.

GOVERNMENT ASSISTANCE

Considered his country's greatest racing talent after dominating its long-distance road races, Juan Manuel was propelled into single-seaters with support from the government as President Peron was keen to build Argentina's reputation abroad. After taking on Europe's best in races in Buenos Aires, he and compatriot Oscar Galvez headed to Europe and he did so well then and in 1949 that Alfa Romeo signed him for the first year of F1.

FALLING AT THE FIRST

Juan Manuel had already tried his hand racing in Europe in 1948 and was back from his native Argentina to contest the inaugural World Championship in 1950. Racing for Alfa Romeo, he was part of an all-Alfa Romeo front row for the British GP at Silverstone. After running third in the opening stages behind Giuseppe Farina and Luigi Fagioli, he was up to second with seven laps to go when an oil pipe burst.

Below The German crowd hails Juan Manuel after he'd hunted down and passed the Ferraris in 1957.

THE FACE OF EXPERIENCE

Racing drivers tended to be older in the early days and Juan Manuel was 38 when the World Championship started in 1950. Armed with the experience of making cars last in the rough, long-distance races held on open roads in Argentina, he allied speed with mechanical sympathy and landed his first world title at the age of 40 in 1951. His final title, in 1957, came when he was 46.

⚐ STUCK ON THE SIDELINES

Fangio wasn't able to defend his first world title, as he didn't contest a single World Championship round in 1952 after being thrown from his own Maserati in the non-championship Monza GP.

⬤ SHOPPING AROUND

Juan Manuel didn't sit still in his quest for F1 titles. Indeed, his five crowns were won with four different teams. His first, in 1951, was with Alfa Romeo who then quit the sport. Back from injury for 1953, he started the year with Maserati but transferred to Mercedes-Benz when the German team's cars were ready. He won with Mercedes again in 1955 before winning for Ferrari in 1956 then rounding it off with Maserati in 1957.

Above After starting with Alfa Romeo, Juan Manuel kept changing teams.

BOUNCING RIGHT BACK

After the disappointment of Silverstone, Juan Manuel Fangio bounced back to win at the second attempt in 1950. This was at Monaco, where he placed his Alfa Romeo 158 on pole position, set the race's fastest lap and led all the way for his first win. Fortune had smiled on him as there had been a nine-car pile-up behind him on the opening lap but he managed to thread his way through the wreckage on lap 2.

Right Juan Manuel's wins flowed from Monaco in 1950.

Right Max got used to winning in 2023 – he triumphed in 19 of the 22 grands prix, obliterating multiple records in the process.

MAX VERSTAPPEN

Max Verstappen leapt from karting to Formula One in a little over 12 months, with the unprecedented rise leaving him competing in the big time aged 17. He quickly proved he was no fish out of water, setting a string of 'youngest ever' records and emerging as a front-runner and contender. A sequence of championships through the early 2020s, and a staggering rate of victories, accelerated Max's surge up the record books and he now has fewer wins than only Michael Schumacher and Lewis Hamilton, despite still being in his mid-20s.

FACT FILE

Name:	Max Verstappen
Nationality:	Dutch
Date of birth:	30/9/97
F1 career span:	2015 – present
Teams:	Toro Rosso 2015–2016, Red Bull 2016–present
Races contested:	209
Wins:	63
Poles:	40
Fastest laps:	33
Points:	3,023.5
Championships:	2021, 2022, 2023, 2024

A WAIT FOR A POLE

Max's rise was rapid but while he claimed his first victory in 2016, he had to wait another three years before he actually started at the very front of the field for a race. Having qualified on the front row of the grid on seven occasions Max finally went one better at the Hungarian GP, in 2019, to tick off that particular milestone.

Above As with many legends of the sport wet weather brought Max's skillset to the forefront, with his display in Brazil in 2016 captivating spectators.

MAKING AN IMPRESSION

In only his second season, Max wowed on occasion, and sometimes irritated rivals with his assertive style. At a rain-soaked Interlagos circuit Max dazzled onlookers by passing rivals with ease before saving a near-certain accident after losing control at high speed. Max tumbled to 16th place with 15 laps to go to take on fresh tyres but charged his way forwards to finish on the podium in third position.

2021 BREAKTHROUGH

Max had to make do with a smattering of wins across 2017 to 2020 amid Mercedes' dominance but Red Bull re-emerged as a title challenger in 2021, laying the foundations for one of the greatest championship battles in history. Max and Lewis Hamilton duelled all season, winning 18 of the 22 races between them, and came to blows on several occasions too. In a contentious decider in Abu Dhabi, Max passed Hamilton on the final lap to snatch the race victory and the world championship.

Above Max and Lewis Hamilton were embroiled in a titanic tussle through 2021, which ended with Max's first world title.

RED BULL VETERAN

Max has been under the Red Bull umbrella for his entire F1 career. Having done 23 races with junior team Toro Rosso, he has competed for Red Bull since partway through the 2016 campaign, taking all of his victories with the operation. It is the second-longest driver/team partnership in F1 history, behind only Lewis Hamilton and Mercedes, with Max having started 186 grands prix in Red Bull colours.

WINNING FROM BEHIND

Max has regularly shown his versatility when it comes to racecraft and that was perhaps best witnessed across successive races in his title-winning 2022 season. Max qualified only 10th in Hungary but, despite an uncharacteristic 360 spin in the race, carved through the pack to win. At the next race in Belgium Max started 14th after a penalty due to a change of engine, but still had pace in hand to breeze through the field to pocket the victory.

Above Max Verstappen made a habit of surging through the pack in 2022.

Above Max was only 18 years old when he first climbed onto the top step of the F1 podium.

CAREER STATS

YEAR	TEAM	RACES	WINS	POINTS	RANKING
2015	Toro Rosso	19	0	49	12th
2016	Toro Rosso/Red Bull	21	1	204	5th
2017	Red Bull	20	2	168	6th
2018	Red Bull	21	2	249	4th
2019	Red Bull	21	3	278	3rd
2020	Red Bull	17	2	214	3rd
2021	Red Bull	22	10	395.5	1st
2022	Red Bull	22	15	454	1st
2023	Red Bull	22	19	575	1st
2024	Red Bull	24	9	437	1st

THE FIRST WIN

Red Bull had swiftly been convinced by Max's potential and after four races of the 2016 season promoted him to Red Bull's senior team, in place of the struggling Daniil Kvyat. On his Red Bull debut, at Spain's Barcelona circuit, Max picked up the pieces when Mercedes pair Lewis Hamilton and Nico Rosberg collided early on to lead the race – his first laps at the front in Formula One. Max stayed calm and claimed the victory, which was also his first podium, at the age of 18 years and 228 days.

THE YOUNGEST EVER

The son of two-time podium finisher Jos, Max's name had been banded about for years due to his success in the karting scene. In 2014 he jumped straight from karts to Formula 3, contended for the title, and was picked up as a Red Bull junior driver, and parachuted straight into F1 for 2015, with Red Bull's junior team, Toro Rosso. At the age of 17 years and 166 days Max took to the grid in Melbourne and became Formula One's youngest racer.

NOT NINETEEN FOREVER

Max and Red Bull dominated the 2023 season, with driver and machine firmly the class of the field. Having set a new record for wins in a season in 2022, with 15, Max pushed that benchmark even higher as he cantered to an astonishing 19 victories from 22 starts, including 10 in a row. Max led 1,003 racing laps – over 75 per cent of the season – and scored 575 points from a possible 620, a winning margin of 290 points. He sealed his third title in the Sprint Race in Qatar, with six races left to run that season.

Below Max Verstappen clinched his fourth title in Las Vegas in 2024.

FERNANDO ALONSO

Fernando Alonso deposed Michael Schumacher to win two titles, in 2005 and 2006, and had several near-misses across the following years, with Ferrari and McLaren. Performances in sub-par machinery has enhanced his already glowing reputation, and he is now the most experienced Formula One driver in history, with an unshakeable desire to succeed.

Above Alonso celebrates a podium finish in 2023.

FACT FILE

Name:	**Fernando Alonso**
Nationality:	**Spanish**
Date of birth:	**29/7/81**
F1 career span:	**2001, 2003–2018, 2021 onwards**
Teams:	**Minardi 2001, Renault 2003–2006, McLaren 2007, Renault 2008–2009, Ferrari 2010–2014, McLaren 2015–18, Alpine 2021–2022, Aston Martin 2023 onwards**
Races contested:	**401**
Wins:	**32**
Poles:	**22**
Fastest laps:	**26**
Points:	**2337**
Championships:	**2005, 2006**

Above It was all smiles as Lewis Hamilton helped Fernando celebrate his first McLaren win at Sepang in 2007, but it all turned sour.

LOSING OUT BY A POINT

Even before he'd secured the second of his consecutive F1 titles with Renault, Fernando had decided to move on to McLaren. This was for 2007 and he would be partnered by rookie Lewis Hamilton. A win in the second round, in Malaysia, suggested great things would follow, but Hamilton began to push. Fernando thought the team was supporting his number two, not him, and the atmosphere soured. Then, at the final round in Brazil, they were overhauled by Ferrari's Kimi Räikkönen, both losing out by a point.

Left Fernando didn't win the drivers' title in 2012, but he pushed Red Bull's Sebastian Vettel all the way with wins like this one at Valencia.

FLYING FOR FERRARI

Fernando won race after race with Ferrari between 2010 and 2015, but no drivers' titles. Had his time with Ferrari not corresponded with the ascendancy of Red Bull Racing, he certainly would have added to his two titles. In 2010, he ended up just four points behind Sebastian Vettel, stymied in the final round by Vitaly Petrov. Then in 2012, Fernando's displays were better still as he ended up just three points behind Vettel after perhaps the best performances of his career. He was second again in 2013, but only sixth in 2014 as Mercedes and Lewis Hamilton dominated.

KARTING GLORY

Almost all F1 drivers have won karting championship titles along the way, but few have been crowned World Kart Champion. Fernando claimed kart racing's most prestigious title in 1996. Then, for good measure, he also won the Spanish junior title, the Spanish senior one, twice, plus the Italian senior title, all by the age of 16.

A YEAR TO LEARN F1

Placed with Minardi for 2001 to learn the circuits, practices and techniques needed to shine in F1, Fernando did a solid job. He was never going to win for this backmarking team, but he impressed, peaking with 10th place in the German GP at Hockenheim. This was worth no points, as they were only awarded to sixth back then.

FIRST TO 400

Fernando's longevity is such that he is the only driver to have raced in F1 in his teens, twenties, thirties and forties and – despite a two-year absence in which he twice won the Le Mans 24 Hours, and tackled the Indianapolis 500 and Dakar Rally – became the first driver to start 400 races. Fernando reached the milestone at the Qatar Grand Prix in 2024, 23 years after his debut, with some current racers not even born when he burst onto the scene!

Left Fernando has started over a third of all of the grands prix held in Formula One history, and is still going strong!

ENDING SCHUEY'S FIVE-YEAR RUN

There were times during Michael Schumacher's five-year reign as World Champion that it seemed as though he would never be toppled. When he was, in 2005, the driver to move ahead was Fernando, who bounced back from a winless 2004 season to secure seven wins and the title for Renault, beating Ferrari's Rubens Barrichello by 34 points. This made Fernando the then-youngest World Champion, at 24 years and 59 days, breaking Lotus driver Emerson Fittipaldi's record from 1972. He then added the 2006 title for emphasis.

ROCKETING UP THE LADDER

As soon as Fernando turned 17, he turned to car racing. Former Spanish F1 driver Adrian Campos signed him up to race for his team in Euro Open by Nissan in 1999 after seeing him equal the lap times of more experienced compatriot Marc Gene in testing. Fernando won six of the 15 rounds to become champion. It was then straight up to Formula 3000 in 2000. Racing for Astromega, Fernando ranked fourth, winning at Spa-Francorchamps. Benetton team principal Flavio Briatore swiftly got him under contract, paying for his maiden F1 season.

CAREER STATS

YEAR	TEAM	RACES	WINS	POINTS	RANKING
2001	Minardi	17	0	0	23rd
2003	Renault	16	1	55	6th
2004	Renault	18	0	59	4th
2005	Renault	19	7	133	1st
2006	Renault	18	7	134	1st
2007	McLaren	17	4	109	3rd
2008	Renault	18	2	61	5th
2009	Renault	17	0	26	9th
2010	Ferrari	19	5	252	2nd
2011	Ferrari	19	1	257	4th
2012	Ferrari	20	3	278	2nd
2013	Ferrari	19	2	242	2nd
2014	Ferrari	19	0	161	6th
2015	McLaren	18	0	11	17th
2016	McLaren	21	0	54	10th
2017	McLaren	19	0	17	15th
2018	McLaren	21	0	50	11th
2021	Alpine	22	0	81	10th
2022	Alpine	22	0	81	9th
2023	Aston Martin	22	0	206	4th
2024	Aston Martin	24	0	70	9th

Below The Spanish flag flies as Fernando flashes across the finish line at the Hungaroring in his Renault in 2003 for his first F1 victory.

THREE TIMES A CHARM

'Team Enstone' has been a place of refuge at times for Fernando. After an abortive stint with McLaren in 2007 he returned to Renault for 2008 and 2009, before a five-year spell at Ferrari. To prove that anything is possible in Formula One, he returned to McLaren in 2015 but it coincided with a downturn in the team's performance. After two years racing in other categories Fernando sought a return to Formula One and in 2021 sealed a comeback with Alpine – the Renault team now operating under its sportscar brand.

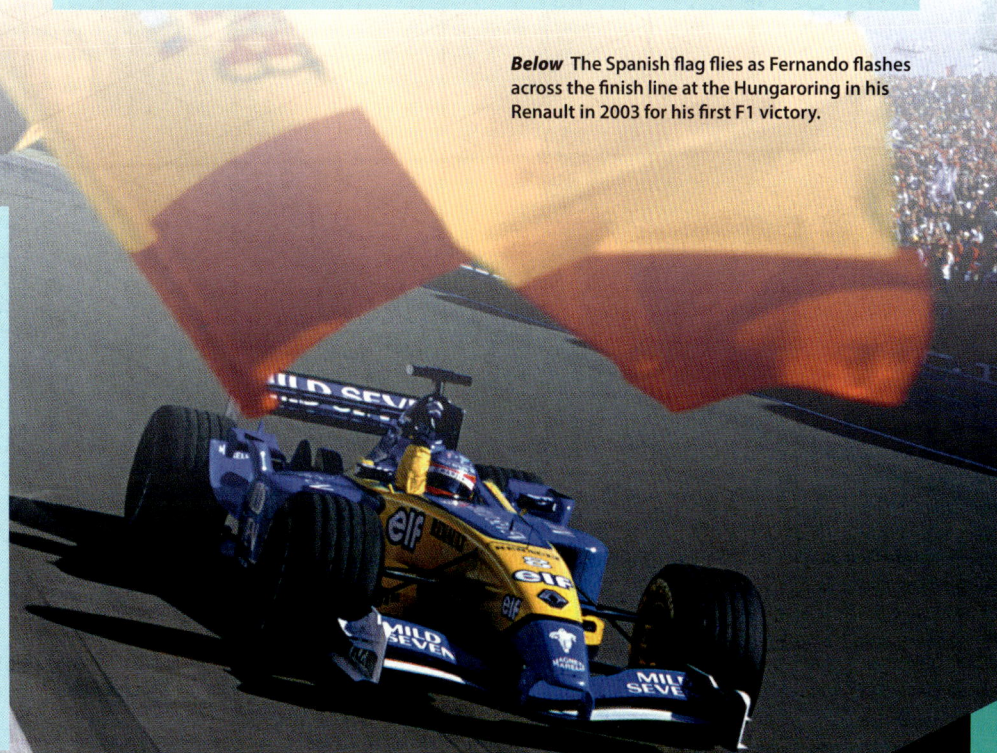

SEBASTIAN VETTEL

Sebastian Vettel set a string of records early in his career as he spearheaded Red Bull Racing's emergence as a front-running force, reeling off four successive titles before he'd even left his mid-20s. Further championships with Ferrari in his next chapter remained elusive, but his achievements undoubtedly leave him as an all-time great, and he has left his mark in the record books.

Above Sebastian Vettel celebrates his win at the 2018 Belgian GP.

FACT FILE

Name:	Sebastian Vettel
Nationality:	German
Date of birth:	3/7/87
F1 career span:	2007–2022
Teams:	BMW Sauber 2007, Scuderia Toro Rosso 2007–2008, Red Bull Racing 2009–2014, Ferrari 2015–2020, Aston Martin 2021–2022
Races contested:	299
Wins:	53
Poles:	57
Fastest laps:	38
Points:	3,098
Championships:	2010, 2011, 2012, 2013

FERRARI TILTS FALL SHORT

Sebastian joined Ferrari in 2015 with the ambition of emulating hero Michael Schumacher, and won on only his second outing for the reds. Further victories followed, and in 2017 and 2018 Sebastian and Ferrari mounted a championship challenge, but fell short on both occasions to Lewis Hamilton and Mercedes. They never came close again, with Sebastian's triumph in Singapore in 2019 the last of his 14 with Ferrari – and the 53rd and final win of his career – and he left in 2020.

THE BEST OF THE REST

Sebastian marked his first season with Red Bull in 2009 by finishing as runner-up, beating his more experienced team-mate, Mark Webber (who finished fourth), by two places. Not only did Sebastian give Red Bull its first GP win, in the third round, but he then added three more, which left him second only to Brawn GP's Jenson Button, who won six of the first seven rounds to build a 32-point lead that Sebastian cut to 11 points by the season's end.

Above Sebastian's breakthrough win for Toro Rosso came at Monza in 2008, after mastering a wet race.

UNEXPECTED VICTORY

Sebastian was emerging as a star during 2008, his first full season with Scuderia Toro Rosso. However, this was always seen as a way of earning a seat with the senior team, Red Bull Racing, for 2009. However, Sebastian didn't wait that long to secure his first Formula One win, as he proved the master of wet conditions to qualify on pole at Monza, then was unsurpassed in a wet race to win unchallenged. It was a massive advance as his previous best finishes had been fifth places at Monaco and Spa.

MAKING IT FOUR IN A ROW

When Sebastian wrapped up his second F1 crown at the 2011 Japanese GP, he became the ninth driver to achieve back-to-back titles, following the example of Alberto Ascari, Juan Manuel Fangio, Jack Brabham, Alain Prost, Ayrton Senna, Mika Häkkinen, Michael Schumacher and Fernando Alonso. At 24 years and 98 days, Sebastian was the youngest, taking almost a year off Alonso's record, set in 2006. In 2013, he became the second driver to win four in a row, at 26 years and 116 days.

Below Sebastian congratulates team-mate Mark Webber after the Australian won the 2011 Brazilian GP.

Above Sebastian powers past Indianapolis's grandstands en route to a point on his 2007 debut.

STRAIGHT INTO THE POINTS

It took injury to Robert Kubica in the 2007 Canadian GP for Sebastian to get his Formula One break a week later at Indianapolis. Taking the Pole's place at BMW Sauber, Sebastian made an immediate impact by qualifying seventh and recovering from falling to 11th in a first lap melée to finish eighth and so record a point first time out. He went on to race for Scuderia Toro Rosso later in the year. Sebastian became the youngest driver to lead a race later that season, in the Japanese GP.

UP FRONT CONTROL

Sebastian was renowned as a qualifying specialist and that meant he often had a clear view of the front of the field when the starting lights went out. Of Sebastian's 53 grand prix victories, he started from the front row of the grid for 47 of them. The other six were achieved from third place on the grid, and he never won a race starting fourth or lower.

LEAVING IT TO THE LAST

The first of Sebastian's four drivers' titles came at the final round of the 2010 championship in Abu Dhabi. He arrived third on points behind Ferrari's Fernando Alonso and Red Bull team-mate Mark Webber. Sebastian led throughout, except for when Jenson Button moved ahead by making his one pit stop later. With Alonso finishing only seventh and Webber eighth, the title was his. In 2012, he also clinched the title at the final round despite being spun on the first lap.

CAREER STATS

YEAR	TEAM	RACES	WINS	POINTS	RANKING
2007	BMW Sauber/ Toro Ross	8	0	6	14th
2008	Toro Rosso	18	1	35	8th
2009	Red Bull	17	4	84	2nd
2010	Red Bull	19	5	256	1st
2011	Red Bull	19	11	392	1st
2012	Red Bull	20	5	281	1st
2013	Red Bull	19	13	397	1st
2014	Red Bull	19	0	167	5th
2015	Ferrari	19	3	278	3rd
2016	Ferrari	21	0	212	4th
2017	Ferrari	20	5	317	2nd
2018	Ferrari	21	5	320	2nd
2019	Ferrari	21	1	240	5th
2020	Ferrari	17	0	33	13th
2021	Aston Martin	22	0	43	12th
2022	Aston Martin	20	0	37	12th

KING OF THE FLYING LAP

Sebastian's ability to set the fastest flying lap in qualifying resulted in 45 pole positions between the 2008 Italian GP and the end of the 2013 season. As he honed his skills and Red Bull's Adrian Newey-designed cars became ever more competitive, Sebastian started to record runs of pole positions. His best to date is five in a row from the 2010 season finale in Abu Dhabi to the 2011 Turkish GP, and then again in 2011 from the Hungarian to Japanese GPs.

Right The most recent of Sebastian's 46 pole positions came with Ferrari in Singapore in 2015.

Below Lewis Hamilton has won seven titles and over 100 races in F1, including at his most successful circuit, Silverstone, in an emotional 2024 race.

LEWIS HAMILTON

Lewis Hamilton burst onto the scene with McLaren, coming agonizingly close to the title as a rookie, before making amends in his sophomore season. A fallower spell followed but a move to Mercedes ushered in an era of dominance for Lewis, who won six world championships in seven seasons to match Michael Schumacher as a seven-times World Champion. With over a century of victories, and pole positions, and more than 200 podiums, the knighted Lewis sits at the top of a litany of F1 records.

FACT FILE

Name:	Lewis Hamilton
Nationality:	British
Date of birth:	7/1/85
F1 career span:	From 2007
Teams:	McLaren 2007–2012, Mercedes 2013–2024, Ferrari 2025–onwards
Races contested:	356
Wins:	105
Poles:	104
Fastest laps:	67
Points:	4862.5
Championships:	2008, 2014, 2015, 2017, 2018, 2019, 2020

BECOMING A FORMULA ONE WINNER

From the charge to the first corner at the opening grand prix of his F1 career – the Australian GP in Melbourne in 2007 – it was clear Lewis had no fear of anyone. He threatened not just his McLaren team-mate Fernando Alonso, but everyone. Third place in Australia was followed by second in the next four grands prix. Most would have been happy with this, but Lewis felt he was held back in Monaco. Next time out, in Canada, it all came good and Lewis became what was then F1's second youngest winner, at 22 years and 154 days.

Above After four near misses, Lewis won his first Grand Prix at the sixth attempt in the 2007 Canadian GP.

SUPPORT FROM HIGH PLACES

Lewis was a hot ticket in karting, from the time that he won the British Cadet Karting title in 1995 at the age of 10. What marked him out as he gathered increasingly senior titles up to the European Formula A title in 2000, was that he'd already landed the financial input of what was then one of the top F1 teams: McLaren. This came after a cheeky request at an awards dinner bore fruit a while later and gave Lewis' father Anthony a welcome rest from chasing finance.

FOUR LAST ROUND LOSSES

Lewis has an extraordinary seven titles but has also missed out on four occasions in last-round deciders. Lewis challenged for the title as a rookie in 2007 but placed seventh in a finale won by Kimi Räikkönen, ensuring the Finn was crowned champion. In 2010, in Abu Dhabi, Lewis was the extreme outsider, while in 2016 he won the race but team-mate Nico Rosberg sealed the title. In 2021 Lewis expertly dominated the race but was overtaken on the final lap for the win, and for the championship, by Max Verstappen, in one of the most contentious finishes to any sporting seasons.

Below Lewis has missed out at the finale four times, none so more controversially than in 2021, when he was robbed of the win and the title.

BECOMING A CENTURION

Lewis had been racking up a double-digit number of victories across several seasons and Michael Schumacher's tally of 91 gradually homed into view. In the pandemic-hit 2020 season Lewis matched Michael's record at the Eifel Grand Prix at the Nürburgring, before going one better next time out in Portugal, in a year in which he won 11 times from just 16 races. Lewis subsequently became the first driver to reach a century of victories at Russia's Sochi Autodrom in 2021, meaning he has won more races than most drivers have ever started.

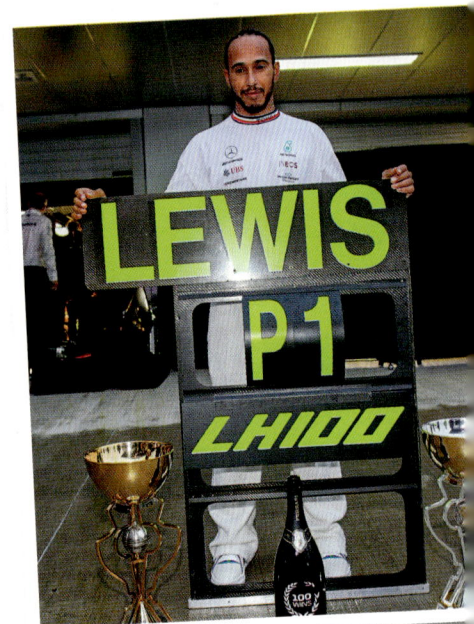

Above Lewis reached 100 wins at the 2021 Russian Grand Prix – and he has raised the benchmark even further since then.

CAREER STATS

YEAR	TEAM	RACES	WINS	POINTS	RANKING
2007	McLaren	17	4	109	2nd
2008	McLaren	18	5	98	1st
2009	McLaren	17	2	49	5th
2010	McLaren	19	3	240	4th
2011	McLaren	19	3	227	5th
2012	McLaren	20	4	190	4th
2013	Mercedes	19	1	189	4th
2014	Mercedes	19	11	384	1st
2015	Mercedes	19	10	381	1st
2016	Mercedes	21	10	380	2nd
2017	Mercedes	20	9	368	1st
2018	Mercedes	21	11	408	1st
2019	Mercedes	21	11	413	1st
2020	Mercedes	16	11	347	1st
2021	Mercedes	22	8	387.5	2nd
2022	Mercedes	22	0	240	6th
2023	Mercedes	22	0	234	3rd
2024	Mercedes	24	2	223	7th

FOUR YEARS, NO PRIZES

World Champion at just 23, Lewis must have thought that he had years of success ahead, but his run was stopped when Brawn GP found a technical advantage in 2009 and Lewis won but twice to rank fifth. Any hope that matters would improve for Lewis in 2010 were knocked when Red Bull Racing came on strong and Sebastian Vettel started a run of four titles on the trot. Lewis kept winning races, but never rose above fourth in the championship before he elected to quit McLaren at the end of 2012.

SECOND TIME AROUND

The pain of being beaten in 2007 gave way as Lewis won four races in the first half of 2008. With Felipe Massa flying for Ferrari, a win at the penultimate race left Lewis with a seven-point lead going to Brazil. The outcome was extremely dramatic as Lewis was slow to change to rain tyres and fell to sixth, one place too low as Massa swept to victory. Luckily, Toyota's Timo Glock had stayed on slicks and Lewis got by him coming out of the final corner of the last lap to win the title by a point.

BACK-TO-BACK

Mercedes dominated under new engine regulations in 2014 and Lewis battled all season long against team-mate Nico Rosberg. Lewis won 11 races to Rosberg's five and clinched the title in the finale in Abu Dhabi, when quirkily double points were awarded for one race only. Lewis' 2015 season was a little more straightforward, winning his third world title with three rounds to spare, in a year in which he matched idol Ayrton Senna for victories and championships. In doing so he became the first British driver to win successive titles.

MATCHING MICHAEL

Having missed out to team-mate Nico Rosberg at the finale in 2016, Lewis went on a run of four successive titles. Lewis beat Sebastian Vettel in 2017 and 2018 before Mercedes moved clear across 2019 and 2020, allowing Lewis easier runs at the championship, moving on to seven titles to match Michael Schumacher. Lewis gunned for a record eighth in 2021 but was controversially defeated by Max Verstappen in the finale in Abu Dhabi, ending his reign at the top of the standings.

Right Lewis' masterful display at a grip-less Istanbul Park netted him the 2020 title, joining Michael Schumacher on seven world titles

123

PART 3

FAMOUS TEAMS

There have been dozens of Formula One teams throughout history, with some lasting mere races, and others going on to become iconic marques in the championship. The likes of Ferrari and McLaren have been in the mix for decades, others such as Red Bull Racing and Mercedes have risen this side of the millennium, while some have had their moment in the limelight and are now consigned to history, recalled only by the most fanatical of fans.

Below Different eras of F1 have witnessed different teams enjoying spells of dominance, with the likes of Ferrari, Red Bull Racing and Mercedes all enjoying stints atop the tree.

FERRARI

The most famous brand in motorsport? Ferrari has been in Formula One throughout the championship's history, with the occupants of its scarlet red machines idolized by its faithful fanbase. Its most dominant spell came with the virtuoso Michael Schumacher in the early 2000s and while most recent seasons have been leaner, Ferrari remains the most successful team in F1 by nearly every metric.

Above The list of icons to have raced for Ferrari now includes Lewis Hamilton.

FACT FILE

Founded:	1946
Years in F1:	1950 onwards
Country:	Italy
HQ:	Maranello, Italy
Constructors' titles:	1961, 1964, 1975, 1976, 1977, 1979, 1982, 1983, 1999, 2000, 2001, 2002, 2003, 2004, 2007, 2008

TWO IN ONE GO

It took until the fourth round of the second World Championship for Ferrari to start a grand prix from pole position for the first time. This was thanks to the efforts of chunky Argentinian Jose Froilan Gonzalez for the 1951 British GP, and that wasn't the end of his glory at Silverstone as he then raced to Ferrari's first victory after swapping the lead with compatriot Juan Manuel Fangio before pulling clear to win by 51s.

Right Gilles Villeneuve was a star for Ferrari between 1977 and 1982.

TITLE NUMBER ONE

Alberto Ascari clinched the first of his two world titles in 1952 and this was the first of the 15 drivers' championship titles earned by nine Ferrari drivers through to Kimi Räikkönen's title in 2007. He wrapped up the championship after just five of the seven rounds, at the German GP at the Nürburgring, when he scored his fourth win in a row and then backed that up by winning the final two rounds.

15 OUT OF 18

Ferrari made it six constructors' titles in succession in 2004, and did it in truly dominant style as it won 15 of the 18 rounds, almost exclusively through the efforts of World Champion Michael Schumacher who won 13. Team-mate Rubens Barrichello won twice to be runner-up and this helped Ferrari finish with more than double the score of its closest rival, BAR.

CAREER STATS

YEAR	RACES	WINS	POINTS	RANKING	YEAR	RACES	WINS	POINTS	RANKING	YEAR	RACES	WINS	POINTS	RANKING
1950	5	0	N/A	N/A	1975	14	6	72.5	1st	2000	17	10	170	1st
1951	7	3	N/A	N/A	1976	15	6	83	1st	2001	17	9	179	1st
1952	7	7	N/A	N/A	1977	17	4	95	1st	2002	17	15	221	1st
1953	8	7	N/A	N/A	1978	16	5	58	2nd	2003	16	8	158	1st
1954	8	2	N/A	N/A	1979	15	6	113	1st	2004	18	15	262	1st
1955	6	1	N/A	N/A	1980	14	0	8	10th	2005	19	1	100	3rd
1956	7	5	N/A	N/A	1981	15	2	34	5th	2006	18	9	201	2nd
1957	7	0	N/A	N/A	1982	16	3	74	1st	2007	17	9	204	1st
1958	10	2	40	2nd	1983	15	4	89	1st	2008	18	8	172	1st
1959	7	2	32	2nd	1984	16	1	57.5	2nd	2009	17	1	70	4th
1960	8	1	26	3rd	1985	16	2	82	2nd	2010	19	5	396	3rd
1961	7	5	40	1st	1986	16	0	37	4th	2011	19	1	375	3rd
1962	5	0	18	5th	1987	16	2	53	4th	2012	20	3	400	2nd
1963	10	1	26	4th	1988	16	1	65	2nd	2013	19	2	354	3rd
1964	10	3	45	1st	1989	16	3	59	3rd	2014	19	0	216	4th
1965	10	0	26	4th	1990	16	6	110	2nd	2015	19	3	428	2nd
1966	7	2	31	2nd	1991	16	0	55.5	3rd	2016	21	0	398	3rd
1967	10	0	20	4th	1992	16	0	21	4th	2017	21	5	552	2nd
1968	11	1	32	4th	1993	16	0	28	4th	2018	21	6	571	2nd
1969	10	0	7	5th	1994	16	1	71	3rd	2019	21	3	504	2nd
1970	13	4	52	2nd	1995	17	1	73	3rd	2020	17	0	131	6th
1971	11	2	33	4th	1996	16	3	70	2nd	2021	22	0	323.5	3rd
1972	12	1	33	4th	1997	17	5	102	2nd	2022	22	4	554	2nd
1973	13	0	12	6th	1998	16	6	133	2nd	2023	22	1	406	3rd
1974	15	3	65	2nd	1999	16	6	128	1st	2024	24	5	652	2nd

SUCCESS ON A SAD DAY

The 1961 Italian GP at Monza will always be remembered as the race that claimed the life of popular German Ferrari driver Wolfgang von Trips. However, Ferrari also remembers it for another reason, as this was the race at which it landed its first constructors' title. This came through Phil Hill giving the team a home win. As his only rival for the title at the final round at Watkins Glen was von Trips, he too was crowned.

Right Phil Hill runs his Sharknose Ferrari high around the Monza banking in 1961, to win the race and the title, but team-mate Wolfgang von Trips had died earlier in the race.

STARTING WITH A BANG

Ferrari didn't contest the first round of the inaugural World Championship in 1950, but it was at Monaco for the second one. Not only that, the Italian team came away with its first podium finish and first points as Alberto Ascari finished second behind Juan Manuel Fangio's Alfa Romeo. The fact that he was a lap behind showed that Ferrari wasn't ready for that first win.

TEAM WINS, DRIVER LOSES

Although Kimi Räikkönen won the drivers' crown in 2007, Ferrari's most recent constructors' title came in 2008 when the combined talents of Felipe Massa and Kimi Räikkönen were enough to help Ferrari outscore the team that fielded champion Lewis Hamilton, McLaren, as Heikki Kovalainen didn't score much in the second McLaren car. Ferrari clinched the crown at the dramatic final race at Interlagos. Although Massa won the race, it was Hamilton who grabbed the drivers' prize.

IT'S NOT GLORY ALL THE WAY

Ferrari is the most successful team but it has had leaner seasons. Its worst campaign came in 1980, when it was only 10th overall, while most recently a woeful chassis and dreadful engine restricted it to just sixth in 2020.

FERRARI'S GREATEST RUN

Although Michael Schumacher gave Ferrari a huge number of wins in the 2000s, scoring eight in a row from 2003 into 2004, it was more than half a century before that Ferrari scored its best winning sequence. This was 14 races in a row, from Piero Taruffi's victory in the 1952 season-opener at Bremgarten to Alberto Ascari at the same Swiss circuit in 1953, with Ascari winning 11 of these and bagging two drivers' titles.

Left Schumacher and Ferrari dominated F1 in the early 2000s.

McLAREN

Founded by racer and engineer Bruce McLaren, the team started winning in the late 1960s, took titles in the 1970s, was reinvented by Ron Dennis in the 1980s, and went on to be a regular front-runner. Having faded from the sharp end in the mid-2010s a massive upheaval followed and the 2020s have brought McLaren back to the fore as a competitive proposition once more.

Left McLaren climbed back to the top the order in 2024, with Lando Norris winning in Miami.

BACK ON TOP!

McLaren gradually improved through the early 2020s and by 2024 was ready to mount a title challenge. A difficult year for Red Bull's Sergio Perez opened the door for McLaren and Ferrari, and it was the guys and girls in papaya that clinched the deal by just 14 points. McLaren pair Lando Norris and Oscar Piastri scored six wins, and took 46 points' finishes from 48 starts, to end a 26-year wait for Constructors' glory.

Right McLaren clinched the 2024 constructor's title with victory in Abu Dhabi.

THE BOSS TAKES THE FIRST WIN

Two years after McLaren's World Championship debut, having had Denny Hulme finish second at the 1968 Spanish GP, the team landed its first win at the next race in Belgium. Fittingly, this came at the hands of Bruce McLaren, who started that race from sixth, fell to 11th on the opening lap but then guided his M7A to victory when Jackie Stewart's Matra ran out of fuel on the final lap.

NEAR FLAWLESS

McLaren's Honda-powered MP4/4 was a technical masterpiece and the team won 15 of the 16 races in 1988, missing out only in Italy. Its drivers, Ayrton Senna and Alain Prost, contested that year's Drivers' title, with the Brazilian beating his rival, a season before their relationship turned acrimonious. McLaren went on to win the Constructors' Championship in each of the next three seasons, though now Ferrari driver Prost denied Senna the Drivers' title in 1989.

RETURNING TO ROOTS

Different eras of fans will associate McLaren with certain liveries. From 1974 to 1996 it ran in red and white, with backing from Marlboro, before spending two decades in silver and black, associated with Mercedes. When Zak Brown took over as McLaren Racing's new CEO in 2017 he returned the team to its roots, adorning the new MCL monikered cars in the papaya first sported way back when.

Above McLaren out-scored its rivals in 2007 but was disqualified from the Constructors' Championship.

MOST POINTS, BUT NO TITLE

McLaren scored more points than any other team in the 2007 season through the combined efforts of Lewis Hamilton and Fernando Alonso, but it did not win the Constructors' Championship. McLaren was excluded from the standings due to the Spygate scandal, in which it was judged to have had technical drawings from rival Ferrari. Some wanted a harsher punishment, including a suspension, but the drivers were permitted to keep their points, and McLaren was allowed to continue competing.

McLAREN'S FIRST 11

Beating your rivals is always gratifying, but asserting dominance throughout a season is extra satisfying. McLaren had an amazing campaign in 1988 as its MP4/4 was the pick of the crop and, with Ayrton Senna and Alain Prost, the team had the best drivers. The team won 11 on the trot, from the season-opening Brazilian GP in April all the way through to the Belgian GP at the end of August.

TAKING TO THE STREETS

Bruce McLaren gave his team its first grand prix outing at Monaco in 1966 and qualified 10th out of 16. Sadly, its Ford V8 was not only down on power but broke down. A different engine was sought for the next race, at Spa, and this was the start of a team that would be a winning outfit within two years.

WINS FIRST, POLES SECOND

Despite taking its first win at the start of its third year in F1, McLaren didn't claim its first pole until the end of its seventh year. This breakthrough came at the 1972 Canadian GP at Mosport Park when Peter Revson scored the fastest lap and team-mate Denny Hulme helped the team take its first one-two on a grid. Sadly, Jackie Stewart soon propelled his Tyrrell to the front and the McLarens had to settle for second and third.

Below Mika Häkkinen in his 1998 championship-winning MP4/13.

Above Just six weeks after Bruce McLaren raced to second place at Jarama in 1970, he was killed when testing at Goodwood.

TRAGEDY AT GOODWOOD

McLaren was dealt a mighty blow in June 1970 when its founder Bruce McLaren was killed when testing at Goodwood. He was driving one of the Can-Am sportscars that helped finance the team's F1 programme.

CAREER STATS

YEAR	RACES	WINS	POINTS	RANKING
1966	6	0	3	9th
1967	6	0	3	10th
1968	12	3	59	2nd
1969	11	1	49	4th
1970	12	0	36	4th
1971	11	0	13	6th
1972	12	1	66	3rd
1973	15	3	68	3rd
1974	15	4	87	1st
1975	14	3	65	3rd
1976	16	6	88	2nd
1977	17	3	65	3rd
1978	16	0	16	8th
1979	15	0	15	7th
1980	14	0	11	7th
1981	15	1	28	6th
1982	16	4	69	2nd
1983	15	1	34	5th
1984	16	12	143.5	1st
1985	16	6	90	1st
1986	16	4	96	2nd
1987	16	3	76	2nd
1988	16	15	199	1st
1989	16	10	141	1st
1990	16	6	121	1st
1991	16	8	139	1st
1992	16	5	99	2nd
1993	16	5	84	2nd
1994	16	0	42	4th
1995	17	0	30	4th
1996	16	0	49	4th
1997	17	3	63	4th
1998	16	9	156	1st
1999	16	7	124	2nd
2000	17	7	152	2nd
2001	17	4	102	2nd
2002	17	1	65	3rd
2003	16	2	142	3rd
2004	18	1	69	5th
2005	19	10	182	2nd
2006	18	0	110	3rd
2007	17	8	0*	-
2008	18	6	151	2nd
2009	17	2	71	3rd
2010	19	5	454	2nd
2011	19	6	497	2nd
2012	20	7	378	3rd
2013	19	0	122	5th
2014	19	0	181	5th
2015	19	0	27	9th
2016	21	0	76	6th
2017	20	0	30	9th
2018	21	0	62	6th
2019	21	0	145	4th
2020	17	0	202	3rd
2021	22	1	275	4th
2022	22	0	159	5th
2023	22	0	302	4th
2024	24	6	666	1st

* All points annulled for alleged spying infringement

RED BULL RACING

Energy drinks producer Red Bull entered Formula One in 1995 when it sponsored the Sauber team, but its presence skyrocketed in 2005 when it purchased the underachieving Jaguar Racing team. Following the right investment, and recruitment, it emerged as a front-runner within a few seasons. It has enjoyed two periods of supremacy in Formula One, with Sebastian Vettel in the early 2010s, and with Max Verstappen in the early 2020s, ruffling a few feathers along the way.

Above Red Bull only joined F1 in 2005 but the eras of Sebastian Vettel and Max Verstappen have solidified the team as an all-time great.

FACT FILE

Founded:	1997*
Years in F1:	2005 onwards
Country:	England
HQ:	Milton Keynes, England
Constructors' titles:	2010, 2011, 2012, 2013, 2022, 2023

* Raced as Stewart Grand Prix before becoming
Jaguar Racing in 2000 then Red Bull Racing in 2005

Above David Coulthard raced to fourth place on the team's debut in the 2005 Australian GP.

FIRST RACE, FIRST POINTS

Red Bull Racing's first grand prix after being rebranded from Jaguar Racing was the 2005 opener in Melbourne. David Coulthard and team-mate Christian Klien qualified fifth and sixth and raced to fourth and seventh to score seven points, which amounted to 70 per cent of Jaguar Racing's 2004 total points tally in one race. By the year's end, they had scored 34 points, to rank seventh, as Fernando Alonso and Renault combined to lift both titles.

FROM BACKING TO OWNING

Dietrich Mateschitz made a considerable fortune from marketing the Red Bull energy drink around the world and his desire to promote it as a brand associated with adrenaline sports drew him to Formula One. At first he sponsored Sauber, but as he wanted to increase control over his involvement, he expanded his operations and took over the team that had been Jaguar Racing for 2005. Having started life as Stewart Grand Prix in 1997, this was the team's second change of identity and the one that would move it from the midfield to the front.

BACK ON TOP

Red Bull's first reign was ended by Mercedes, as the Silver Arrows hit their stride in the mid-2010s, but the two teams battled tooth and nail for honours in 2021. While Max Verstappen won the Drivers' crown, Red Bull had to settle for second in the Constructors' championship, 28 points behind Mercedes, the first time since 2008 that respective titles had been won by different teams. But Red Bull finally ended Mercedes' eight-year rule in 2022, besting Ferrari by a margin of 205 points.

BECOMING AN ENGINE MANUFACTURER

Red Bull has always been a customer team, spending brief spells powered by Cosworth and Ferrari, before taking Renault engines. A falling out led to their being branded by sponsor TAG Heuer, until Red Bull forged a partnership with Honda. But from 2026, Red Bull will go its own way, having created Red Bull PowerTrains, in partnership with American car company Ford, meaning for the first time it will be its own works operation.

CAREER STATS

YEAR	RACES	WINS	POINTS	RANKING	YEAR	RACES	WINS	POINTS	RANKING
2005	19	0	34	7th	2015	19	0	187	4th
2006	18	0	16	7th	2016	21	2	468	2nd
2007	17	0	24	5th	2017	20	3	368	3rd
2008	18	0	29	7th	2018	21	4	419	3rd
2009	17	6	153.5	2nd	2019	21	3	417	3rd
2010	19	9	498	1st	2020	17	2	319	2nd
2011	19	12	650	1st	2021	22	11	585.5	2nd
2012	20	7	460	1st	2022	22	17	759	1st
2013	19	13	596	1st	2023	22	21	860	1st
2014	19	3	405	2nd	2024	24	9	589	3rd

Above Red Bull will become its own power unit manufacturer from the 2026 season.

SUPER SEB

Red Bull's encouraging 2009 campaign proved to be the launchpad for a spree of success, as it won four consecutive Constructors' Championships across 2010 to 2013, with Sebastian Vettel taking the Drivers' title on each occasion. There were close-run affairs in 2010 and 2012, but in 2011 and 2013 Vettel dominated, taking all of Red Bull's 13 wins in his last title-winning campaign, including nine in a row to round out the season.

Right Sebastian Vettel ruled the roost in the early 2010s and rounded out his fourth title campaign with nine successive victories.

TRAINING GROUND

A year after it entered Formula One Red Bull bought the ailing Minardi team, renamed it Toro Rosso, and used it as a launchpad for prospective future Red Bull drivers. Not every driver made the grade, but the likes of Sebastian Vettel, Daniel Ricciardo and Max Verstappen all graduated through the scheme, while Carlos Sainz and Pierre Gasly raced for Toro Rosso and went on to have successful careers elsewhere. Toro Rosso was renamed AlphaTauri in 2020, and then Visa Cash App RB in 2024, as the entity evolves beyond just being a junior outfit.

BEATEN BY JUNIOR

It was always assumed that Red Bull Racing would lead the way and that its junior team, Scuderia Toro Rosso, would follow. However, after Sebastian Vettel's shock win for Toro Rosso at Monza in 2008, Red Bull Racing had to wait until the third round of the following season before it claimed its first victory. This came at Shanghai, with Vettel the driver to do it, again in very wet conditions. For good measure, team-mate Mark Webber made it a Red Bull Racing one-two.

SMASHING RECORDS

Red Bull smashed a host of records during its phenomenally successful 2023 season. The RB19 was the class of the field in the races, with Max Verstappen winning 19 times, and Sergio Perez twice, to give Red Bull a return of 21 wins from 22 starts. It also broke McLaren's record from 1988 of successive victories, raising the benchmark to 15 straight victories. Red Bull's final points tally of 860 was more than double that of second-placed Mercedes in the championship.

Left Red Bull won an impressive 17 races from 22 in 2022. Somehow, it went even better in 2023, winning all but one of the 22 grands prix.

WILLIAMS

Sir Frank Williams had a couple of abortive attempts to run his own team before a collaboration with engineer Patrick Head transformed his prospects. Williams emerged as a title-winning powerhouse of the 1980s and 1990s before a steady decline prompted the Williams family to sell up in 2020. Now, under fresh ownership and leadership, long-term plans are in place to restore Williams to its rightful position.

FACT FILE

Founded:	1968
Years in F1:	1972 onwards
Country:	England
HQ:	Grove, England
Constructors' titles:	1980, 1981, 1986, 1987, 1992, 1993, 1994, 1996, 1997

Above Williams has nine Constructors' titles, but none since 1997. Alex Albon leads the charge to get Williams back towards the front of the grid.

MALDONADO'S SHOCK

Pastor Maldonado was a mercurial driver who in the right circumstances could be as fast as anyone. In Spain, in 2012, Maldonado converted a shock pole position – having been promoted after Lewis Hamilton was excluded – into an unlikely win. Neither Williams nor Maldonado claimed a single top four finish across the rest of the season. It was Williams' first win since Juan Pablo Montoya (right) won in 2004, and it remains its most recent triumph.

Right Juan Pablo Montoya won at Interlagos in 2004 but it wasn't until 2012 that the team won again.

PROVING IT WAS NO FLUKE

After Clay Regazzoni took the team's first victory at the British GP in 1979, Alan Jones won the next race, in Germany. Having got the jump on Jean-Pierre Jabouille's pole-sitting Renault, Jones then led every lap to take victory. Clay Regazzoni completed Williams' first one–two finish.

FRANK'S BAD BREAK

Frank Williams' life took an unwanted turn in 1986 when he was involved in a car crash on the way back from testing at Paul Ricard that broke his neck, leaving him wheelchair-bound.

MADE IN BRITAIN

Alan Jones was Williams' lead driver in 1979, but it was team-mate Clay Regazzoni who claimed the team's first grand prix victory. This came at the British GP at Silverstone. Up until lap 38 of 68 it looked as though the pole-starting Australian would be winner, but then his water pump failed and Regazzoni was free to canter home. As the team had a Saudi sponsor, Regazzoni had to decline the champagne celebration.

HANGING ON TO HIS DRIVE

Williams is a team that likes to keep its drivers on their toes – it famously let both Nigel Mansell and Damon Hill know during their title-winning campaigns (1992 and 1996) that they would not be needed for the following year. So Riccardo Patrese, Williams' longest-serving driver, did well to stay for five full seasons. The Italian clocked-up 80 grand prix starts between 1988 and 1992 before being replaced by Hill.

Below Riccardo Patrese (trailing team-mate Nigel Mansell) enjoyed two victories in 1991.

⚙ IT CAME TO A SUDDEN STOP

When Williams secured the 1997 constructors' championship title at the European GP at Jerez, it was the team's fifth title in six years, so more were sure to follow. Amazingly, as McLaren came back to form, Williams' form faded and the 1997 success, shaped by champion Jacques Villeneuve and team-mate Heinz-Harald Frentzen, remains the most recent time that Williams reached the top of the pile.

⚫ A TROUBLED BEGINNING

Frank Williams fielded cars as long ago as 1969. However, the first time he entered a car that was unique to his team came in 1972, at the British GP at Brands Hatch, when Henri Pescarolo was slowest of the qualifiers in his Politoys FX3. Unfortunately, it was written-off on the third lap and it would be another seven years until Williams scored its breakthrough win.

Left After over 500 grands prix the Williams family sold up in 2020, but its legacy is comfortably assured, with new owners eager to revive its fortunes.

REGRESSION AND FAREWELL

Sir Frank scaled back his day-to-day involvement with Williams in the 2010s, with daughter Claire taking on the role of Deputy Team Principal. After a brief revival in 2014/15, scoring regular podiums, Williams regressed through the mid-pack, slumping to last in 2018. Amid financial concerns the Williams family sold up mid-2020 to Dorilton Capital, and the remarkable Sir Frank died in November 2021, aged 78. Ex-Mercedes strategist James Vowles took the helm in 2023, tasked with rejuvenating the team's prospects.

Below Career stats: Nigel Mansell has scored most victories for Williams, with 28 spread across three spells with the team.

CAREER STATS

YEAR	RACES	WINS	POINTS	RANKING	YEAR	RACES	WINS	POINTS	RANKING	YEAR	RACES	WINS	POINTS	RANKING
1972	1	0	0	-	1990	16	2	57	4th	2008	18	0	26	8th
1973	15	0	2	10th	1991	16	7	125	2nd	2009	17	0	34.5	7th
1974	15	0	4	10th	1992	16	10	164	1st	2010	19	0	69	6th
1975	12	0	6	9th	1993	16	10	168	1st	2011	19	0	5	9th
1976	13	0	0	-	1994	16	7	118	1st	2012	20	1	76	8th
1978	16	0	11	9th	1995	17	5	118	2nd	2013	19	0	5	9th
1979	15	5	75	2nd	1996	16	12	175	1st	2014	19	0	320	3rd
1980	14	6	120	1st	1997	17	8	123	1st	2015	19	0	257	3rd
1981	15	4	95	1st	1998	16	0	38	3rd	2016	21	0	138	5th
1982	15	1	58	4th	1999	16	0	35	5th	2017	21	0	83	5th
1983	15	1	38	4th	2000	17	0	36	3rd	2018	21	0	7	10th
1984	16	1	25.5	6th	2001	17	4	80	3rd	2019	21	0	1	10th
1985	16	4	71	3rd	2002	17	1	92	2nd	2020	17	0	0	10th
1986	16	9	141	1st	2003	16	3	144	2nd	2021	22	0	23	8th
1987	16	9	137	1st	2004	18	1	88	4th	2022	22	0	8	10th
1988	16	0	20	7th	2005	19	0	66	5th	2023	22	0	28	7th
1989	16	2	77	2nd	2006	18	0	11	8th	2024	24	0	17	9th
					2007	17	0	33	4th					

LOTUS

This team was the one to watch through the 1960s and 1970s. Team founder Colin Chapman's ideas revolutionized F1, leading to periods of domination with Jim Clark and then, in the late 1970s, with Mario Andretti. However, Chapman died and the team fell away after a late flurry with Ayrton Senna. Its name has been revived twice, but these teams have no link to the original Lotus and the Lotus name dropped out of F1 again at the end of the 2015 season.

Left Jim Clark spearheaded Lotus' charge during its glory days, seen here in a Lotus Cosworth 49 at the South African Grand Prix in 1968.

A HOLLOW VICTORY

Lotus was left reeling when Jim Clark was killed in early 1968, but Graham Hill galvanized the team and helped it to that year's title double. Cruelly, in 1970, Lotus' hopes were sent crashing when championship leader Jochen Rindt was killed at Monza. Yet, Rindt was to end the year as F1's only posthumous champion, as second-placed Jacky Ickx failed to beat his points score.

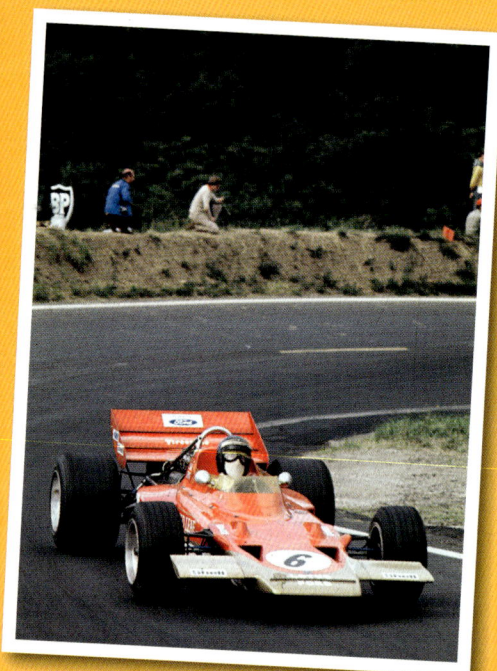

Above Jochen Rindt guides his Lotus 72 to victory in the 1970 French GP. He was later killed at Monza.

BLAZING A TRAIL

It was always a question of when, not if, Lotus was going to land a constructors' title. Having finished second three years in a row, it all came right in 1963. And how! Almost entirely through the efforts of Jim Clark, who won seven of the 10 rounds, and with the advances wrought by Lotus introducing F1's first monocoque, both team and driver wrapped up their titles with victory at Monza with three rounds still to run.

Above Both Jim Clark and team boss Colin Chapman (on car) had reason to celebrate at Monza in 1963.

STARTING WITH A WHIMPER

When Cliff Allison and Graham Hill turned up at Monaco for the second grand prix of 1958, qualifying their Lotus 12s 13th and 15th, they were both roughly 5s off the pace. Allison finished 13 laps down on Maurice Trintignant's winning Cooper and Hill not at all, revealing few signs that this new marque was going to be the lead team of the following decade, but fate knew differently.

BEATING THE WORKS TEAM

Statisticians can be confused by Lotus' very early days in F1 as the most successful Lotus entry wasn't fielded by the works team, but by privateer Rob Walker instead. He had Stirling Moss as his driver and Moss scored not only the first pole position (Monaco 1960) and first win at the same race, but the marque's first fastest lap as well at the following race at Zandvoort. Then the works Lotus team got up to speed.

THE END OF THE LINE

When a team is at the top of its game, it's hard to imagine its winning ability coming to an end. Jim Clark's death in 1968 knocked Lotus back, but Ayrton Senna's departure to McLaren for 1988 sealed the team's fate, with the final Lotus win coming at the 1987 Detroit GP when Senna made his tyres last to outwit Williams' Nigel Mansell. His best results in the remaining 11 rounds were a pair of second places.

ELIO HANGS AROUND

In terms of years, Jim Clark was the longest-serving Lotus driver, racing with the team from 1960 to the start of 1968 – 72 grands prix up to his death. Mario Andretti was at Lotus for five years in the 1970s and managed three more, 75. Then along came Elio de Angelis in 1980 and he raced for Lotus on a record 90 occasions before moving on to Brabham in 1986.

Left De Angelis took his final win for Lotus in the 1985 San Marino GP after Alain Prost was disqualified.

CAREER STATS

YEAR	RACES	WINS	POINTS	RANKING	YEAR	RACES	WINS	POINTS	RANKING	YEAR	RACES	WINS	POINTS	RANKING
1958	9	0	3	6th	1971	11	0	21	5th	1983	15	0	11	7th
1959	8	0	5	4th	1972	12	5	61	1st	1984	16	0	47	3rd
1960	8	0	34	2nd	1973	15	7	92	1st	1985	16	3	71	3rd
1961	8	3	32	2nd	1974	15	3	42	4th	1986	16	2	58	3rd
1962	9	3	37	2nd	1975	14	0	9	7th	1987	16	2	64	3rd
1963	10	7	58	1st	1976	16	1	29	4th	1988	16	0	23	4th
1964	10	3	40	3rd	1977	17	5	62	2nd	1989	16	0	15	6th
1965	10	6	56	1st	1978	16	8	86	1st	1990	16	0	3	7th
1966	9	1	21	5th	1979	15	0	39	4th	1991	16	0	3	9th
1967	11	4	50	2nd	1980	14	0	14	5th	1992	16	0	13	5th
1968	12	5	62	1st	1981	15	0	22	7th	1993	16	0	12	6th
1969	11	2	47	3rd	1982	16	1	30	5th	1994	16	0	0	-
1970	12	6	59	1st										

Left Emerson Fittipaldi took nine wins and the 1972 world title for Lotus.

🏆 HATS OFF TO THE WINNER

Team founder Colin Chapman had a trademark celebration for any win in the 1970s – he would climb over the pitwall, onto the track and hurl his black corduroy cap into the air.

TRIUMPH AND TRAGEDY

Lotus's most recent title came off the back of one of Colin Chapman's many technical innovations. Having introduced ground effects in 1977, Mario Andretti and Ronnie Peterson took control in 1978. With win following win, the team landed the title by the 12th of the 16 rounds. Sadly, Peterson would die two races later.

Below Triumph and tragedy: Ronnie Peterson raced to a dominant win in Austria in 1978, but he died two races later.

MERCEDES GP

Mercedes-Benz entered a team in 1954 and 1955 but disappeared for decades before re-emerging as an engine supplier. But in 2010 the Silver Arrows returned to F1, acquiring the team that had competed as Honda and Brawn Grand Prix, and set about plotting its path to the top. Once it got there it enjoyed a period of unprecedented rule, winning eight successive Constructors' Championships between 2014 and 2021, and seven Drivers' titles, six for Lewis Hamilton and one for Nico Rosberg.

Below Mercedes is striving to return to the top of a sport they dominated during the 2010s, with George Russell leading the charge.

FACT FILE

Founded:	1999
Years in F1:	1999 onwards
Country:	England
HQ:	Brackley, England
Constructors' titles:	2009, 2014, 2015, 2016, 2017, 2018, 2019, 2020, 2021

FIFTY IN THREE YEARS

New engine regulations in 2014 brought Mercedes to the fore, as its 1.6 litre V6 turbo remained the class of the field for several years, boosting an already strong chassis. Between them Lewis Hamilton, who replaced Michael Schumacher in 2013, and Nico Rosberg claimed 56 pole positions and 51 wins from the 59 races held from 2014 to 2016, with Hamilton defeating Rosberg in 2014 and 2015, before Rosberg turned the tables in 2016 – and promptly stunned Mercedes and Formula One by retiring a few days later.

SHOWING ITS BRAWN

Honda Racing dwindled as fast as it soared and the onset of a global recession forced it to close its doors at the end of 2008. Amazingly, not only did an eleventh-hour revival and renaming after technical director Ross Brawn put it back on the grid for 2009, but Button and Rubens Barrichello were given a performance advantage as the car exploited a loophole to run a double-decker diffuser and so Brawn GP took eight wins and romped to both titles.

MERCEDES TAKES OVER

Having supplied engines to McLaren for years, Mercedes decided that it wanted to try and win with cars bearing its name, so Brawn GP was bought and the name changed to Mercedes GP for 2010. Michael Schumacher came out of retirement, but could do nothing as Red Bull, McLaren and Ferrari fought over the title. By 2012, though, Mercedes GP had its first win when Nico Rosberg triumphed in China.

ONE-TWO, ONE-TWO

Mercedes' dominance across three seasons enabled Lewis Hamilton and Nico Rosberg to set a new record, taking the most 1-2 finishes by team-mates. The pair were first and second in 31 races between 2014 and 2016, with Hamilton leading the way 20 times to Rosberg's 11. That surpassed the previous record of 24 achieved by Michael Schumacher and Rubens Barrichello at Ferrari.

NEW NAME, NEW FORTUNE

Honda's involvement in the team continued to increase to the point that BAR became Honda Racing for 2006. Honda got its reward, too, when Button mastered changing conditions to win a rain-hit Hungarian GP, giving him his first win after 113 races without victory.

Below BAR morphed into Honda Racing in 2006 and Jenson Button gave the team its first win, at the Hungarian GP.

MUCH FANFARE, BUT NO POINTS

Launched with the motto "a tradition of excellence", BAR failed to score a point in its debut season. However, changes were made, most notably the improvement of the Honda engines it used from 2000 and then the arrival of Jenson Button in 2003. Together, they made great strides and the Geoff Willis-designed chassis was good enough for Button to press Ferrari's Michael Schumacher in 2004 when BAR finished as runners-up to the Italian team, with Button third overall.

PIECES OF EIGHT

Mercedes faced a renewed threat from Ferrari in 2017 and 2018 but continued its title spree, as Valtteri Bottas adeptly took Rosberg's place, before it moved clear once more in 2019 and 2020, with that year's title ensuring it broke its opponent's record of six straight Constructors' championships. Mercedes moved the benchmark further in 2021, clinching its eighth successive crown at the final round in Abu Dhabi, but with Lewis Hamilton losing the Drivers' title in agonizing circumstances very few were in the mood to celebrate.

Right Mercedes won eight successive world titles between 2014 and 2021.

CAREER STATS

YEAR	RACES	WINS	POINTS	RANKING	YEAR	RACES	WINS	POINTS	RANKING
1999	16	0	0	N/A	2012	20	1	142	5th
2000	17	0	20	=4th	2013	19	3	360	2nd
2001	17	0	17	5th	2014	19	16	701	1st
2002	17	0	7	8th	2015	19	16	703	1st
2003	16	0	26	5th	2016	21	19	765	1st
2004	18	0	119	2nd	2017	20	12	688	1st
2005	19	0	38	6th	2018	21	11	655	1st
2006	18	1	86	4th	2019	21	15	739	1st
2007	17	0	6	8th	2020	17	13	573	1st
2008	18	0	14	9th	2021	22	9	613.5	1st
2009	17	8	172	1st	2022	22	1	515	3rd
2010	19	0	214	4th	2023	22	0	409	2nd
2011	19	0	165	4th	2024	24	4	468	4th

* As BAR 1999–2005, Honda Racing 2006–2008, Brawn F1 2009

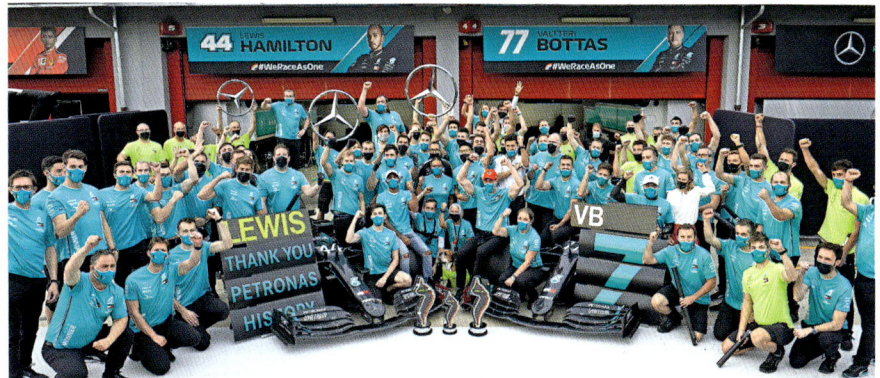

FROM A VETERAN TO A ROOKIE

Mercedes has favoured longevity and experience with its driver line-ups, but for 2025 has turned to youth. Lewis Hamilton's move to Ferrari opened a vacancy alongside George Russell and Mercedes has filled the breach with Andrea Kimi Antonelli. Aged 18, he will become the third-youngest racer in history, the youngest to ever race for the Silver Arrows, and the first time a complete novice has been put in one of its race cars. There's just a gap of 21 years and 356 grands prix between Antonelli and his predecessor!

Left Mercedes brought in Andrea Kimi Antonelli to replace Lewis Hamilton.

RENAULT

Renault won the first ever grand prix, the French GP of 1906, and made its first World Championship appearance in 1977 when it introduced turbocharged engines. Renault became a winning team in 1979 but bowed out after 1985. It returned in 2002 when it took over the Benetton team, running as Renault until rebadging as Lotus for 2012, then being changed back again to Renault for the 2016 season.

Below Winning at home was always important for Renault, so Rene Arnoux delighted the bosses when he led home Alain Prost in a Renault one-two at Paul Ricard in 1982.

FACT FILE

Founded:	1977
Years in F1:	1977–1985, 2002–2011, 2012–2015 as Lotus, 2016–2020
Country:	France
HQ:	Enstone, England
Constructors' titles:	2005, 2006

151

ALPINE ENTERS THE FRAY

Renault returned to Formula One as a works team in 2016, but its five-year plan to contend for titles ended only with a trio of podiums, scored by Daniel Ricciardo and Esteban Ocon in 2020. From 2021, Renault rebranded the team as Alpine, in deference to the sportscar arm of the company it sought to grow. Ocon pulled off a shock win for himself and Alpine in Hungary, in 2021, but Alpine has remained entrenched in the midfield, or worse.

Right Renault morphed into Alpine for 2021 – the team remained the same, but the name changed as part of a wider branding exercise.

A REALLY LONG WAIT

Although the French hosted the first grand prix, back in 1906 (won by a Renault incidentally) the nation really took its time to get going in F1. Indeed, although Bugatti, Gordini and Talbot tried to win for the glory of France in the 1950s, it took until 1979 for that first race win and a further 26 years for the first title to be won by a French team. Mind you, by this point, it was a French team operating out of Britain.

AT HOME AND AWAY

Renault's two spells in F1 are distinct as the first, from 1977 to 1985, was based in France and the second spell, from 2002, based in Britain, taking over the Benetton team premises and personnel.

BEING DOUBLY HONOURED

Despite Renault's successes in the late 1970s and early 1980s in the days when the team was wholly French, it took until 2005 for the now British-run team representing the French marque to take its first constructors' championship. Then, like buses, a second title came along straight after it, with Fernando Alonso's second place behind Ferrari's Felipe Massa in the 2006 Brazilian GP at Interlagos sealing the deal.

NOW THAT'S SOMETHING NEW

There was considerable interest when Renault made its F1 debut midway through 1977. This wasn't just because an all-new team arrived for the British GP at Silverstone with an all-new car, but also because the yellow racer was powered by the first turbocharged engine in F1. Jean-Pierre Jabouille qualified 21st and was making progress when the car pulled off with, you've guessed it, turbo-charger failure…

Below Jean-Pierre Jabouille at Silverstone in 1977.

FIRST POINTS, BUT ONLY JUST

The almost ceaseless mechanical failures that blighted Renault's debut season in 1977 were reduced for its second campaign and Jean-Pierre Jabouille claimed the team's first points at the 1978 US GP at Watkins Glen. He qualified ninth but advanced as others fell off and was fourth at flagfall. It could have been third but his engine spluttered with eight laps to go. He let Jody Scheckter's Wolf by, then just limped home.

DOING IT IN STYLE

When Renault scored its breakthrough victory, it did so in style. This wasn't simply because it did so on home ground when Jean-Pierre Jabouille was first to the chequered flag in the 1979 French GP at Dijon-Prenois, but because the battle over second place was all but explosive in the closing laps, with team-mate Rene Arnoux and Ferrari's Gilles Villeneuve changing places at almost every bend and entertaining royally.

Below Rene Arnoux lost out to Gilles Villeneuve in the 1979 Franch GP, but he did set the fastest lap.

LANDMARK FLYING LAPS

Renault brought turbocharged engines into F1 in 1977 and their power soon made them almost untouchable around a lap. For races, the boost had to be turned down, not just to reduce fuel consumption, but to ensure they didn't blow. So, although Renault's first pole came at the 1979 South African GP, it took another five races before it took its first fastest lap, through Rene Arnoux in the French GP, a race won by team-mate Jean-Pierre Jabouille.

Right Fernando Alonso took the drivers' titles in 2005 and 2006.

CAREER STATS

YEAR	RACES	WINS	POINTS	RANKING	YEAR	RACES	WINS	POINTS	RANKING	YEAR	RACES	WINS	POINTS	RANKING
1977	5	0	0	-	2003	16	1	88	4th	2014	19	0	19	8th
1978	14	0	3	12th	2004	18	1	105	3rd	2015	19	0	78	6th
1979	15	1	26	6th	2005	19	7	191	1st	2016	21	0	8	9th
1980	14	3	38	4th	2006	18	8	206	1st	2018	21	0	122	4th
1981	15	3	54	3rd	2007	17	0	51	3rd	2019	21	0	91	5th
1982	16	4	62	3rd	2008	18	2	80	4th	2020	17	0	181	5th
1983	15	4	79	2nd	2009	17	0	26	8th	*2021	22	1	155	5th
1984	16	0	34	5th	2010	19	0	163	5th	*2022	22	0	173	4th
1985	16	0	16	7th	2011	19	0	73	5th	*2023	22	0	120	6th
2002	17	0	23	4th	2012	20	1	303	4th	*2024	24	0	65	6th
					2013	19	1	315	4th	*As Alpine				

BENETTON

The team was born out of the Toleman team after it ran into financial difficulties in 1985 and was bailed out by the Benetton knitwear company. Racing as Benetton from 1986, they took Michael Schumacher to titles in 1994 and 1995 but disappeared when taken over by Renault for 2002. In 2012, it changed its name again, to Lotus, but changed back to being Renault for the 2016 World Championship, adopting corporate colours once more.

Below Benetton's peak came in the mid-1990s, with Michael Schumacher driving the team to the title.

FACT FILE

Founded:	1986
Years in F1:	1986–2001
Country:	England
HQ:	Enstone, England
Constructors' title:	1995

TOP OF ALL THE LISTS

Not only was Michael Schumacher Benetton's longest-serving driver, with 68 starts between his transfer from Jordan towards the end of the 1991 season and the end of 1995, but he was the team's most successful driver by some margin. His tally, before he left to race for Ferrari in 1996, was two drivers' titles, 19 wins, 10 pole positions, 24 fastest laps and 313 points.

Left Berger surprised everyone when he came back from missing three races in 1997 to win the German GP for what would be Benetton's final grand prix success.

Above Gerhard Berger used his tyres sensibly in the Mexican heat in 1986 to give Benetton its first victory one race before the end of its maiden campaign.

FIRST YEAR WINNERS

It took until the penultimate grand prix of its first season racing as Benetton (after its development years racing as Toleman) for the team to secure its first win. This came at the Mexican GP in 1986 when Gerhard Berger qualified fourth, gained a place at Nigel Mansell's expense on the opening lap, then kept his cool to run non-stop to victory on his Pirelli tyres while his Goodyear-shod rivals had to pit for fresh rubber.

THE FIRST AND THE LAST

Not only did Gerhard Berger score Benetton's first win in 1986, but he returned to the team after nine years away racing for Ferrari (twice) and McLaren to be the driver who gave Benetton its last. This came in 1997 at the German GP at Hockenheim. Early-season form hadn't suggested such an outcome would be possible, and he missed three races with a sinus problem, before bouncing back with this popular win from pole.

END OF YEAR, END OF NAME

The record books show that Benetton's last grand prix was at the final round of the 2001 World Championship, the Japanese GP, as Renault's buy-in meant that the Enstone-based team would be known as Renault from 2002 onwards. It hadn't been a good season for either Giancarlo Fisichella or Jenson Button, and although they qualified sixth and ninth at Suzuka, neither scored, with Button seventh and Fisichella on the sidelines.

Right Jenson Button was the last driver to finish a race in a Benetton car, finishing seventh at Suzuka in the 2001 season finale.

STRAIGHT INTO THE POINTS

Benetton wasn't a brand new team when it made its debut at the 1986 season-opener in Brazil, rather a re-badged version of the team that had finished 1985 as Toleman. However, the investment that poured in over the close-season resulted in a superior car and Gerhard Berger qualified 16th before racing through the field to score a point for sixth, four places up on team-mate, Teo Fabi. More points would follow.

LIGHT THE TOUCHPAPER

Very few teams show pace-setting speed in their first season, but Benetton did. Propelled by turbocharged BMW engines, the green cars with multi-coloured flashes on their engine covers certainly had ample power, most especially with the boost turned up for qualifying. This resulted in the team's first pole position at the 1986 Austrian GP, when Teo Fabi and Gerhard Berger shared an all-Benetton front row.

GIFTED A VICTORY

Benetton's second win came at Suzuka in 1989, but Alessandro Nannini was only able to celebrate after McLaren's Ayrton Senna was disqualified for rejoining incorrectly after a clash with Alain Prost.

Below Michael Schumacher's victory in Germany in 1995 was an important ingredient in his second title and the team's first.

CAREER STATS

YEAR	RACES	WINS	POINTS	RANKING	YEAR	RACES	WINS	POINTS	RANKING
1986	16	1	19	6th	1994	16	8	103	2nd
1987	16	0	28	5th	1995	17	11	137	1st
1988	16	0	39	3rd	1996	16	0	68	3rd
1989	16	1	39	4th	1997	17	1	67	3rd
1990	16	2	71	3rd	1998	16	0	33	5th
1991	16	1	38.5	4th	1999	16	0	16	6th
1992	16	1	91	3rd	2000	17	0	20	4th
1993	16	1	72	3rd	2001	17	0	10	7th

Left Nelson Piquet claimed both of Benetton's wins in 1990 then added another in 1991.

FIRST DRIVER THEN TEAM

Michael Schumacher won the drivers' championship for Benetton in a controversial 1994 season, but the team had to wait until he secured the championship again in 1995 before it could celebrate its own crown. This constructors' championship was wrapped up at the Japanese GP when Schumacher qualified on pole and then led every lap (apart from when pitting). He had already claimed the drivers' title two races earlier.

TYRRELL

Once a racer, then a team manager, Ken Tyrrell helped Matra to succeed in F1 before founding his own marque in 1970. Jackie Stewart grabbed two drivers' and one constructors' title over its first four years to establish the team, but it was never as competitive again and was bought by British American Racing in 1998.

Above Jackie Stewart in action during the 1972 season in a Tyrrell 006. Tyrrell had won the constructor's title the year before.

FACT FILE

Founded:	1960
Years in F1:	1970–1998
Country:	England
HQ:	Ockham, England
Constructors' title:	1971

SIX WHEELS FOR VICTORY

With its typically sensible and somewhat workmanlike cars, Tyrrell wasn't considered to be a team that pursued revolution in design until it launched the P34 in 1976. It had four small wheels at the front to give the car a lower frontal area in order to reduce its drag co-efficient, and it worked well enough for Jody Scheckter to lead Patrick Depailler home in a one-two in the Swedish GP at Anderstorp. But no other team saw fit to copy it.

Right Patrick Depailler stayed with Tyrrell from 1974 to 1978. This is the French ace in the team's P34 six-wheeler in 1976.

VICTORY RUN THWARTED

Although Tyrrell started 1970 running a March chassis for Jackie Stewart, it wasn't until the Canadian GP, the 11th of 13 races, that the Scot was sent out to race in the team's first chassis, the Tyrrell 001. Stewart delighted the team by qualifying on pole, something he'd managed three times in the March with which they'd started the year. Then, heading to victory, his stub-axle failed just before half distance.

STAYING CLOSE TO HOME

F1 standards have changed greatly, but even in its day it came as a shock to learn that Ken Tyrrell ran his successful team from sheds alongside his family's timber yard business.

WITHDRAWAL HITS TITLE HOPE

Tyrrell was on course for its second constructors' title in 1973 after a battle with Lotus. However, Francois Cevert's death in qualifying for the final round, the United States GP, led Ken Tyrrell to withdraw the team. This left the way clear for Ronnie Peterson to win for Lotus to gift them the crown, meaning that Tyrrell's final title was the drivers' one that Jackie Stewart claimed three races earlier at the Austrian GP.

GETTING BACK ON TRACK

With Jackie Stewart's retirement at the end of 1973, and Francois Cevert's tragic death, it was left to Tyrrell's new guard of Patrick Depailler and Jody Scheckter to keep the team at the front. It all came together for the pair in the seventh round, the Swedish GP at Anderstorp, when they claimed the team's first one-two in qualifying before the South African got the jump on the Frenchman and led all the way.

Below After giving Tyrrell its first win of 1974 in Sweden, Jody Scheckter was a winner again three races later in the British GP at Brands Hatch.

IMPRESSING THE BOSSES

If you're powered by Ford, winning the Detroit GP isn't a bad way to impress the right people on the streets of the world's automotive capital. This is what happened to Tyrrell in 1983 when Michele Alboreto worked his way forward from sixth to third then gained a place when Rene Arnoux retired his Ferrari from the lead. When new leader Nelson Piquet's Brabham picked up a puncture, Alboreto secured the team's 23rd and final win.

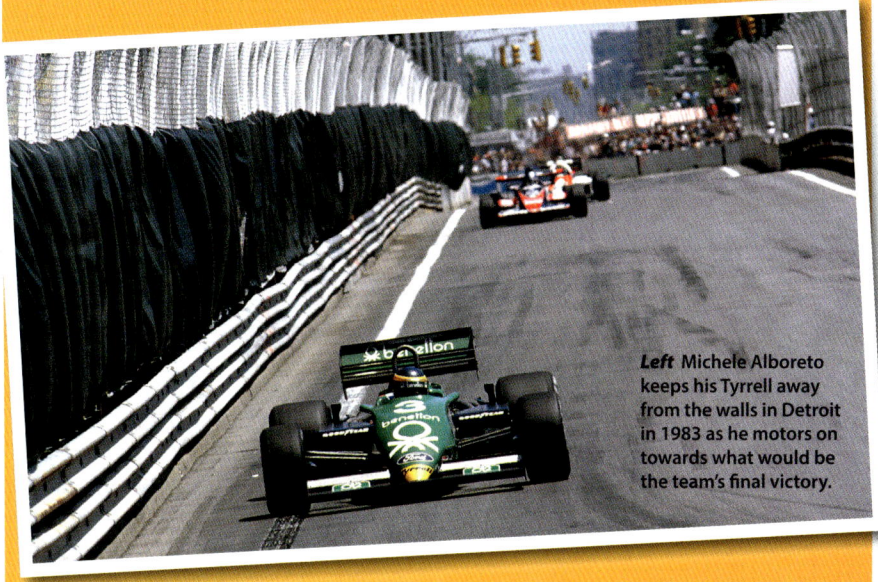

Left Michele Alboreto keeps his Tyrrell away from the walls in Detroit in 1983 as he motors on towards what would be the team's final victory.

MAKING YOUR OWN LUCK

Jackie Stewart raced to five wins and a second in the first seven rounds of 1971. So great was his advantage that he secured the drivers' title and Tyrrell wrapped up the constructors' title at the eighth round of 11. Ironically, the team's first title was claimed at the Austrian GP, in which Stewart retired, albeit because he lost a wheel just a few laps after his closest rival, Ferrari's Jacky Ickx, had dropped out, leaving BRM's Jo Siffert to win.

ENDING WITH A WHIMPER

Tyrrell's time in F1 came to an end at the 1998 Japanese GP at Suzuka after 29 years. Sadly, this once proud team, whose World Championship entry was taken over by BAR, went out with a whimper when Ricardo Rosset failed to qualify and Toranosuke Takagi crashed out just after mid-distance in a collision with Minardi's Esteban Tuero. That they were scrapping over last place emphasized how far the team had fallen.

Right Jackie Stewart helped Tyrrell to its only constructors' championship in 1971 by winning six of the 11 rounds, in Spain, Monaco, France, Britain, Germany and Canada.

CAREER STATS

YEAR	RACES	WINS	POINTS	RANKING	YEAR	RACES	WINS	POINTS	RANKING	YEAR	RACES	WINS	POINTS	RANKING
1970	3	0	0	-	1980	14	0	12	6th	1990	16	0	16	5th
1971	11	7	73	1st	1981	15	0	10	8th	1991	16	0	12	6th
1972	12	4	51	2nd	1982	16	1	25	6th	1992	16	0	8	6th
1973	14	5	82	2nd	1983	15	1	12	7th	1993	16	0	0	-
1974	15	2	52	3rd	1984	12	0	0*	-	1994	16	0	13	6th
1975	14	1	25	5th	1985	16	0	7	9th	1995	17	0	5	8th
1976	16	1	71	3rd	1986	16	0	11	7th	1996	16	0	5	8th
1977	17	0	27	5th	1987	16	0	11	6th	1997	17	0	2	10th
1978	16	1	38	4th	1988	15	0	5	8th	1998	16	0	0	-
1979	15	0	28	5th	1989	16	0	16	5th					

* All results were stripped from the team in 1984 as illegal fuel was found in its cars at the Detroit GP

COOPER

This was the team that bucked traditional thinking when it entered cars with an engine behind the driver rather than in front and proved that big wasn't best. However, after title glory in 1959 and 1960, its form rather dropped away and instead made its money from selling chassis for others to drive.

FACT FILE

Founded:	1946
Years in F1:	1953–1968
Country:	England
HQ:	Surbiton, England
Constructors' titles:	1959, 1960

Above Jack Brabham in a Cooper-Climax T51 at the British Grand Prix in 1959. Cooper were constructors' champions in both 1958 and 1959.

OVER AND ALMOST OUT

The last grand prix entered by Cooper Car Co was the 1968 Mexican GP. Vic Elford and Lucien Bianchi qualified 17th and 21st, but only Elford was able to finish, in eighth place. With money tight, that was the end of the works team. A Cooper made one last visit to a World Championship round in the Monaco GP the following year when Elford finished seventh for Colin Crabbe's Antique Automobiles Ltd team.

ONE, TWO, NOTHING

Cooper won two constructors' titles, in 1959 and 1960. Jack Brabham led the team's attack, winning the drivers' championship in both those years, ably supported by Bruce McLaren. However, the Australian left Cooper and Kiwi McLaren soldiered on. The rise of Lotus and resurgence of Ferrari left it fighting for the minor point-scoring places through until Cooper's demise at the end of 1968.

Right One, two, nothing: Brabham had good reason to smile in both 1959 and 1960.

BEATEN BY A CUSTOMER

Imagine the mixed feelings you'd experience if your marque defeated the big guns to score its maiden victory, yet the car wasn't run by your works team but a private entry. This was what happened to Cooper in 1958 when Rob Walker Racing's Stirling Moss went to the season-opener in Argentina in a Cooper and came away victorious. It would take just over a year for Jack Brabham to win for Cooper Car Co, at Monaco.

Left Stirling Moss gave Cooper its first win, for Rob Walker Racing in Argentina in 1958.

FOLLOWING THE LEADER

You might have thought that Jack Brabham would hold the record as Cooper's longest-serving driver. However, it is Bruce McLaren, his team-mate when Jack won the drivers' titles in 1959 and 1960 who comes out far ahead, 64 to 39. The Kiwi joined Cooper at the tail end of 1958 and stayed on until the close of the 1965 season before he, like Brabham before him, headed off to found his own marque.

Right Bruce McLaren steers his Cooper T60 Climax to first place at Monaco in 1962. McLaren was Cooper's longest-serving driver.

A FOOT IN THE DOOR

Harry Schell's family team entered a Cooper in the 1950 Monaco GP and assorted privateers ran Coopers in 1952. However, it was in 1953 that the Cooper Car Co finally entered a works team, starting by running a car for Adolfo Schwelm-Cruz in the season-opening race in Buenos Aires. He was the first to retire, when his car shed a wheel, and team-mates John Barber and Alan Brown finished a distant eighth and ninth.

COOPER'S HIGH FIVE

Cooper's best winning sequence came in the second year in which it won the constructors' championship, 1960. Much of the momentum required to vanquish Lotus came from this five-race winning streak that started when Jack Brabham won the Dutch GP, then added the next four in Belgium, France, Britain and Portugal.

A SOARAWAY SALES SUCCESS

Cooper did more than run a successful team, as the sale of its F1 chassis enabled many privateers to enter the World Championship. The greatest number fielded was 16 at the 1959 British GP.

Below A privately-entered Cooper driven by John Love was heading for victory in the 1967 South African GP until it had to pit for fuel and Pedro Rodriguez came through to win for the works team.

CAREER STATS

YEAR	RACES	WINS	POINTS	RANKING	YEAR	RACES	WINS	POINTS	RANKING
1953	3	0	N/A*	N/A*	1963	10	0	25	5th
1955	1	0	N/A*	N/A*	1964	10	0	16	5th
1957	5	0	N/A*	N/A*	1965	10	0	14	5th
1958	9	2	31	3rd**	1966	9	1	30	3rd
1959	8	5	40	1st**	1967	11	1	28	3rd
1960	8	6	48	1st	1968	12	0	14	6th
1961	8	0	14	4th					
1962	9	1	29	3rd					

* There was no constructors' championship until 1958
** Including the results of privateer Cooper-fielding team Rob Walker Racing as the constructors' series points were awarded according to the make of car rather than the team running it

Above Jack Brabham won two races on his way to the 1959 title with Cooper.

A WIN/WIN SITUATION

The season-opening 1967 South African GP is a race remembered for a 'what if' performance as it was the most famous upset in F1 history. John Love, a driver from neighbouring Rhodesia (now Zimbabwe) was heading for victory in a privately-entered Cooper when he had to pit for fuel with seven laps to go. Love's hiccough left the way clear for one of the works cars, driven by Pedro Rodriguez, to come through to victory.

PART 4

GREAT TRACKS

Formula One's calendar has gradually expanded as the championship seeks to tap into fresh markets while retaining the core events that have contributed to its rich history. The likes of Silverstone, Spa-Francorchamps, Suzuka, Monaco, Melbourne and Monza have been cornerstones of the schedule for generations, each possessing ribbons of tarmac that are laced with memories. They are venues relished annually by the teams and drivers as they seek to imprint their mark on these places.

Above Suzuka is regarded as one of the finest circuits in the world; the drivers plunge downhill into Turn 1 before tackling a sequence of high-speed esses.

MONZA

This historic parkland circuit has always been blessed with superlatives, from the fastest race average speed, fastest straightline speed, the closest group finish and even the greatest number of lead changes during a grand prix. And, being in Italy, every second of Ferrari action at Monza is cheered on by the fanatical tifosi.

ONE FOR TORO, TWO FOR JOY

Monza may be all about Ferrari, but Red Bull's second team RB has operated out of Italian town Faenza since 1985. In 2008, when it was Toro Rosso, Sebastian Vettel dominated a rain-hit weekend to claim a shock victory, the first of his 53 in Formula One. Toro Rosso was rebranded as AlphaTauri for 2020 and remarkably Pierre Gasly claimed a surprise maiden win at Monza. It means both of the entrant's wins have come on home soil.

A ROYAL APPOINTMENT

Motor racing circuits tend to be built on greenfield sites, but Monza is a little different, as it was built in 1922 on the parkland surrounding Monza royal palace, which explains the mature trees that surround it, adding to its appeal.

FANGIO'S HAT-TRICK

Juan Manuel Fangio is the only driver to have achieved three wins in a row at Monza, the great Argentinian achieving this hat-trick between 1953 and 1955. He took the first of these for Maserati, hitting the front out of the final corner when race-leader Giuseppe Farina crashed out. Fangio then added the next two while leading the Mercedes-Benz attack, albeit with a fortunate win in 1954 when others retired and a clear run in 1955.

Left Pierre Gasly took a shock victory for home team AlphaTauri in 2020.

TRACK FACTS

Opened: 1922

Country: Italy

Location: 10 miles north-west of Milan

Active years in F1: 1950–1979, 1981 onwards

Most wins/driver: Michael Schumacher, 5 (1996, 1998, 2000, 2003, 2006); Lewis Hamilton, 5 (2012, 2014, 2015, 2017, 2018)

Most wins/team: Ferrari, 20 (1951, 1952, 1960, 1961, 1964, 1966, 1970, 1975, 1979, 1988, 1996, 1998, 2000, 2002, 2003, 2004, 2006, 2010, 2019, 2024)

Lap length: 3.600 miles

Number of turns: 11

Lap record: 1m21.046s, 159.909mph, Rubens Barrichello (Ferrari), 2004

Above Monza is located in a royal park to the north-west of Milan and its lay-out can be made out, as well as that of the oval circuit cutting the through the trees.

MERCEDES' MID-2010s STREAK

Mercedes enjoyed a streak of successes in the mid-2010s, becoming the first team to claim five straight victories at Monza. Lewis Hamilton kick-started the run in 2014, doubling up in 2015, before Nico Rosberg's triumph in 2016. Hamilton added another pair of back-to-back wins across 2017 and 2018 until the spree was snapped in 2019 by Ferrari's Charles Leclerc – much to the delight of the Tifosi.

Right Mercedes dominated through the mid-2010s as it silenced the raucous home crowd.

ALFA COMPLETES DOMINATION

The pattern was set when the World Championship came to Monza for the first time in 1950 to round out its inaugural season: Alfa Romeo would win as it had in the previous five races. Indeed, Giuseppe Farina controlled proceedings, but Ferrari challenged for the first time, with Alberto Ascari running second until his engine overheated. After taking over team-mate Dorino Serafini's car, Ascari recovered to bag second place.

Below Lewis Hamilton chases Fernando Alonso through the Parabolica corner in 2007.

HAMILTON'S RECORD 2020 LAP

Monza has always been a high speed circuit thanks to its long straights and fast curves, and speeds reached a peak during qualifying in 2020. Mercedes driver Lewis Hamilton set a time of 1m 18.887 to secure pole position, lapping the circuit at an average speed of 164.268mph. It was the fastest ever qualifying lap in Formula One history, and all of the top 10 fastest qualifying laps have come at Monza.

USING THE FAMOUS BANKING

Monza is still considered fearsome, but it was far more so in 1955, 1956, 1960 and 1961 when the Italian GP was held on a layout that included an extra loop with massive banked corners at either end, bringing its lap length up to 6.214 miles. After 1961, when 14 spectators were killed when Wolfgang von Trips crashed into the crowd, the World Championship reverted to Monza's 3.573-mile layout, cutting out the banking.

DELIGHTING THE TIFOSI

Fangio, Moss, Peterson, Piquet, Prost and Vettel have all won three grands prix at Monza. Rubens Barrichello has claimed four victories, but the driver who really put Ferrari back on the map from the late 1990s, Michael Schumacher, is joint top of the pile, with five wins. These came in 1996, 1998, 2000, 2003 and 2006. To the delight of the Tifosi, Ferrari is the team with the greatest winning record, having taken 20 wins.

EXIT OF PARABOLICA

The final corner of Monza's lap, the Parabolica, is a long, long corner. Approached at 210mph, this is a fourth gear bend, with drivers still travelling at 130mph as they turn through this right-hander. Exit speed is critical, and drivers should be changing up to fifth gear and hitting 150mph by the exit, as they need to carry as much speed as possible onto the start/finish straight past the grandstand and on down to the first chicane.

MONACO

By rights, there shouldn't be a grand prix at Monaco, as its streets are too narrow for contemporary F1 cars to find space to overtake, but to discard it would strip the World Championship of the race with the strongest identity. The yachts and beautiful people add glamour, and F1 would be the poorer without it.

WINNING FROM FOURTEENTH

Almost half of Monaco's grands prix have been won from pole position – unsurprisingly – but the lowest starting place for a winner has been from way down in 14th place. In 1996 Ligier's Olivier Panis avoided the trouble that befell the majority of the grid to claim his sole Formula One triumph in wet conditions. Panis and his fellow podium finishers, David Coulthard and Johnny Herbert, were the only three cars still circulating at the end.

EVERY WHICH WAY BUT...

There has been some enthralling racing at Monaco, but Nigel Mansell's pursuit of Ayrton Senna in 1992 was debatably even more exciting than Jochen Rindt's successful chase of Jack Brabham in 1970. Mansell had led from the start, but what made it Monaco's most memorable race was when a wheel weight came loose and Mansell had to pit for new tyres. On rejoining, with six laps to go, he was 5s down on Senna, then closed right in and was all over him but just couldn't find a way past.

IN A CLASS OF HIS OWN

Juan Manuel Fangio was very much the star of the show at Monaco's first World Championship race in 1950. Not only did he put his Alfa Romeo 158 on pole position by 2.6s from team-mate Giuseppe Farina but he also shot off to win the race by a lap, setting fastest lap as he went. His advantage over the slowest of the 20 qualifiers, Johnny Claes in Ecurie Belge Talbot was 20.8s...

A TRULLI GREAT DAY

Jarno Trulli started 252 grands prix across a career that spanned 15 years, and had a reputation as a formidable qualifier. That was put to great effect in 2004 when he claimed a stunning pole position and backed it up 24 hours later, beating Jenson Button by less than half a second. Trulli went on to take three more poles in his career but never again mounted the top of the podium.

Below Denny Hulme drifts his Repco-powered Brabham BT20 as he turns right across the brow onto the descent to Mirabeau during his winning drive in 1967.

CASINO SQUARE

One of the most glamorous of Monaco's glamorous spots, Casino Square, passes in a flash for the drivers when the grand prix circus comes to town. The cars arrive over a brow into the preceding corner, Massenet, then feel funnelled by crash barriers and a patch of shade before bursting back into the sunlight as they enter the square.

TRACK FACTS

Opened: 1922

Country: Monaco

Location: Monte Carlo

Active years in F1: 1950, 1955–2019, 2021–present

Most wins/driver: Ayton Senna, 6 (1987, 1989, 1990, 1991, 1992, 1993)

Most wins/team: McLaren, 15 (1984–1986, 1988–1993, 1998, 2000, 2002, 2005, 2007–2008)

Lap length: 2.074 miles

Number of turns: 19

Lap record: 1m12.909s, Lewis Hamilton (Mercedes), 2021

Above The way in which the circuit has to thread its way between Monaco's buildings and harbour is clear from this view.

McLAREN'S MONTE MAGIC

One might have thought, given its lengthy history in F1, that Ferrari would be the team with the most wins at Monaco, but the Italian team has underachieved there by its own standards. For, while it has 19 wins on home ground at Monza, it has won only 11 times at Monaco since 1950. McLaren is way clear at the top of the pile at Monaco, having recorded 15 wins up to and including the 2024 season.

Above Charles Leclerc had heartbreak several times, sweetening the feeling of a first home triumph in 2024.

LECLERC'S HOME RUN

Monaco had one of its own from 2018 when Charles Leclerc stepped up to Formula One. Fortune was not on Leclerc's side for several years, amid incidents and setbacks, but finally in 2024 Leclerc claimed an emotional home victory, cheered on by the locals. He became the first Monegasque to win a world championship Monaco Grand Prix round.

THE PRINCE'S PLEASURE

Like Monza, Monaco has a royal connection. Not only was cigarette manufacturer Antony Noghes given permission to stage racing on a street circuit by Prince Louis II, but the Grimaldis' castle overlooks the circuit from on high.

Above When Alain Prost won at Monaco in 1988, McLaren had no way of knowing that it would triumph in the next five races there as well.

SIX IN SUCCESSION

McLaren enjoyed an amazing run at Monaco when its drivers won in the principality six years running from 1988 to 1993. Alain Prost inherited victory in the first of these when team-mate Ayrton Senna crashed inexplicably out of a clear lead. Senna then made amends and won the next five races here. Incredibly, Senna's victory at Monaco in 1987 for Lotus was the only non-McLaren win in the 10 years from 1984.

SILVERSTONE

The site of the first ever World Championship round in 1950, Silverstone is more than the home of the British GP. It's one of the true homes of motor racing, not just because of its long history but also because the majority of the teams are based in England, making this their home race.

DRESSED TO THE NINES

Lewis Hamilton has thrived at Silverstone and set a new record in 2024 when he claimed his ninth victory at the circuit – the most by any driver at one venue. Hamilton took his first Silverstone win in 2008, recording an astonishing victory in the wet by 68 seconds, before a streak of four-in-a-row across 2014 to 2017. Further wins came in 2019, 2020 and 2021, while the ninth win in 2024 ended Hamilton's longest drought in Formula One. Hamilton also has 15 podiums at Silverstone – another record – more than double any other driver, and seven pole positions – four more than any other driver.

AND THEY'RE OFF...

Silverstone had the honour of hosting the first round of the first World Championship in 1950. Watched by the royal family from a private grandstand, the race was an Alfa Romeo benefit as not only did its cars fill the first four places on the grid but Giuseppe Farina led home an Alfa one-two-three ahead of Luigi Fagioli and Reg Parnell, with team-mate Juan Manuel Fangio dropping out with a connecting rod failure.

FLYING ROUND THE TRACK

Silverstone set something of a trend when its circuit was marked out around the perimeter roads of an airfield in 1948. The airfield had become disused in the wake of the Second World War and the race circuit gave it a new lease of life.

Left No driver in history has had greater success than Lewis Hamilton at Silverstone, with nine victories.

TRACK FACTS

Opened: 1948

Country: England

Location: 16 miles south-west of Northampton

Active years in F1: 1950–1954, 1956, 1958, 1960, 1963, 1965, 1967, 1969, 1971, 1973, 1975, 1977, 1979, 1981, 1983, 1985, 1987 onwards

Most wins/driver: Lewis Hamilton, 9 (2008, 2014–17, 2019–21, 2024)

Most wins/team: Ferrari, 14 (1951–1954, 1958, 1990, 1998, 2002–2004, 2007, 2011, 2018, 2022)

Lap length: 3.659 miles

Number of turns: 18

Lap record: 1m27.097s, Max Verstappen (Red Bull Racing), 2020

Above Silverstone's origins as an airfield are clear to see from an aerial shot, with the main runway running from Copse (bottom left) to Stowe (top right).

WINNING ON THREE WHEELS

Sadly due to the Covid-19 pandemic there were no fans in the grandstands to witness an extraordinary finish in 2020, when several drivers were slowed by tyre failures at the high-energy circuit. That included long-time race leader Lewis Hamilton, who suffered a left-front failure halfway around the final lap. Remarkably, coaxed by race engineer Pete Bonnington, Hamilton guided his wounded car across the remaining half lap to take the win on only three fully inflated tyres.

Right Lewis Hamilton suffered a tyre failure on the final lap of the race in 2020 but still managed to claim victory.

WINNING BY MILES

The greatest winning margin for a British GP at Silverstone was an entire lap, and this has happened three times. This first occurred in 1969 when Matra racer Jackie Stewart trounced the field, with Jacky Ickx the best of the rest for Brabham. The previous biggest winning margin had been in 1956 when Juan Manuel Fangio had beaten his Ferrari team-mates Peter Collins and Alfonso de Portago by 1 min 32 secs.

WINNING FOR BRITAIN

There have been many great races at Silverstone and the 1987 British GP was one of the most memorable. This was in a period of Williams' superiority and the battle within the team between Nigel Mansell and Nelson Piquet was as fierce as it was with rivals. With the packed crowd urging him on, Mansell's jinking move to take the lead with two laps to go was brilliant.

SKITTLES AT SILVERSTONE

When Jody Scheckter hit F1, he was desperate to make an impression and his over-exuberance at the start of the 1973 British GP led to an accident that certainly won't be forgotten. Having started sixth in his McLaren, the young South African ran wide coming out of Woodcote at the end of lap 1 scattering those behind, leaving seven cars unable to take the restart and Andrea de Adamich with leg injuries.

BUTTONED UP

Jenson Button claimed 15 wins and 50 podiums, and contested 17 grands prix at Silverstone – but never managed to finish inside the top three on home turf. Button came close on a handful of occasions by finishing third, in 2004, 2010 and 2014 – in 2010 Button trailed Nico Rosberg by just six-tenths of a second, and four years later crossed the line a similarly agonizing nine-tenths of a second behind Daniel Ricciardo.

APPROACH TO STOWE

Silverstone is an open track and feels particularly broad on the Hangar Straight where the drivers race down towards the grandstands and the fast right-hander at Stowe. Arriving at 190mph, the drivers have to drop down two gears to fifth and try to stop themselves from running wide as the track kinks back slightly on itself and drops into the dip known as the Vale.

Below Jenson Button was a fan favourite for 17 years at the British Grand Prix but never quite managed to score a podium finish.

SPA-FRANCORCHAMPS

A win at this Belgian circuit is a feather in any driver's cap. It's a real drivers' circuit, challenging them like few others as it follows the route of much of the circuit that opened in 1921. It has gradient change, it has fast corners and it often has changeable weather to add that extra twist.

🏆 FANGIO DRAWS FIRST BLOOD

The fourth round of the inaugural World Championship in 1950 brought the teams to Spa-Francorchamps, and Giuseppe Farina and Juan Manuel Fangio shared a lap time to be equal fastest in qualifying. It was the Argentinian who led away and records show that Raymond Sommer led in his Talbot-Lago, but this was only when Alfa Romeo's star duo pitted for fuel. Thereafter, Fangio came back to score his second win.

⚙ VICTORY WITH TIME TO SPARE

Despite the fastest lap of the 1963 Belgian GP being covered in just under 4 mins, Jim Clark's winning margin over Cooper driver Bruce McLaren was 4 mins 54 secs. This was the largest winning margin in the history of the race and was achieved after rain hit late in the race once the Lotus driver had made his break and McLaren was just a fraction under a lap behind as they completed the circuit at a reduced pace.

ALL TOGETHER NOW...

Some accidents involve a driver throwing his car off the circuit, others one car hitting another. Then there are pile-ups, and the 1998 Belgian GP produced one of these. It happened, as most do, on the first lap and was triggered by David Coulthard after his McLaren had been tagged by a Ferrari. In all, 12 cars were involved and four were too damaged to take the restart, which also resulted in a first corner accident...

HAMILTON'S LOSS AND WIN

Lewis Hamilton is the only driver in history to have crossed the line first and not won the race, and not crossed the line first but won the race, at the same circuit. In 2008 Hamilton finished first on the road but was harshly issued a 25-second post-race penalty for a track limits infringement, relegating him to third. In 2024 Hamilton finished second to team-mate George Russell, but a few hours later Russell was disqualified due to his Mercedes being underweight, and Hamilton inherited the win.

A RACE A LAP LONG

Persistent heavy rain and mist caused havoc in 2021. Several attempts were made to start the race, to no avail, and after a wait of over three hours it officially began. But it did so behind the safety car and on the third lap the race was suspended and not resumed. Per the regulations, which count back two laps, the result was taken at the end of lap one. Consequently Max Verstappen's winning time was three minutes and 27 seconds – the shortest race in history.

Below Bad weather wrecked the race in 2021, creating the shortest race ever.

TRACK FACTS

Opened: 1921

Country: Belgium

Location: 20 miles south-east of Liege

Active years in F1: 1950–1956, 1958, 1960-1968, 1970, 1983, 1985–2002, 2004–2005, 2007 onwards

Most wins/driver: Michael Schumacher, 6 (1992, 1995–1997, 2001–2002)

Most wins/team: Ferrari, 14 (1952–1953, 1956, 1961, 1966, 1996–1997, 2001–2002, 2007–2009, 2018, 2019)

Lap length: 4.352 miles

Number of turns: 19

Lap record: 1m 44.701s, Sergio Perez (Red Bull Racing), 2022

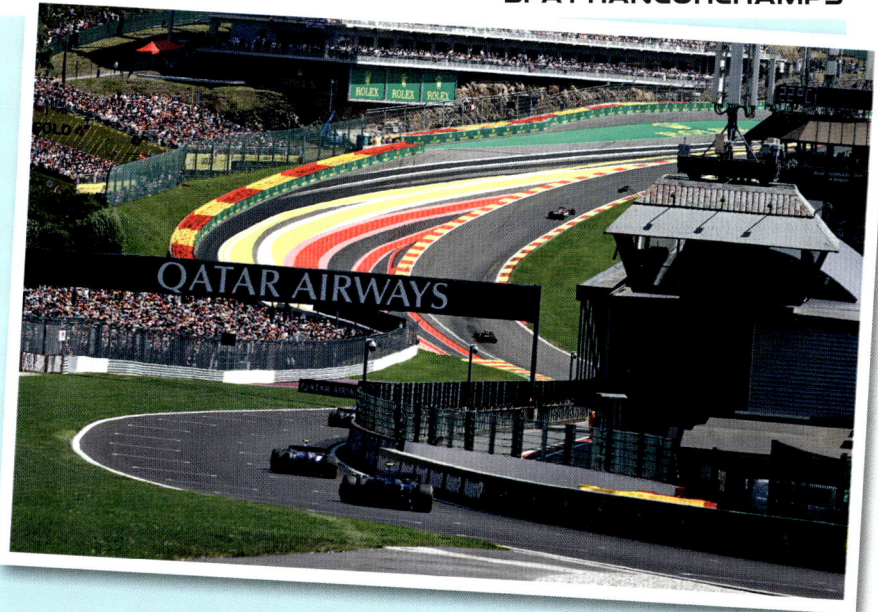

Above Spa-Francorchamps is the longest circuit on the current calendar.

SPA'S UPS AND DOWNS

Not a lot of circuits offer much in the way of gradient changes, but Spa-Francorchamps does. What made the original circuit so unusual, though, was that its 9.2-mile long lap spanned not one but two valleys, cresting the hill in between.

TOP 10 WINNERS

In 2024, the top 10 finishers at Spa-Francorchamps were all previous race winners – the first time that such a situation had unfolded in Formula One history, in what was the 1,115th grand prix to be held. They were (in order): Lewis Hamilton, Oscar Piastri, Charles Leclerc, Max Verstappen, Lando Norris, Carlos Sainz, Sergio Perez, Fernando Alonso, Esteban Ocon, and Daniel Ricciardo. That was even achieved after the exclusion of original first-on-the-road driver Russell!

EAU ROUGE

Spa-Francorchamps is home to one of the most revered and iconic complexes on the calendar: the Eau Rouge-Raidillon. After a downhill section the drivers hit a compression at a left-hand kink before swiftly ascending rightwards up a ribbon of tarmac 30 metres high, finishing with another left-hand bend that leads them onto the Kemmel Straight. The section is now easily flat out – at least in dry conditions – in modern Formula One machinery.

SCHUMACHER LOVES SPA

The closest grand prix circuit to Michael Schumacher's childhood home in Kerpen is actually in Belgium, rather than Germany, and it was a venue where he thrived. Schumacher debuted at Spa-Francorchamps in 1991, claimed his maiden win in 1992, and added five more across the following decade. Schumacher also clinched his seventh and final world title at Spa-Francorchamps, in 2004, and in 2012 made his 300th grand prix start at the race.

Right Several of Michael Schumacher's milestones came at Spa-Francorchamps across his career, and with six wins he is the most successful driver at the circuit.

Above The Circuit de Spa-Francorchamps rises and falls a hundred metres across the Belgian countryside, and the steepest section is the climb of Eau Rouge.

ZANDVOORT

The Dutch Grand Prix was a firm fixture of Formula One's calendar through its first three decades but fell by the wayside after 1985. A revival looked improbable, until the emergence of Dutch superstar Max Verstappen, and in 2021 Formula One returned to the old-school circuit nestled in the North Sea dunes.

SUPER MAX

The grandstands were a sea of orange for Zandvoort's return in 2021 and Max Verstappen duly delivered, converting pole position into victory to become the first Dutch driver to win the Dutch Grand Prix. Verstappen doubled up in 2022, and made it a three-peat in 2023, before McLaren's Lando Norris halted his streak in 2024. Jim Clark remains out in front, on four Dutch Grand Prix wins, which he achieved in 1963, 1964, 1965 and 1967.

Right National hero Max Verstappen is the only Dutch driver to have claimed victory at the Dutch Grand Prix.

A SWEDE DAY FOR BONNIER

Jo Bonnier enjoyed a 15-year career in Formula One, starting over 100 grands prix, but the Swede's finest weekend came at Zandvoort in 1959. Driving a BRM P25, Bonnier scored his sole pole position and went on to claim his maiden victory, which turned out to be the only win of his career, and the first by a Swedish driver in Formula One.

LAUDA'S LAST

Three-time champion Niki Lauda claimed 25 career victories – and his final moment atop the podium came at Zandvoort in 1985. In a difficult last season Lauda finished only three of that year's 16 races and the high point came around the Dutch dunes, rising from tenth on the grid to beat McLaren team-mate Alain Prost to victory by just 0.232s.

TRACK FACTS

Opened: 1948

Country: Netherlands

Location: 15 miles west of Amsterdam

Active years in F1: 1952, 1953, 1955, 1958-1971, 1973-1985, 2021-present

Most wins/driver: Jim Clark, 4, (1963, 1964, 1965, 1967)

Most wins/team: Ferrari, 8 (1952, 1953, 1961, 1971, 1974, 1977, 1982, 1983)

Lap length: 2.646 miles

Number of turns: 14

Lap record: 1m 11.097s, Lewis Hamilton (Mercedes), 2021

Above Zandvoort winds its way around the sand dunes next to the North Sea.

BANKING ON IT

When Formula One returned in 2021 two corners – Hugenholtzbocht and Arie Luyendykbocht – were heavily reprofiled to include banking. At both turns banking of 18 per cent – or 32 degrees – was included on the corners, providing an extra challenge for teams and drivers, while also promoting different racing lines. They are the steepest corners of any track on the calendar.

Above Banking is more associated with oval circuits in America, but two of Zandvoort's corners have the unusual challenge.

ON YER BIKE

Zandvoort is a town of around 20,000 citizens, so each day there is a five-fold increase in the number of people when Formula One is around. The circuit makes no parking available for fans, and instead there are 12 trains an hour carting spectators from central Amsterdam to Zandvoort. Alternatively, the Dutch inclination for cycling is maximized to full effect, with bicycle parking for tens of thousands of bikes available at the track!

LEAST AND MOST

In the 1961 race not one pit stop was recorded at Zandvoort – the only full-distance grand prix where this has happened. It was also the first F1 race at which all starters – 15 – reached the finish, a situation which wasn't repeated until 2005. Conversely, in a grand prix hit by showers in 2023 there were a record 84 pit stops (excluding a red flag phase in which all drivers had to pit).

A DARK PAST

The Dutch Grand Prix was overshadowed twice in the early 1970s by fatal accidents. In 1970 Piers Courage was killed after a car failure caused an accident, while in 1973 Roger Williamson crashed and became trapped in the burning wreckage. Fellow driver David Purley heroically sprinted to the scene but his efforts were in vain, and Williamson died from asphyxiation. Purley, for his bravery, was awarded the George Medal.

A SUCCESSFUL HUNT FOR HESKETH

Hesketh was only around for a handful of years in the 1970s, and regularly fielded just one car, and in its short existence the team gained a reputation for its flamboyant approach to the sport, especially with James Hunt as its lead driver. At a damp Zandvoort in 1975 Hunt started third but was among the early stoppers for slick tyres, and the gamble paid off. Hunt went on to take his maiden victory, which proved to be the first and only win for Hesketh.

Right James Hunt and Hesketh upset the order in 1975 and claimed a maiden – and only – victory for the underdog operation.

SINGAPORE

As Formula One expanded its roster of events in the 2000s it sought new markets and landed upon Singapore, at the crossroads of Asia, with a street track designed around the heart of the city. And, for the first time in history, action took place at night.

⚙ UNDER THE GRANDSTAND

A unique element of the original Marina Bay layout was a section of track – a short spurt between Turns 18 and 19 – which passed underneath an enormous grandstand. But city officials wanted to use the space to create a public square and ahead of the 2023 round the section between Turns 16 and 19 was removed and instead bypassed, creating a longer straight between Turn 15 and the new Turn 16. The removal of four turns cut out just 130 metres, but made each lap over five seconds faster.

🏆 HITTING THE LIMIT

Marina Bay is one of the slowest circuits on the calendar, meaning it is among the longest races of the season. On four occasions – in 2012, 2014, 2017 and 2022 – the slow average speed, exacerbated by either prolonged Safety Car periods or wet weather, meant the races did not last the full scheduled distance and instead hit the two-hour time limit. In 2022 Sergio Perez's winning time of two hours and two minutes was 42 minutes longer than the preceding race at Monza!

Above The fiddly chicane, with its high kerbs, caught out several drivers before it was replaced in 2013.

SLUNG AWAY

When Singapore joined the calendar in 2008, one of its notorious sections was an awkward high-kerbed left-right-left chicane. The narrow complex, dubbed the Singapore Sling, frustrated drivers and errors through the section often resulted in cars being launched skywards, with a handful of competitors pitched into the wall after a mistake. It was, sadly, replaced in 2013 with a single left-hand corner – though is still a challenge, with George Russell crashing out there in 2023.

A BIG START SMASH

One of Singapore's most dramatic moments came in 2017, when rain hit the race for the first time. Three of the top four starters, Sebastian Vettel, Max Verstappen and Kimi Räikkönen, collided off the start line and were eliminated. Vettel's title rival, Lewis Hamilton, picked his way through the melee to rise from fifth to first, taking a win few expected prior to the rain.

Below A dramatic opening few metres in 2017 eliminated several contenders and cleared the path for Lewis Hamilton to grab victory.

TRACK FACTS

Opened: 2008

Country: Singapore

Location: Marina Bay, downtown Singapore

Active years in F1: 2008-19, 2022–present

Most wins/driver: Sebastian Vettel, five (2011–13, 2015, 2019)

Most wins/team: Ferrari, 4, (2010, 2015, 2019, 2023); Red Bull, 4, (2011–13, 2022); Mercedes 4, (2014, 2016–18)

Lap length: 3.070 miles

Number of turns: 19

Lap record: 1m34.486, Daniel

Above The bright lights of the Marina Bay Street Circuit show a layout that winds its way around key landmarks in the Lion City.

HOT AND SWEATY

The heat and humidity in Singapore, which has a tropical climate, makes the weekend among the toughest of them all for drivers. To prepare for the sweat bucket of a city drivers have been known to use exercise bikes in saunas – while wearing jumpers. During the race weekend there are ice buckets aplenty, to keep core temperature as cool as possible, and drivers can lose up to four kilos through the course of a race.

LIGHTS UP

F1 now has six night or twilight races, but Singapore held the inaugural night race in 2008. Approximately 1,600 lights are set up along the perimeter of the circuit 10 metres above the ground, and each light has a brightness of about 3,000 lux – roughly four times the brightness of football stadium lighting. The lighting structures are erected in a way that maximizes brightness while ensuring drivers do not suffer from glare.

CRASHGATE

Singapore's inaugural race in 2008 is remembered for the 'Crashgate' scandal. Renault's Nelson Piquet Jr. crashed at Turn 16, deploying the Safety Car, and the timing aided the pit stop strategy of team-mate Fernando Alonso, who went on to win. The full details only came to light a year later, after Piquet left the team, as he revealed he had been instructed by Renault to deliberately crash at the corner. The architects of the scandal resigned from Renault.

LESS THAN THREE TENTHS IN IT

Fernando Alonso and Sebastian Vettel were levels above the rest in 2010. Alonso secured the first Grand Chelem of his career, setting pole position, recording fastest lap, and leading every lap on his way to victory, but he was hounded relentlessly by Vettel. After 61 laps just 0.293s separated the Ferrari and Red Bull as they flashed across the finish line – with third-placed Mark Webber half a minute behind the duelling pair.

SAINZ SPOILS THE PARTY

Red Bull won 21 of the 22 grands prix held in the 2023 season – a new record – but the only blot on its copybook came in Singapore. The Red Bull was ill-suited to Marina Bay's layout and its cars struggled for pace. Instead it was left to Ferrari's Carlos Sainz to control the grand prix, resisting McLaren's Lando Norris and Mercedes' Lewis Hamilton, with the top three covered by just 1.2 seconds.

Right Red Bull swept the 2023 season, except for in Singapore, with Carlos Sainz delivering a well-received win for Ferrari.

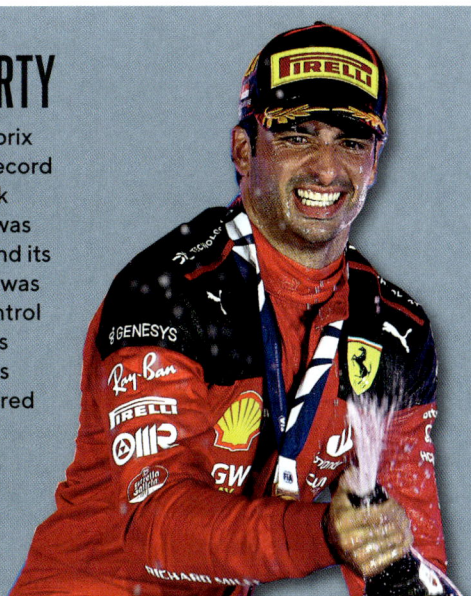

179

MONTREAL

The Circuit Gilles Villeneuve is one of the very best examples of a circuit close enough to a metropolis to attract a capacity crowd. Over the years this circuit, on an island in a river, has produced great racing, but it is better known for being a car-breaker and having a chicane that bites.

LEWIS LOVES MONTREAL

Lewis Hamilton has taken over a century of wins in Formula One, and Montreal is among his most successful venues. Hamilton claimed his maiden victory – from his first pole position – at Montreal in 2007, for McLaren, and added further wins for the team in 2010 and 2012. In his time at Mercedes Hamilton won in 2015, 2016, 2017, and then again in 2019, levelling Michael Schumacher on seven Montreal wins.

THE DREAM START

Imagine the excitement when Quebec welcomed its greatest star to its greatest city, as Montreal did for its first grand prix in 1978. Gilles Villeneuve qualified his Ferrari third behind Jean-Pierre Jarier's Lotus and Jody Scheckter's Wolf. Having slipped behind Alan Jones' Williams, he regained third when Jones had a puncture. Then he passed Scheckter. Jarier held a 30s lead but retired, leaving Villeneuve to score his first win.

ISLAND OF ADVENTURE

The Circuit Gilles Villeneuve has one of the sport's most unusual settings. Not only is it built on an island, but it runs alongside the rowing lake used at the 1976 Olympics and surrounds the futuristic pavilions built on the site of world trade show, Expo 67.

Left Lewis Hamilton (yellow helmet) claimed his maiden win in Canada in 2007.

TRACK FACTS

Opened: 1978

Country: Canada

Location: Ile de Notre Dame, Montreal

Active years in F1: 1978–1986, 1988–2008, 2010–2019, 2022 onwards

Most wins/driver:
Michael Schumacher, 7 (1994, 1997–1998, 2000, 2002–2004); Lewis Hamilton 7, (2007, 2010, 2012, 2015–17, 2019)

Most wins/team: Ferrari 11 (1978, 1983, 1985, 1995, 1997, 1998, 2000, 2002–2004, 2018)

Lap length: 2.710 miles

Number of turns: 14

Lap record: 1m 13.078s Valtteri Bottas (Mercedes,) 2019

Above The Circuit Gilles Villeneuve, located on the man-made Ile Notre Dame, is surrounded by water, including the Olympic rowing basin and Saint Lawrence river.

RAIN, RAIN, GO AWAY

Safety car deployments are all too common in grands prix held at the Circuit Gilles Villeneuve and Jacques Laffite's winning average in his Ligier was just 85.310mph in 1981, more than 22mph down on the previous year. Slowed by torrential rain, this was still much faster than Jenson Button's 46.518mph average in 2011 when the race was not only run on a slick and treacherous circuit but endured a two-hour stoppage too.

Right Jacques Laffite splashes his Ligier through the wet en route to victory at an average of just 85mph in 1981.

BY THE SMALLEST OF MARGINS

The closest finish to a grand prix held here came in 2000 when Michael Schumacher won by 0.174s from Ferrari team-mate Rubens Barrichello. The race was hit by rain midway and Barrichello worked his way past Giancarlo Fisichella to second but wasn't allowed to challenge for the lead. All too often, races here have been close in their first half before the circuit's car-breaking characteristics thinned the field.

A VIOLENT BARREL-ROLL

Thanks to the endless efforts to make racing cars safer, drivers today unlike their predecessors stand every chance of surviving accidents. Robert Kubica had reason to thank those responsible for these advances after the 2007 Canadian GP when his BMW Sauber clipped Jarno Trulli's Toyota on the approach to the hairpin, cannoned off a wall and disintegrated as it rolled back across the track. He escaped with just bruising.

FERRARI LEADS THE WAY

Seven-time World Champion Michael Schumacher won seven times – once with Benetton and then six times with Ferrari – at the Circuit Gilles Villeneuve and this helped Ferrari to become the team that has won the most frequently here, with a tally of 11 triumphs. McLaren and Williams also have a strong record at the Canadian circuit, having claimed seven wins here apiece.

THE JEAN AND ONLY

Jean Alesi took 32 podiums during a distinguished 201-race career that involved stints with several iconic teams. But of those 32 visits to the podium just one came with Alesi gracing the top step, which happened in Montreal in 1995. The enigmatic Alesi, driving the #27 Ferrari associated with local legend Gilles Villeneuve, finally broke his duck to triumph – and on the occasion of his 31st birthday.

FINAL CHICANE (TURN 13)

All a driver can see straight ahead as they accelerate up to 200mph down the final straight from L'Epingle is the pit entry. The track disappears to the right into this very tight chicane. Getting the braking just right is very difficult, with few sighting points to judge it by. The exit is blind at this point and many drivers get the second (left-hand) part of the sequence wrong and then slam into the wall beyond.

Below Ayrton Senna negotiates the final chicane during the 1988 Canadian Grand Prix at the Circuit Gilles Villeneuve in Montreal, on his way to victory.

INTERLAGOS

Although rough around the edges, Interlagos remains one of the world's great racing circuits, with its dipping, twisting lap providing scope for the brave to overtake. Often a late-season race, Interlagos has been made all the more exciting by hosting some classic title shoot-outs.

A POPULAR HOME WIN

After holding a non-championship race in 1972, a Brazilian GP at Interlagos had World Championship blessing for 1973. Emerson Fittipaldi was the nation's hope and he qualified second behind his Lotus team-mate Ronnie Peterson. Fittipaldi took the lead at the start and fellow Brazilian Carlos Pace leapt into second in his Surtees, but was soon demoted. Fittipaldi was untouchable though and his was a popular win.

SENNA, BUT ONLY JUST

Ayrton Senna had won plenty of races but never at home, and it was starting to get to him. Having won 1991's opening race in Phoenix, he put his McLaren on pole at Interlagos (as he had in the three preceding years). Senna made the race truly memorable for the home fans as he led every lap, until he hit gearbox trouble and had to run the final seven laps in sixth gear, just holding off Riccardo Patrese's Williams.

FIVE IN A ROW

Interlagos wasn't always the final round of the season in the mid-late 2000s, but despite that it still played host to five successive title-clinching races. Fernando Alonso secured his two world titles at Interlagos in 2005 and 2006, before Kimi Räikkönen's victory earned him the crown in 2007. The 2008 title went Lewis Hamilton's way at the final corner of the last lap while in 2009 Jenson Button sealed his world championship at Interlagos.

FERRADURA

There is gradient change aplenty at the home of the Brazilian GP, and Ferradura is one of the trickiest of these. It's approached up the climb from Descida do Lago, then the track arcs gently to the right, but it's made difficult by the fact that it's at the crest of this hill before a level run from its exit to the next turn, Laranja. Taken in fifth gear, it's easy for drivers to carry too much speed in and spin.

Below This long right-hander with its uphill entry and downhill exit remains a true test of driving skill.

Above Jenson Button was crowned world champion at Interlagos in 2009.

TRACK FACTS

Opened: 1940

Country: Brazil

Location: 9 miles south of Sao Paulo

Active in F1: 1973–77, 1979–80, 1990–2019, 2021 onwards

Most wins/driver: Michael Schumacher, 4 (1994, 1995, 2000, 2002)

Most wins/team: Ferrari, 9 (1976, 1977, 1990, 2000, 2002, 2006, 2007, 2008, 2017)

Lap length: 2.677 miles

Lap record: 1m 10.540s, Valtteri Bottas (Mercedes), 2018

Above The circuit sits in a natural amphitheatre as is clear when viewing from above the Curva do Sol and looking back towards the Senna S.

LIKE FATHER, LIKE SON

Father and son Jos and Max Verstappen have had wildly different career successes, but are both linked by unusual incidents at Interlagos. In 2001 Jos, while being lapped by leader Juan Pablo Montoya, collided with the Williams driver, putting them both out of the race. In 2018 Jos' son Max, leading the race for Red Bull, tangled with Esteban Ocon while lapping him, spinning off and ceding a likely win.

HALF A SECOND, TWO BROTHERS

The closest finish to a Brazilian GP at Interlagos was when Michael Schumacher won in 2002 ahead of his brother Ralf whose Williams had chased him home, losing out by just 0.588s. It was the first outing for the Ferrari F2002 and although Ralf could close in on the Ferrari he simply couldn't find a way past, perhaps wisely being wary as Michael had clashed with Ralf's team-mate Juan Pablo Montoya on lap 1. Emerson Fittipaldi won in 1973 and 1974, then Michael Schumacher in 1994 and 1995, Mika Häkkinen in 1998 and 1999 and Juan Pablo Montoya in 2004 and 2005. Two teams have won three in a row, though: Ferrari from 2006 to 2008, then Red Bull from 2009 to 2011.

NINE PODIUMS, NO WINS

Double World Champion Fernando Alonso has taken nine podiums at Interlagos – second only to Michael Schumacher's 10 – but has not yet taken to the top step. No driver has scored that many podiums at one venue without taking a win. Alonso finished third in 2003, 2005, 2007, 2010, 2013 and 2023, and second in 2006, 2008 and 2012 across spells with four different teams.

BETWEEN THE LAKES

The name Interlagos means 'between the lakes' and the original 4.946-mile circuit lay-out crossed the lake at the foot of its hillside site twice. The shorter track, introduced in 1990 crosses the lake only once, at Descida do Lago.

HAMILTON'S LAST TO FIRST

Lewis Hamilton was excluded from qualifying in 2021 due to a technical infringement but surged from last to fifth in the sprint race, before climbing from 10th on the grid to a remarkable victory in the grand prix. It meant Hamilton had gained 24 positions across the course of the two races, widely regarded as one of the finest performances of a distinguished career.

Left Lewis Hamilton – who was granted honorary Brazilian citizenship – claimed an iconic victory in 2021.

MELBOURNE

The trip to Melbourne may be the longest of the season for Formula One drivers but any jet leg or travel fatigue is soon discarded once they get to savour the high-speed parkland circuit just a stone's throw away from the centre of the popular city.

Below Melbourne's 2023 race featured several interruptions.

A THRICE STOPPED RACE

A new record was set at Melbourne's race in 2023 as it was red-flagged three times. Alex Albon's crash on lap seven of 58, and Kevin Magnussen's accident on lap 54, both caused stoppages. With just a couple of laps remaining there was some clumsy driving at the restart and due to a spate of incidents the red flags appeared once more. As the lap counter had ticked down that was that, and the chequered flag flew soon after.

⏱ FIRST TURN FARRAGOS

The first corner of the lap of the Albert Park circuit is a 75-degree right-hander that feeds almost immediately into a similarly open left. In their own right, they are not a tricky combination. On the opening lap of a grand prix, however, they have proved to be harder to negotiate than expected, with Ralf Schumacher having a huge airborne accident in 2002 in his Williams and then Fernando Alonso coming a cropper there in 2016.

DOUBLE TROUBLE

In the late 1990s, it was thankfully unusual for any car to catch fire, even in the case of an accident. So, it was eye-opening when Rubens Barrichello's Stewart caught fire on the grid for the 1999 Australian GP, and even more so as team-mate Johnny Herbert's did too.

TRACK FACTS

Opened: 1996

Country: Australia

Location: Albert Park, 1.5 miles south of central Melbourne

Active years in F1: 1996–2019, 2022 onwards

Most wins/driver: Michael Schumacher, four (2000, 2001, 2002, 2004)

Most wins/team: Ferrari, 10 (1999, 2000, 2001, 2002, 2004, 2007, 2017, 2018, 2022, 2024)

Lap length: 3.280 miles

Number of turns: 16

Lap record: 1m 19.183 Charles Leclerc (Ferrari), 2024

Above An aerial view of the Melbourne circuit as the grid forms. This temporary street track has only a few demanding corners.

SHINING ON HOME TURF

Mark Webber was delighted to have made it to F1 in 2002, but he didn't hold high hopes of making much of a splash, as he was with the tailend Minardi team. However, the gritty Australian had every reason to celebrate after his debut on home ground, as he kicked off his campaign with fifth place, up from 18th on the grid, in a race of unusual attrition, as only eight finished and Mark was two laps down.

Above Mark Webber holds off Mika Salo's Toyota to take two championship points on his F1 debut in front of the exultant fans in the Albert Park grandstands.

HAPPY HUNTING FOR McLAREN

Australia finally joined the World Championship in 1985, with a race in Adelaide. In all, 11 races were held there, with McLaren winning five of them. McLaren's winning form down under continued after the move to Melbourne, too, with David Coulthard and Mika Häkkinen triumphing in 1997 and 1998 respectively before Coulthard won again in 2003, Lewis Hamilton in 2008, and Jenson Button in 2010 and again two years later.

A GIFT FOR HÄKKINEN

There was a curious result the third time that Albert Park hosted a World Championship round, in 1998. Mika Häkkinen was leading when he peeled into the pits. He thought that he had heard a message to pit over his radio. As none had been issued, he was flagged through, emerging second behind team-mate David Coulthard. As the pair had agreed that whoever led into Turn 1 on lap 1 ought to win, the Scot had to wave Häkkinen back past.

MELBOURNE MAESTROS

Victories in Melbourne have been shared out across its history, with Michael Schumacher taking the most wins, with four. Jenson Button and Sebastian Vettel both picked up three victories apiece, while Lewis Hamilton has 'only' two. That's because Hamilton has scored eight pole positions in Melbourne, a record, including six in a row between 2014 and 2019.

RACING IN THE FIFTIES

Australia had hosted its own grand prix since 1928, with Phillip Island its home until 1935, after which time it moved from state to state. In 1953, a circuit was laid out around the lake in Melbourne's Albert Park and Doug Whitehead won in a Lago-Talbot. Three years later, it hosted another non-championship grand prix, this time with a more international field. Victory went to Stirling Moss in a works Maserati 250F ahead of team-mate Jean Behra.

BRUNDLE'S LUCKY ESCAPE

Martin Brundle deserved more than he managed in terms of results, especially early in his F1 career with Tyrrell in the mid-1980s and again with Benetton in 1992. By 1996, though, it was thought that his move to Jordan might be his last roll of the dice. To say that his season started spectacularly is an understatement, not because he qualified well, as he was only 19th out of 22 starters, but because he was launched into a sequence of barrel rolls as David Coulthard took evasive action at Turn 3. He scrambled out as soon as his car came to rest, inverted, and then took the spare car for the restart.

Above Flight time: Ralf Schumacher goes airborne after colliding with Rubens Barrichello at the first corner in 2002. This coming together ended the race for both of them.

SUZUKA

Suzuka is the only figure-of-eight circuit on the Formula One calendar and is adored by drivers for its combination of fast and challenging corners, which winds and wraps its way through the undulating Mie countryside. It has also hosted some transfixing grands prix and eye-catching showdowns.

STARTING WITH A BANG

The first World Championship round held at Suzuka was in 1987 – the only two previous Japanese GPs had been held at the Fuji Speedway in 1976 and 1977. The 1987 race saw drama as early as qualifying when Nigel Mansell crashed and ended his title challenge by injuring his back. This took the pressure off his Williams team-mate Nelson Piquet, who was cruising to fourth place when his Renault engine failed. Victory was taken by Gerhard Berger for Ferrari, with Ayrton Senna second for Lotus.

SHINING AT HOME

No Japanese driver has yet won a round of the World Championship, and only twice has a Japanese driver finished on the podium. So, it was with a strong sense of occasion that Aguri Suzuki guided his Larrousse to third place in the 1990 Japanese GP, advancing from 10th on the grid. Takuma Sato finished fifth at Suzuka for Jordan in 2002 and then improved on that by finishing third for BAR at Indianapolis in 2004, while Kamui Kobayashi had a spectacular charge up the order to seventh for Sauber at Suzuka in 2010.

S-CURVES

Suzuka is an extremely difficult circuit, but the S-Curves are rated as being even more technically difficult than the fabled, high-speed 130R bend. This stretch of track early in the lap includes two left-hand bends and two rights, alternating, on a steepening upward slope as the track climbs the hillside beyond a pair of lakes behind the paddock. The final corner of the sequence, the second right-hander, is the tightest of all and the nature of the layout is such that any mistake is magnified through each of the corners as it becomes ever harder to get back onto the racing line.

A WIN AT 33MPH

Wet weather impacted Suzuka's 2022 race and proceedings were halted shortly after the start. A two-hour delay followed and once conditions improved the three-hour window for competition was encroaching closer. Winner Max Verstappen managed 28 of 53 scheduled laps before the chequered flag flew and thanks to a quirk in the rules was awarded full points – the shortest race for which they were allocated. The lengthy delay meant Verstappen's average winning speed was just 33mph!

Below Wet weather can strike Suzuka – as happened in a rain-shortened race in 2022.

Above Driving on tiptoes: Suzuka's uphill "S" Curves is a really testing sequence of corners, with drivers having to balance finding some grip and with going fast.

Below Suzuka is the only F1 circuit overlooked by a Ferris wheel, and this is the view to the starting grid.

TRACK FACTS

Opened: 1962

Country: Japan

Location: 30 miles south-west of Nagoya

Active years in F1: 1987–2006, 2009–2019, 2022 onwards

Most wins/driver: Michael Schumacher, 6 (1995, 1997, 2000, 2001, 2002, 2004)

Most wins/team: Ferrari, 7 (1987, 1997, 2000, 2001, 2002, 2003, 2004)

Lap length: 3.608 miles

Number of turns: 18

Lap record: 1m 30.983s Lewis Hamilton (Mercedes), 2017

BACK IN THE BEGINNING

The first Japanese GP was held back in 1963, at Suzuka, just a year after the circuit was opened. It wasn't a Formula One event, but a sportscar one, with victory being taken by the best of a field of European drivers brought over to Japan to bolster the race entry. The winner was British driver Peter Warr in a Lotus 23, who went on to become Lotus founder Colin Chapman's righthand man and, after Chapman's death in 1982, the team principal.

Left Ayrton Senna waves to his besotted fans after winning in 1993, but other years weren't so kind.

HIGHS AND LOWS

Ayrton Senna was supported with a passion by Japanese fans, but his all-attack attitude that they loved led not only to victories in 1988 and 1993, but disqualification after winning in 1989, penalized for his McLaren having received a pushstart from the marshals as it sat across the track after being hit by Alain Prost. He exacted revenge on Prost a year later and drove the Ferrari driver off the circuit at the first corner.

MIGHTY MICHAEL

Michael Schumacher holds the record for scoring the most grand prix wins at Suzuka, with six victories from his first in 1995, to his last in 2004. Michael was also in the mix in 1994 before being beaten by Damon Hill in a wet race. In 1998, he started from the back of the grid after stalling on pole and raced up to third before getting a puncture, enabling Mika Häkkinen to land the drivers' title. In 2006, he retired with engine failure while leading. He finished second in 1994, 1996 and 1999.

TYPHOON DELAYS

Suzuka's event has been beset by severe storms and typhoons, most notably in 2010 and 2019, when Saturday activity was cancelled, and qualifying instead shifted to Sunday morning. Heavy rain caused disruption to races in 1994, 2014 and 2022. The scheduled distances were not reached on those occasions, with 2014's encounter red-flagged after an accident involving Jules Bianchi, who died from his injuries nine months later. Such a situation has finally been alleviated with Suzuka's event moving from autumn to spring in 2024.

FORMULA ONE STATISTICS

Lewis Hamilton's phenomenal Formula One career has vaulted him to the top of most of the record tables, but the likes of Michael Schumacher and Max Verstappen also hold their own across a plethora of statistics. Through Formula One's 75-year history there have been a host of drivers and constructors who have at times shone brightly, emphasizing how the world's most spectacular sport has ebbed and flowed over the decades. Note: Statistics correct through the end of 2024.

DRIVER RECORDS

STARTS

402 Fernando Alonso	175 Graham Hill	147 Charles Leclerc	
356 Lewis Hamilton	171 Niki Lauda	146 Eddie Irvine	
350 Kimi Räikkönen	166 Lance Stroll	146 Derek Warwick	
323 Rubens Barrichello	163 Jacques Villeneuve	146 Carlos Reutemann	
308 Michael Schumacher	163 Thierry Boutsen	144 Emerson Fittipaldi	
308 Jenson Button	161 Mika Häkkinen	134 Jean-Pierre Jarier	
299 Sebastian Vettel	161 Johnny Herbert	132 Eddie Cheever	
281 Sergio Perez	161 Ayrton Senna	132 Clay Regazzoni	
269 Felipe Massa	158 Martin Brundle	128 Mario Andretti	
257 Daniel Ricciardo	158 Olivier Panis	128 Adrian Sutil	
256 Riccardo Patrese	156 Esteban Ocon	128 Lando Norris	
252 Jarno Trulli	156 Heinz-Harald Frentzen	128 George Russell	
246 David Coulthard	153 Pierre Gasly	123 Jack Brabham	
246 Valtteri Bottas	152 John Watson	123 Ronnie Peterson	
229 Giancarlo Fisichella	149 Rene Arnoux	119 Pierluigi Martini	
227 Nico Hulkenberg			
215 Mark Webber			
210 Gerhard Berger			
209 Max Verstappen			
208 Andrea de Cesaris			
206 Carlos Sainz			
206 Nico Rosberg			
204 Nelson Piquet			
201 Jean Alesi			
199 Alain Prost			
194 Michele Alboreto			
187 Nigel Mansell			
185 Kevin Magnussen			
183 Nick Heidfeld			
180 Ralf Schumacher			
179 Romain Grosjean			
176 Jacques Laffite			

Above Lewis Hamilton overtook Michael Schumacher's record victory tally in 2020 and now has over a century of wins.

POLE POSITIONS

104 Lewis Hamilton	18 Mario Andretti		
68 Michael Schumacher	Rene Arnoux		
65 Ayrton Senna	Kimi Räikkönen		
57 Sebastian Vettel	17 Jackie Stewart		
40 Max Verstappen	16 Felipe Massa		
33 Jim Clark	Stirling Moss		
Alain Prost	14 Alberto Ascari		
32 Nigel Mansell	Rubens Barrichello		
30 Nico Rosberg	James Hunt		
29 Juan Manuel Fangio	Ronnie Peterson		
26 Mika Häkkinen	13 Jack Brabham		
26 Charles Leclerc	Graham Hill		
24 Niki Lauda	Jacky Ickx		
Nelson Piquet	Juan Pablo Montoya		
22 Fernando Alonso	Jacques Villeneuve		
20 Damon Hill	Mark Webber		
Valtteri Bottas			

FASTEST LAPS

77 Michael Schumacher	19 Damon Hill		
67 Lewis Hamilton	Stirling Moss		
46 Kimi Räikkönen	Ayrton Senna		
41 Alain Prost	Mark Webber		
38 Sebastian Vettel	Valtteri Bottas		
33 Max Verstappen	18 David Coulthard		
30 Nigel Mansell	17 Rubens Barrichello		
28 Jim Clark	Daniel Ricciardo		
26 Fernando Alonso	15 Felipe Massa		
25 Mika Häkkinen	Clay Regazzoni		
24 Niki Lauda	Jackie Stewart		
23 Juan Manuel Fangio	14 Jacky Ickx		
Nelson Piquet	13 Alberto Ascari		
21 Gerhard Berger	Alan Jones		
20 Nico Rosberg	Riccardo Patrese		

WINS

105	Lewis Hamilton	22	Damon Hill		Felipe Massa
91	Michael Schumacher	21	Kimi Räikkönen		Jacques Villeneuve
63	Max Verstappen	20	Mika Häkkinen	10	Gerhard Berger
53	Sebastian Vettel	16	Stirling Moss		James Hunt
51	Alain Prost	15	Jenson Button		Ronnie Peterson
41	Ayrton Senna	14	Jack Brabham		Jody Scheckter
32	Fernando Alonso		Emerson Fittipaldi		Valtteri Bottas
31	Nigel Mansell		Graham Hill	9	Mark Webber
27	Jackie Stewart	13	Alberto Ascari	8	Denny Hulme
25	Jim Clark		David Coulthard		Jacky Ickx
	Niki Lauda	12	Mario Andretti		Charles Leclerc
24	Juan Manuel Fangio		Alan Jones		Daniel Ricciardo
23	Nelson Piquet		Carlos Reutemann	7	Rene Arnoux
	Nico Rosberg	11	Rubens Barrichello		Juan Pablo Montoya

WINS IN ONE SEASON

19	Max Verstappen 2023		Michael Schumacher 1995, 2000 & 2001	
15	Max Verstappen 2022	8	Lewis Hamilton 2021	
13	Michael Schumacher 2004		Mika Häkkinen 1998	
	Sebastian Vettel 2013		Damon Hill 1996	
11	Lewis Hamilton 2020		Michael Schumacher 1994	
	Lewis Hamilton 2019		Ayrton Senna 1988	
	Lewis Hamilton 2018	7	Fernando Alonso 2005	
	Lewis Hamilton 2014		Fernando Alonso 2006	
	Michael Schumacher 2002		Jim Clark 1963	
	Sebastian Vettel 2011		Alain Prost 1984 & 1988	
10	Max Verstappen 2021		Alain Prost 1993	
	Lewis Hamilton 2015		Kimi Räikkönen 2005	
	Lewis Hamilton 2016		Ayrton Senna 1991	
9	Max Verstappen 2024		Jacques Villeneuve 1997	
	Lewis Hamilton 2017			
	Nigel Mansell 1992			
	Nico Rosberg 2016			

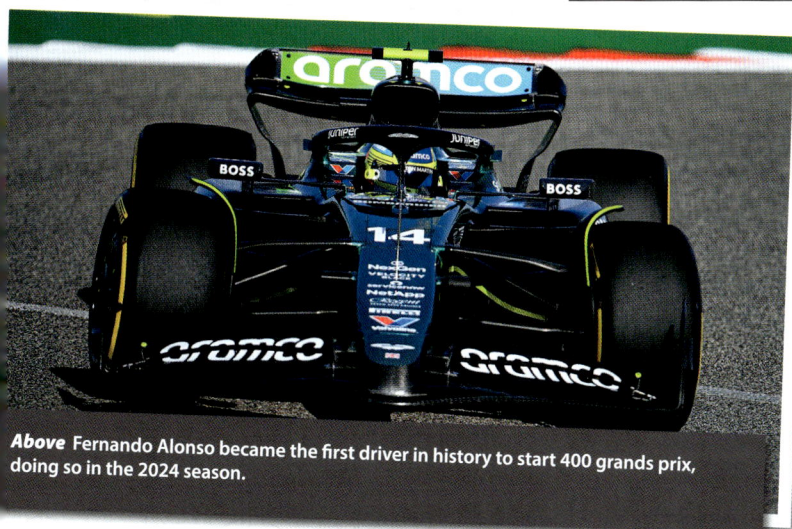

Above Fernando Alonso became the first driver in history to start 400 grands prix, doing so in the 2024 season.

Above Juan Manuel Fangio leads his Mercedes team-mate Stirling Moss on his way to victory in the 1955 Dutch GP, the year he claimed the third of his five titles.

POINTS

4862.5	Lewis Hamilton	1007	Lando Norris	360	Damon Hill
3098	Sebastian Vettel	798.5	Alain Prost		Jackie Stewart
3023.5	Max Verstappen	658	Rubens Barrichello	389	Oscar Piastri
2337	Fernando Alonso	714	George Russell	329	Ralf Schumacher
1873	Kimi Räikkönen	614	Ayrton Senna	310	Carlos Reutemann
1797	Valtteri Bottas	571	Nico Hulkenberg	307	Juan Pablo Montoya
1638	Sergio Perez	535	David Coulthard	292	Lance Stroll
1594.5	Nico Rosberg	485.5	Nelson Piquet	289	Graham Hill
1566	Michael Schumacher	482	Nigel Mansell	281	Emerson Fittipaldi
1329	Daniel Ricciardo	445	Esteban Ocon		Riccardo Patrese
1430	Charles Leclerc	420.5	Niki Lauda	277.64	Juan Manuel Fangio
1235	Jenson Button	420	Mika Häkkinen	275	Giancarlo Fisichella
1272.5	Carlos Sainz	436	Pierre Gasly	274	Jim Clark
1167	Felipe Massa	391	Romain Grosjean		Robert Kubica
1047.5	Mark Webber	385	Gerhard Berger		

TITLES

7	Michael Schumacher	1	Mario Andretti
	Lewis Hamilton		Jenson Button
5	Juan Manuel Fangio		Giuseppe Farina
4	Alain Prost		Mike Hawthorn
	Sebastian Vettel		Damon Hill
	Max Verstappen		Phil Hill
3	Jack Brabham		Denny Hulme
	Niki Lauda		James Hunt
	Nelson Piquet		Alan Jones
	Ayrton Senna		Nigel Mansell
	Jackie Stewart		Kimi Räikkönen
2	Fernando Alonso		Jochen Rindt
	Alberto Ascari		Keke Rosberg
	Jim Clark		Nico Rosberg
	Emerson Fittipaldi		Jody Scheckter
	Mika Häkkinen		John Surtees
	Graham Hill		Jacques Villeneuve

CONSTRUCTOR RECORDS

STARTS

1098	Ferrari
970	McLaren
851	Williams
761	Renault* (nee Toleman, then Benetton then, Renault* then Lotus II, then Alpine)
715	Visa Cash App RB (nee Minardi, then Toro Rosso, then AlphaTauri)
625	Aston Martin (nee Jordan then Midland then Spyker then Force India then Racing Point)
600	Sauber (BMW Sauber, Alfa Romeo Racing, Kick Sauber)
527	Red Bull (nee Stewart then Jaguar Racing)
492	Lotus
492	Mercedes GP (+ BAR + Honda Racing + Brawn)
430	Tyrrell
409	Prost (+ Ligier)
394	Brabham
291	Arrows

NB. The Lotus stats are based on the team that ran from 1958 to 1994, whereas those listed as Renault* are for the team that started as Toleman in 1981, became Benetton in 1986 then Renault in 2002 and ran as Lotus 2012–15. The Renault listings are from its first spell in F1 between 1977 and 1985. The stats for Red Bull Racing include those of the Stewart GP and Jaguar Racing teams from which it evolved. Likewise, Force India's stats include those of Jordan and Midland plus Spyker; and Scuderia Toro Rosso those of Minardi.

POLE POSITIONS

253	Ferrari	39	Brabham	10	Maserati		Shadow
164	McLaren	34	Renault* (+ Toleman + Benetton + Lotus II)	9	Ligier		Toyota
141	Mercedes GP (+ Honda Racing & Brawn GP)			8	Mercedes		2 Lancia
		31	Renault	7	Vanwall	1	Arrows
		14	Tyrrell	5	March		BMW Sauber
128	Williams	12	Alfa Romeo	4	Matra		Toro Rosso
107	Lotus	11	BRM	4	Force India (+ Jordan + Racing Point)		Haas
104	Red Bull (+ Stewart)		Cooper				

Above Rubens Barrichello leads Fernando Alonso through the first corner at Monza in 2004, having started on pole.

Below Williams has nine F1 titles to its name, but ranked only fourth in 1982, when Keke Rosberg landed the drivers' crown despite winning only one of the year's 16 GPs.

TITLES

16	Ferrari			Renault
9	McLaren	1	Benetton
	Williams		Brawn
8	Mercedes GP		BRM
7	Lotus		Matra
6	Red Bull		Tyrrell
2	Brabham		Vanwall
	Cooper		

WINS

248	Ferrari	16	Cooper	2	Honda
189	McLaren	15	Renault	1	BMW Sauber
138	Mercedes GP (+ HondaRacing + Brawn GP)	10	Alfa Romeo		Eagle
		9	Ligier		Hesketh
123	Red Bull (+ Stewart)		Maserati		Penske
114	Williams		Matra		Porsche
79	Lotus		Mercedes (1950s Mercedes)		Shadow
49	Renault		Vanwall		Toro Rosso
35	Brabham	4	Jordan		AlphaTauri
23	Tyrrell	3	March		Racing Point
17	BRM		Wolf		Alpine

WINS IN ONE SEASON

21	Red Bull 2023			Williams 1992
19	Mercedes GP 2016			Williams 1993
17	Red Bull 2022	9	Mercedes 2021
16	Mercedes GP 2014		Ferrari 2001
	Mercedes GP 2015		Ferrari 2006
15	Mercedes GP 2019		Ferrari 2007
	Ferrari 2002 & 2004		McLaren 1998
	McLaren 1988		Red Bull 2010
13	Mercedes GP 2020		Williams 1986
	Red Bull 2013		Williams 1987
12	McLaren 1984	8	Benetton 1994
	Mercedes GP 2017		Brawn GP 2009
	Red Bull 2011		Ferrari 2003
	Williams 1996		Lotus 1978
11	Red Bull 2021		McLaren 1991
	Mercedes GP 2018		McLaren 2007
	Benetton 1995		McLaren 2012
10	Ferrari 2000		Renault 2005
	McLaren 2005		Renault 2006
	McLaren 1989		Williams 1997

Above Red Bull enjoyed a record-breaking 2023 season.

ONE-TWO FINISHES

1	Ferrari 87		Lotus 8		Matra 2
2	Mercedes GP 55	9	BRM 5		Renault 2
3	McLaren 49		Mercedes 5	17	BMW Sauber 1
4	Williams 33	11	Alfa Romeo 4		Jordan 1
5	Red Bull 31		Brawn 4		Ligier 1
6	Brabham 8	13	Benetton 2		Maserati 1
	Tyrrell 8		Cooper 2		

POINTS

10,324	Ferrari	1018	Sauber (+ BMW Sauber, Alfa Romeo Racing, Kick Sauber)
8195.5	Mercedes GP (+ BAR + Honda Racing + Brawn GP)		
		886	Toro Rosso (+ AlphaTauri +RB)
7,933	Red Bull (+ Stewart + Jaguar Racing)	854	Brabham
		617	Tyrrell
6957.5	McLaren	439	BRM
3637	Williams	424	Prost (+ Ligier)
2684	Renault* (+Toleman + Benetton + Lotus II + Alpine)	333	Cooper
		312	Renault (1980s Renault)
2105	Aston Martin (+ Jordan + Midland + Spyker + Force India + Racing Point)	307	Haas
		278.5	Toyota
1514	Lotus	171.5	March

FASTEST LAPS

263	Ferrari	71	Lotus	15	BRM	10	Aston Martin (+ Jordan +Force India)	4	RB (+ Toro Rosso, +AlphaTauri)
172	McLaren	61	Renault* (+ Toleman + Benetton + Lotus II)		Maserati	9	Mercedes	3	Surtees
133	Williams			14	Alfa Romeo	7	March		Toyota
104	Mercedes GP (+ Brawn GP)	40	Brabham	13	Cooper		Vanwall	2	Haas
		22	Tyrrell	12	Matra	5	Sauber		
99	Red Bull	18	Renault	11	Prost				

PICTURE CREDITS

The publishers would like to thank the following sources for their kind permission to reproduce the pictures in this book.

Alamy: Justin Long 136B
Getty Images: Allsport 171BR; Nelson Almeida/AFP 183B; Vanderlei Almeida/AFP 38T; Jerry Andre 116-117, 174; Sam Bagnall/LAT 30T; Lars Baron 178B; Lorenzo Bellanca/LAT 114TL, 148B, 169B; Sam Bloxham/LAT 30B, 134-135, 138-139, 146-147, 177T, 184B; Frederic J. Brown/AFP 10-11; Gareth Bumstead/Sutton Images 27T; Giuseppe Cacace 67B; Bernard Cahier 158-159, 162-163; Marco Canoniero/LightRocket 110B; Rudy Carezzevoli 5R, 42-43, 71T, 78-79, 189L; Timothy A. Clary/AFP 180T; Charles Coates/LAT 34, 59B, 140T, 152B, 183T, 185T; Mike Cooper 99T; Benjamin Cremel/AFP 172T; Glenn Dunbar/LAT 40TR, 49T, 53BL, 66B, 118B; Nicolas Economou/NurPhoto 74B; Steve Etherington/LAT 33B, 77T, 80-81, 119T, 122BL, 133C, 149T, 153B, 188, 190C, 191; Evening Standard/Hulton Archive 100-101; Andrew Ferraro/LAT 45T, 47T, 76B, 114TR, 118T, 122T; Peter Fox 12-13, 22T, 122BR, 152T, 171BL, 186B; Simon Galloway/LAT 45B, 61B; Paul Gilham 20T, 39B, 137T; Gongora/NurPhoto 108-109; Patrick Hertzog/AFP 82T; Mike Hewitt/Allsport 154-155; Andy Hone/LAT 28T, 36B, 110TL, 173T; Kym Illman 69T; Dan Istitene 21T, 26B, 46, 61T, 148T; Jeroen Jumelet/AFP 176B; Keystone-France/Gamma-Keystone 104-105; Toshifumi Kitamura/AFP 17T; LAT 4BR, 14B, 16B, 17B, 19B, 21B, 22B, 23B, 24, 25B, 25B, 26T, 31T, 32B, 35B, 37B, 40TL, 40B, 47B, 49B, 50T, 52B, 54, 56B, 56B, 57T, 58T, 58B, 60T, 62B, 66T, 67T, 68B, 69B, 71L, 71B, 72B, 75B, 82R, 82B, 84-85, 86, 87T, 87L, 87B, 90T, 90B, 91T, 91B, 94T, 94B, 95T, 95B, 98T, 98B, 98B, 99B, 102TL, 102TR, 102B, 103, 106, 107T, 107C, 107B, 128, 129T, 133T, 140B, 141C, 144TL, 144TR, 144B, 145T, 145B, 150-151, 153T, 156T, 156L, 156B, 157T, 157B, 160T, 160B, 161T, 161B, 164T, 164L, 164B, 165T, 165B, 181T, 181B, 187B, 189R, 190B; Kirby Lee 68T; Bryn Lennon 72T, 123, 149B, 171T, 180B, 187T; Clive Mason 6-7, 19R, 32T, 55BR, 70, 75T, 132T, 141T, 178T; Zak Mauger/LAT 35T, 114B; Jordan McKean/LAT 111B; Colin McMaster/LAT 37T, 172T; Alessio Morgese/NurPhoto 36C, 126-127; Kazuhiro Nogi/AFP 52T, 137B; David Phipps/Sutton Images 18, 142-143, 177B; Picme/LAT 185B; Ryan Pierse 77B; Joe Portlock 76T, 110TR; Jakub Porzycki/NurPhoto 175T; Mike Powell/Allsport 33T; Roslan Rahman/AFP 179T; Mario Renzi/Formula 1 20B, 176T; Pascal Rondeau 39T, 55T; Clive Rose 23T, 55BL, 73B, 124-125, 129B, 166-167, 179B, 186R; Vladimir Rys/Bongarts 14T; Rainer Schlegelmilch 62T, 96-97, 170; Peter Spinney/LAT 136T; Alastair Staley/LAT 47L; Sutton Images 4-5C, 29T, 29B, 57B, 88-89, 92-93, 168B, 173B, 175BL; James Sutton/Formula 1 175BR; Mark Sutton/Sutton Images 168T, 184T; Steven Tee/LAT 41, 83, 111T, 115, 119B, 182B; Mark Thompson 4-5T, 9, 15B, 31B, 48, 51T, 59T, 64-65, 74T, 112-113, 120-121, 130-131, 132B, 169T, 182T; Simon Wohlfahrt/AFP 38B
PA Images: DPA 28B, 73T; Tom Hevezi 63B; John Marsh 16T, 36T, 51B, 53BR; PA Archive 15T; Martin Rickett 27B; S&G and Barratts 19T
Shutterstock: AP 53T; Victor R. Caivano/AP 63T; Alberto Pellaschiar/AP 50B; Pixathlon 60B
Topfoto.co.uk: 44

Every effort has been made to acknowledge correctly and contact the source and/or copyright holder of each picture. Any unintentional errors or omissions will be corrected in future editions of this book.